BASEBALL AND THE
BABY BOOMER

A History, Commentary, and Memoir

BASEBALL AND THE
BABY BOOMER

A History, Commentary, and Memoir

TALMAGE BOSTON

FOREWORD BY FRANK DEFORD
PREFACE BY LOU BROCK

bright sky press

HOUSTON AND ALBANY, TEXAS

bright sky press

2365 Rice Blvd., Suite 202 Houston, Texas 77005
Box 416, Albany, Texas 76430

10   9   8   7   6   5   4   3   2   1

Library of Congress Cataloging-in Publication Data

Boston, Talmage, 1953-
Baseball and the baby boomer : a history, commentary, and memoir / by Talmage Boston.
p. cm.
Includes bibliographical references and index.
ISBN 978-1-933979-26-7 (jacketed hardcover : alk. paper) 1. Baseball—United States—
History—20th century. 2. Baseball—United States—History—21st century. I. Title.

GV863.A1B644 2008
796.3570973 B—dc22

2008015716

Book and cover design by Ellen Peeples Cregan, Cregan Design
Edited by Dixie Nixon

Printed in the U.S.A. by Ocean-graphics LLC

*This book is dedicated to Bobby Bragan
and Dr. Bobby Brown—*

*Who have kept my baseball fire burning
over the last sixteen years.*

TABLE OF CONTENTS

"Men do not quit playing because they grow old;
They grow old because they quit playing."

~ *Oliver Wendell Holmes*

FOREWORD

I'M SOMETHING OF AN INTERLOPER HERE, because I'm not a Baby Boomer. Rather, I'm a Depression Baby, of which there are not many, so we were all the more precious and appreciated—unlike the Boomers, who were turned out lustfully and indiscriminately in a time of peace and prosperity.

It's also true that my overlooked cohorts, we tweeners who bridged the gap between the so-called Greatest Generation and the Boomers, were the last to be bred at a time when baseball utterly ruled. It was only when the Boomers came along in their vast numbers that the National Pastime forfeited its hegemony and began to share attention with the NFL and the NBA and the ice thing that came down from Canada and even, Lord help us, NASCAR. Not to mention televised poker.

But when I was growing up, baseball strode our American sports world like a colossus. When the schedule officially ended, that only meant that it was time for the Hot Stove League, which featured as much bloviating about baseball as there was in the season itself. Oh, there was the occasional heavyweight championship fight and horses raced so that we might have something to legally bet on in a more puritanical republic and college boys played games of football and basketball, but baseball was the be-all and end-all. Paul Gallico gave up sportswriting and hied to the south of France to be a novelist. Why? "February," he famously replied. What was a sports scribe to do till pitchers and catchers reported? Now, of course, February has the Super Bowl and the Daytona 500 and the NBA All-Star fiesta.

And yet ... And yet ...

It is still so for many of us, irrespective of birthdate, that the world really does not start spinning again until Spring Training begins. Baseball must now share the devotions of American fans, but it still holds a tenderer place in our sports consciousness, and as Talmage Boston points out so poignantly in Chapter Nine, the old ball game seems to work its magic best as a generational glue. And now, it's not just the fathers and sons of Field of Dreams, but mothers and daughters who are in the mix, too.

In another chapter, Talmage writes so nicely about how baseball nurtures friendship. True enough, all sports in all lands encourage bantering and friendly arguments, but because baseball's place is so much more restrained than the back-and-forth games, it allows for more cogitation and conversation. It nurtures friendship more productively. The Boomers were the first generation to come into this world with television, the invention that gave so much more power to the visual. Baseball is the most oral of games. It's just about the last cracker barrel in our society. The Boomers who love baseball are blessed that thereby their sense of hearing and speech is heightened, as it is with us old-timers.

Anybody who grows up at any time with any game is going to have special favorites. Baseball is a team game, and you're always going to incline to the boys who wear the right uniform. And different players are heroes to different people. Talmage's selection of principals about whom he chose to write—from Jackie Robinson to Bart Giamatti—reveals what matters to him probably better than any traditional Rorschach test ever would. He called me up in an absolute pet one day, fearful that the absence of a chapter on Carl Ripken would somehow be sacrilegious. Nonsense. The beauty of the exercise he has set for himself with this book is that he can make up the lineup all by himself, and the devil take the hindmost.

I do think it's instructive—and not the least bit surprising—that most all of the stars he has chosen to feature came some years ago, back when he was more boy than man. He seems to be at his most passionate—and good for him—in defending the feats of Roger Maris and Nolan Ryan from the ravages of the steroid era. But then, it's natural that we are invariably more impressed with the players of our youth. They seem to us to be bigger in every way then, and surely more indelible. Talmage, it's perfectly all right to leave Cal Ripken to the admiration of some budding Gen X writer.

Frank Deford
Westport, Connecticut
August 1, 2008

PREFACE

I N JULY OF 1994, my hero and mentor, Buck O'Neil, wrote the introduction to Talmage Boston's first venture into capturing the spirit of this great game. With a few short sentences, Buck caught the essence of Talmage's first book about baseball in 1939, which happens to be the year I was born. Buck has been a key figure to my own success in baseball, and it is in his honor that I now write this introduction.

When I opened *Baseball and the Baby Boomer* the first time, my expectations were high for another great baseball history book by Talmage. But more than just history, when I read it, I began to think I was reading a love story—love of the game, love for its heroes, and love for the values and lessons the game has taught the Baby Boomer generation.

The memories and competitive spirit conjured up in these pages make me realize how humbled and honored I am to have competed at the major league level when I did. Yes, as you will see in these chapters, there's certainly lots of history and mystery in the baseball world where I got to work, live, and play.

Shortly before he moved on to the real Hall of Fame with the Lord, Buck O'Neil told me, "All the great ones want the ball." The ball is in Talmage's hand with *Baseball and the Baby Boomer,* and I think you'll find his point of view on the subjects in this book to be a real celebration of those of us who played the game after Jackie Robinson leveled the diamond for everyone.

Lou Brock
St. Louis, Missouri
June 8, 2008

INTRODUCTION

BABY BOOMERS ENTERED the kinder and gentler world of America between 1946 and 1964—that is, between the St. Louis Cardinals' winning the World Series behind the seventh game heroics of Enos "Pesky Held the Ball" Slaughter and Bob "Take No Prisoners" Gibson. In those years, America transformed itself from a radio to a television society, and those born then grew up under tough love "Greatest Generation" parents who had weathered the Great Depression and prevailed in World War II. In most Truman-Eisenhower-Kennedy era families, divorce was rare, dads spent their entire careers employed as "company men," and moms stayed home with the kids.

As someone born in early October 1953 during the Yankees-Dodgers World Series, my baseball consciousness started upon entering the world. By the late summer of 1960, a few months shy of my seventh birthday, baseballphilia kicked into high gear, with the arrival of my first trading cards (which my mother didn't throw away—Thank You, Mom!), my first glove (a Japanese import that cost less than $3), and a steady Saturday afternoon diet of Diz and Pee Wee praising the merits of Falstaff beer while broadcasting "The Game of the Week" on our small black-and-white TV.

That year, Ted Williams retired from the game at the end of the season, and seeing the Splendid Splinter in the Red Sox away uniform bearing "Boston" on the front meant the Bosox then and forever had to be my team. In believing Teddy Ballgame's outfit surely must have been named in honor of my family, I was already showing early flashes of having the egocentricity necessary to become a writer.

The significance of my first attractions to baseball came amidst the following circumstances prevalent in 1960 when we mid-Baby Boomers first started paying attention to the game:

- Though all big league managers were Caucasian, integration of African-American players by all teams had occurred (my Red Sox, alas, being the last to integrate in 1959), and the Negro Leagues had essentially disappeared;

- Watching baseball on television happened weekends, and listening to games on the radio happened weeknights;

- No one knew about ballplayers' personal lives except for the glowing accounts found in the pages of *SPORT* and *Sports Illustrated* magazines, meaning most fans believed every major league star was something of a "hero";

- The Reserve Clause kept players tied to one team their entire careers, causing them to change uniforms only through trades over which they had no control;

- No players had facial hair or sideburns, most chewed tobacco, and stars got paid to endorse cigarettes;

- The World Series made up the entirety of post-season play;

- Without a players union, sports agents, arbitration, or free agency, the average big league salary was about $10,000 a year;

- Batters wore no gloves or padding, and helmets had no flaps;

- The only way a starting pitcher earned a "quality start" was to throw and win a complete game, and no one counted pitches;

- Baseball cards cost a penny and came in packages with a thin brittle stick of bubble gum dusted with a sugary white powder;

- No one imagined baseball could ever be played under a roof or on artificial turf.

As of 1960, pro football had started to capture the public's imagination, two years after the nationally televised Johnny Unitas-led overtime NFL championship win by the Baltimore Colts over the New York Giants. The fourteen-year-old NBA had as its main attraction the epic battles won by Bill Russell over Wilt Chamberlain.

On sandlots and school playgrounds below the Mason-Dixon line where I grew up, kids played kickball (which basically had the same rules as baseball) instead of soccer; never heard of lacrosse; and never thought about hockey because ponds never froze and there were no indoor rinks. Each twelve-month year had three and only three sports segments—baseball, football, and basketball seasons.

That's the way it was growing up as a Baby Boomer in America pre-Kennedy-assassination. Then time passed and we went to college, pursued careers, married, and reared our own children. Flattop haircuts came and went, the Beatles made us want to grow our hair as long as our parents would allow until the job interviews commenced, and it became time to clean up our acts. Starting in the 1980's, to our total amazement, the hair on our heads began to recede, turn gray, and/or disappear down the shower drain.

For many of us, despite this aging process, baseball remained an important part of our lives. Of course, childhood memories stayed with us, but every year brought a new baseball season that featured not only the game's enduring patterns, but also new heroes, villains, ballparks, records, statistics, and above all, insights into the game and its connection to life itself.

This book attempts to take the reader on the journey in time many of us born after World War II have now traveled. It is in large part a volume of baseball history, but it's also the memoir of a fan. All of us have our most memorable stories about the National Pastime, and the chapters in this book are the ones that resonated the most for me. Some electrified me; some touched me to the bone; and some involved me.

Many may wonder why certain stories and personalities of the post-war era fail to appear in these pages, and my response to that is, "Sorry, those other events and people just aren't my favorites. What's in this book, quite simply, is what I felt called to sit down and write about in reviewing my lifetime of baseball memories." Who knows? If this book does well enough, a sequel that covers the other great post-war stories of the diamond might well surface.

Almost every chapter in *Baseball and the Baby Boomer* has been the subject of 300-page books written by other authors. My goal here is to tell these stories of the game and some of its greatest characters in streamlined fashion, but with sufficient depth and intensity to interest a serious baseball aficionado, without digging into so much minutiae as to overwhelm the first-time baseball history reader. I like to think my strength as a writer is the ability to synthesize information into complete, concise, and vivid self-contained chapters; readers and critics can determine whether I've succeeded in doing that with this book.

In his selection of short fiction entitled *Eyes to See* (Thomas Nelson, 2008), novelist Bret Lott described the ideal for a writer aspiring to craft a good story—create something "gem-like, that can be read in one sitting, opening a world before the reader's very eyes and revealing secrets in a small pocket of time that allows him to go somewhere else and know something new." Each stand-alone chapter in this book aspires to fulfill Mr. Lott's description of what a well-told story should be, making these subjects open to review for all generations—not just Baby Boomers—so they can read them and "go somewhere else and know something new."

Over the last fifty years, most Baby Boomers have played the game, watched it, coached our kids in it, read about it, and best of all, replayed it in that special place Bart Giamatti named "The Green Fields of the Mind." May those who peruse these pages use them as a means of entering those green fields, where the sun shines on memory and imagination, and makes one yearn to play again..

Talmage Boston
Dallas, Texas
October 1, 2008

Mickey Mantle — an incredible talent tortured by physical and emotional pain.

CHAPTER ONE

MICKEY MANTLE AND JIMMY PIERSALL
The Dark Side of Fathers and Sons Playing Catch

On a sunny Saturday morning in April 1961, my father bought my first baseball glove, and then played catch with me in our front yard. We never played catch together again, which bothered me for years until learning the life stories of Mickey Mantle and Jimmy Piersall, and how in some instances, fathers and sons playing baseball together can have its dark side. My dad may not have been inclined to play baseball with me, but at least he often said the three little words to his children that didn't get said by the fathers in the Mantle and Piersall homes.

S omewhere out there in the dark corner of a bar sits a man drowning his sorrows as he tries to make peace with his deceased father. A movie buff, he puts down his drink, closes his eyes, and in his mind plays the final scene from *Field of Dreams* one more time, where Kevin Costner at last reconciles with his reincarnated dad by playing catch with him; as the ball gets tossed back and forth, music swells in the background, and the closing credits roll.

Flush with insight, the man lifts his drink, and toasts himself for understanding at last how the strained situation with his father got its start, muttering aloud, "If only Dad and I had played more catch when I was a boy, it all would have been so different...."

No one ever played more catch with his son than Mutt Mantle or John Piersall. In fact, both these dads played baseball with their boys for almost twenty years. Despite their good intentions, however, the only dreams their time in the game produced for their sons were of the nightmare variety.

The lives of Mickey Mantle and Jimmy Piersall tell stories of fathers and sons the man in the bar needs to know. The next time he rolls his interior projector, he should add footage from the 2005 HBO documentary on Mantle and the 1957 movie, *Fear Strikes Out* (based on Piersall's autobiography), into the Costner cornfield images, and recognize that the answers to his questions about the father-son relationship are not necessarily found on a mythical ball field. No. He can find his answers to successful generational connection by finding the real (not movie reel) places where fathers and sons engage in that rarest of male pastimes—heart-to-heart communication filled with statements of genuine affirmation and encouragement.

———————

The Mantle story began October 20, 1931. At the age of nineteen, Mutt and his wife, Lovell, met the stork in Spavinaw, Oklahoma, where the plan for their first baby, named in honor of his dad's favorite baseball player, Philadelphia A's star catcher Mickey Cochrane, started with his first breath. The young father soon started rolling a steady stream of balls to his infant son, from the very beginning pursuing the dream—when this boy grows up, Mickey Mantle will have the baseball talent good enough to make the major leagues.

Mutt had played enough baseball to know Mick could improve his chances for success if he became a switch hitter, allowing him to see (and, therefore, hit) a pitcher's curveball better than a right-handed hitter facing a righty hurler or a lefty facing a lefty. With that strategy set, when Mickey reached the age of four, Mutt started a routine he would follow for years—leaving the zinc mines where he worked every afternoon at 4:00, coming home, and pitching right-handed to Mick and having his dad, Grandpa Charlie, throw left-handed while daylight permitted, allowing the boy to get plenty of swings from both sides of the plate.

A natural right-handed hitter, Mickey preferred swinging with his biological stroke no matter who was pitching, and even sneaked in some righty swings against right-handed pitchers in those rare games when his dad wasn't there, but Mutt was in attendance most of the time, and insisted that his son switch hit.

The father's plan worked. In no time, Mickey Mantle perfected a ferocious swing capable of hitting long drives with ambidextrous power, the ball jumping off his bat with a force never seen before in that part of the country. Neighbors marveled at the boy's towering blasts and suspected Mutt's ambitious dream might well come true.

In the midst of this Oklahoma Field of Dreams scenario came the hook that took the story out of the fairy tale realm—the hook that starts the snag in many dysfunctional father-son relationships—the hook known as the force of personality. In the Mantle family, it did as much damage to young Mickey's head as he ever did to a baseball with his quick bat.

The men of Mutt's generation living in the Dust Bowl of the American Midwest embodied what screenwriters call "the strong, silent type." In a word, they were "severe," a natural response to their hard lives. Entering the job market with a grade school education, they scratched out a living throughout the Great Depression with their hands and backs, chain-smoked cigarettes, stayed married to one wife, fathered multiple children, didn't say much, and never

Young Mickey — relaxed and confident on the outside, tied in knots on the inside.

expressed their feelings. Any display of emotion would obviously prove a man's weakness, and strong, silent types would rather die than show weakness.

Boys like Mickey Mantle, raised by severe dads, soon accepted life's harsh realities. The family had food to eat, a roof over its head, hand-me-down clothes, outdoor plumbing, and not much else. Since sparing the rod spoiled the child, kids learned to be seen and not heard, and obeyed mom and dad without asking questions. They knew their parents wanted them to get their high school diplomas and move on to a better life, removing themselves from their upbringing's dire circumstances. These father-son expectations played out in the Mantle family with Mutt believing his oldest boy could become the best baseball player who ever lived. Unlike Babe Ruth and Lou Gehrig, Mick could run fast; unlike Ty Cobb, he had power; and unlike anyone else in baseball history, he had no weakness as a hitter because he could smash the ball with power from both sides of the plate.

Mutt's vision seemed justified. Mickey could run faster, throw harder, and hit the ball farther right-handed or left-handed than anyone else his age in northeastern Oklahoma. Despite his prodigious talents on the diamond, however, like every ballplayer in history, Mick could not field every ball cleanly, make perfect throws each time the baseball came his way, or hit a rocket over the fence with every swing of the bat. And that inability to be flawless caused problems with his dad.

Whenever young Mickey Mantle made a mistake in a game, Mutt's high-powered stare zeroed in on his son. Mick put it this way, "My father could freeze you with a look." After seeing his son make a rare misplay, the dad's eyes locked on the boy and communicated with full force, "You failed me, Mick, and you also failed yourself. And if you fail much more, you're not gonna make it to the big leagues, and you'll end up rotting in the mines the rest of your life just like me." A strong, silent type doesn't have to express these words, but can deliver every nuanced thought in one second with just his eyes.

Mutt's killer stare soon hooked into his son's core and wouldn't turn loose during a ballgame or after it ended. It made Mickey kick water coolers and slam bats into dugout walls. When he got home, it made the boy wet his bed at night until he was sixteen years old. In Mick's mind, everything his dad said and did was right, and if Mutt saw him as a failure, then by golly he must be a failure.

Accepting the clear message from his dad's looks and knowing he was to be seen and not heard kept Mickey from confronting Mutt after a game and pleading his case in the spirit of, "Look, Dad, I know I struck out in the fourth inning. But I did get three hits and knocked in two runs and threw a runner out at home. And if you look around, you can see I'm the best player in the league. And when you were my age, I bet you didn't bat 1.000 and catch every ball hit your way. So come on, I'm not a failure, and you shouldn't look at me like I am." A son couldn't say things like that to a strong, silent, severe dad in the Great Depression. So Mutt's freezing looks kept killing Mickey's self-esteem from his first games all the way through high school, even when the boy's heroics on

NATIONAL BASEBALL HALL OF FAME LIBRARY, COOPERSTOWN, NEW YORK

Mutt Mantle with his son, Mickey, on the front porch of their Dust Bowl home. "My father could freeze you with a look."

the ball field began drawing attention from big league scouts.

In the spring of 1949, Mickey Mantle graduated from Commerce High School, signed a contract with the world champion New York Yankees for an $1100 bonus, and within two years, advanced from the Yanks' Class D minor league team in Independence, Kansas, to the hallowed ground of Yankee Stadium. After a sensational '51 spring training in Arizona where Mick's tape measure blasts prompted sports-writers to compare the "Commerce Comet" with Babe Ruth, followed by a fast start in the season's first two months, the prized rookie lost his sense of the strike zone in June producing strikeouts by the dozens that caused manager Casey Stengel to send him down to the Yanks' AAA farm team in Kansas City, in hopes the rookie could rebuild his confidence away from the pressures of the Big Apple.

Arriving in the minors with his head down, Mick's slump continued, producing one bunt single in his first twenty-three times at bat. Wondering if he'd ever get another solid hit, and whether he had what it took to become a successful ballplayer, Mickey called home and expressed doubts to his dad about his future in the game. Mutt listened long enough to get the gist of the message, jumped in his old car, and drove non-stop from Commerce to Kansas City.

Entering his son's room at the Aladdin Hotel, Mutt had the same look on his face that had frozen Mickey so many times before. Rather than give his despondent son any sign of encouragement, the father stormed over to the dresser, opened the drawers, picked up Mick's battered cloth suitcase, and started jamming clothes into it. After a few seconds of frantic packing, he paused, and spoke with every ounce of contempt he could muster, "I thought I raised a man. But I raised a coward!" As he then resumed stuffing the bag, the dad did something he had never done before in his son's presence. He cried.

To Mutt Mantle, for Mickey to quit baseball and give up on the game before his twentieth birthday would mean more than the end of the family dream. It meant Mutt had failed as a father. For a young man with a $7500 a year contract from the world champion New York Yankees, who had already proved his ability to hit 450-foot home runs from both sides of the plate at the major league level, to consider flushing his unique baseball talents into the ground in exchange for a life in $33 a week zinc mining hell was so far beyond any doomsday scenario Mutt could imagine, it made his insides pour out.

Watching his father, Mickey Mantle saw that contrary to everything he had seen before, strong, silent men could cry, and it didn't mean they were weak. It just meant they had feelings, and no self-imposed stoic defenses were strong enough to block out life-and-death emotions, as Mutt's grief in the Kansas City hotel room came with a force usually reserved for funerals.

For half his life, Mutt had trained Mickey for a better life than his own. Now all that time and effort hung in the balance, and his boy was threatening to quit, and throw it away into a shaft from which it could never be retrieved. As his tears fell on the suitcase, Mutt could surely visualize his blond, chiseled son aging before his eyes into a mirror image of himself—a destitute, coughing, old-before-his-time miner.

When Mickey saw his dad break down, he realized for the first time the effect of what he was considering. Quitting baseball now would mean having to go home to the zinc mines, and coming out of the ground every day covered in filth for the privilege of earning a pittance wage. Worse, it would mean seeing his dad's hard look aimed at him every single day.

All the frustration of being demoted to the minor leagues, the loneliness from months in Arizona and New York, and the guilt over bringing anguish upon his dad, combined to flip a switch inside Mickey Mantle. Tears poured out of Mickey just like they did from his dad, and in a few minutes, they both calmed themselves, talked, and found a way to end the crisis. Mickey would give baseball one last shot.

That one shot turned into an explosion. In the first game after the hotel conversation, Mickey Mantle hit a double, triple, and two home runs, beginning an attack on American Association pitching that went on for sixty days until late August, when the Yankees called him back to the majors.

The Kansas City meeting became Mutt's final show of strength. After returning home to Commerce, Hodgkin's disease attacked his thirty-nine year old frame, and the inner satisfaction of seeing Mickey's return to productivity on the ball field was no match for the sudden onslaught of cancer.

With his days numbered, Mutt Mantle traveled to New York City in October 1951 to watch the Yankees defend their championship in the World Series against Leo Durocher's New York Giants, led by National League Rookie of the Year Willie Mays and "Shot Heard Round the World" playoff hero Bobby Thomson. Casey Stengel started Mickey in right field the first two games, playing alongside the aging Joe DiMaggio in center, this Series becoming the final games in the Yankee Clipper's career.

After the Giants won the first game, in the fifth inning of Game Two, Mays lofted a fly ball into shallow right center, and both Joe and Mickey went for it. As DiMaggio got close to the ball, Mick stopped in his tracks to avoid a collision, but in pulling up, Mickey's spikes caught on an outfield sprinkler head, and he fell down in a heap with what proved to be two torn ligaments in his right knee. Reeling in pain and sensing the injury might cause a premature end to his career, Mickey Mantle lay on the field until the stretcher arrived and cried uncontrollably.

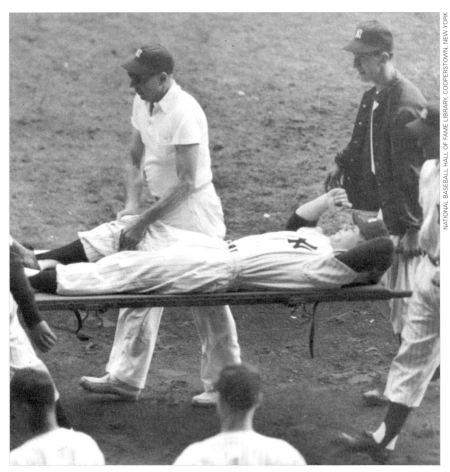

Mickey Mantle is carried off the field in Game Two of the '51 Series, after yielding to DiMaggio on Mays' fly ball, catching his spikes on a sprinkler head, and tearing the ligaments in his right knee. The knee would never be the same after the injury.

The next day, after arriving at Lennox Hill Hospital in a cab with his father, Mick got out of the taxi holding his crutches, and tried to step onto the curb. When Mickey leaned on his dad's shoulder for balance, the elder Mantle crashed to the ground, and the staff immediately rushed both men to the same room. Mick had knee surgery that day while nurses tried to comfort Mutt, and side by side in their hospital beds, they could at least watch the rest of the World Series on television. For the first time since Kansas City, Mick took a hard look at his father and saw a very sick man, a good thirty pounds lighter than he had been three months before at the Aladdin Hotel. Doctors then broke the news to the Yankee rookie that Mutt had terminal cancer and couldn't live much longer.

Between October and his death the following May, Mutt Mantle had one final piece of advice for his eldest son. He asked Mickey to drop his New York girlfriend and return to Oklahoma to marry his high school sweetheart, Merlyn Johnson, because "she's like us." Without objection, Mick accepted his dad's directive, and on December 23, 1951, he and Merlyn married, two months after reaching his twentieth birthday.

Something happened to Mickey Mantle when Mutt died in the spring of 1952. The young ballplayer lost his moral compass, and, believing he was destined to follow in his father's, grandfather's, and uncles' footsteps, and die before reaching the age of forty, Mick decided to reject his family's nose-to-the-grindstone ways, and started turning himself into a full blown hedonist.

Embracing a fast and loose lifestyle in his early years with the Yankees, Mickey soon became the constant companion of teammate Billy Martin, a young man who personified the antithesis of both a moral compass and the strong, silent type. Mickey knew he was veering off course with his new friend when he admitted to Merlyn, "You know, if my dad was alive, he would take one look at Billy and tell him to get back in his frigging car and go back to California." Regardless, Mickey and Billy soon became inseparable, and partied without limits for the next thirty-seven years whenever the opportunity arose, from the time Mutt died until Martin's passing in a 1989 car wreck.

In the years after his dad's death, part of Mutt's dream for Mickey's baseball career came true, as Commerce, Oklahoma's brightest star became one of the game's greatest players, hitting 536 career home runs, winning 3 Most Valuable Player awards, leading the Yankees to 12 American League pennants and 7 world championships, and being a first ballot inductee into the National Baseball Hall of Fame. But in those same years, Mick developed into a raging alcoholic, compulsive philanderer, and absentee father whose bad habits got even worse after his playing days ended, showing leadership in his family only by "leading" Merlyn and his four sons down the rocky road of alcohol addiction, with his boys also ingesting massive quantities of drugs.

Miraculously, in late 1993, when his self-loathing bottomed out after he spewed an expletive into the face of a minister, Mickey Mantle at last began the process of turning his life around. The start of his transformation from boorish drunk to sensitive human being came

After Mutt Mantle's death, Billy Martin served as Mickey's immoral compass for 37 years.

when his third son, Danny, entered the Betty Ford Center in Rancho Mirage, California, for alcohol and drug treatment. Danny achieved sobriety there, as had one of Mick's old drinking cronies, Pat Summerall, and with their encouragement, Mickey entered the Ford Center on December 28, 1993, for a month of treatment.

As Mickey Mantle became acquainted with his fellow alcoholics, he heard them talk about the emotional wounds received from their severe fathers, and how they never felt affirmed or accepted, leading to their fall into the bottle. Hearing each story, Mick could only nod his head.

The toughest part of the treatment came when the staff required every patient to write a letter to his dad. Mickey lost his composure as he started the process and broke down, later telling Bob Costas in a television interview that his tears came from knowing he had wasted his talents, and disappointed his father to the extent that every time he looked into the sky, he envisioned Mutt gazing down from heaven with his piercing look of disapproval, saying, "You failed me, son."

Knowing the high expectations his dad had once had, the pain Mickey felt as he wrote the letter at the Ford Center seemed justified. The son who Mutt Mantle thought should become the greatest ballplayer ever, and grow up to become a good strong, silent man, had not achieved his dad's goals. Hitting a paltry .237 in his final season with the Yankees caused Mickey's career batting average to fall two points below the coveted .300. He hadn't approached 600 home runs because alcohol abuse cut his career short. He had been an irresponsible husband to Merlyn, and hadn't mentored any of his sons into productive lives, confessing to Costas the guilt he felt because, "I wasn't there for my kids, like my dad was for me." In addition, his business ventures—bowling alleys, restaurants, and employment agencies—had all gone bust.

Aware of failures in every facet of his life, Mickey knew, but couldn't understand, the phenomenon of his still being the idol of an entire generation of men who had grown up in the fifties, were now middle-aged, and were happy to wait in lines and pay big bucks just to get his autograph. For the first time since his baseball career ended, Mickey Mantle was making a huge income at card shows in the early nineties, yet the avalanche of hero worship pouring down on him just added to his emotional chaos.

With no intoxicants or medication available at the Ford Center to

In the eighties and early nineties, as the alcoholic Mantle spiraled downward, the demand for his autograph soared.

dull his disappointment, sort out the confusion of his icon status, or reduce his vision for the beginning of a new life, Mickey worked on the letter to his dad and slowly gained composure, finally writing three words to Mutt that neither of them had ever said to the other before— "I love you."

After Mantle left the Ford Center in January 1994, tragedy soon struck. His youngest son, Billy (named for Billy Martin), who had battled alcohol and drugs since his teens, died suddenly of Hodgkin's disease at the age of thirty-six. Then shortly after Billy's death, Mick's mother and biggest fan, Lovell, passed away.

Enduring these deaths in his fragile recovering condition, Mick held fast to his new drink of choice, Diet Coke, and never again broke sobriety. On top of that, Mickey found he could reach out to his three surviving sons for the first time as a father and not just a drinking buddy, show them his real tears of "mea culpa" disappointment, and start getting things between them on a functional track by using the same three words in conversations with his sons that he had written to his dad, words that had been missing from Mantle men's vocabularies for too many generations.

In the summer of 1995, Mickey Mantle's abused liver failed, and during the transplant surgery, doctors found cancer cells in his bile ducts, which proved fatal on August 13, 1995, meaning his time of self-esteem personal transformation was shortened by over forty years' worth of self-inflicted damage flowing from self-hate exacerbated by the excesses of alcohol.

———————

Mutt and Mickey Mantle's story is not unique. At the same time one father drove his son toward big league baseball glory in Commerce, Oklahoma, another dad matched the effort with his boy in Waterbury, Connecticut.

Like Mutt, John Piersall had been a good ballplayer in his youth, and from the time son Jimmy was born on November 14, 1929, John became a man obsessed with one goal—his boy would become a major league star.

As a housepainter, John made a meager living, and had plenty of free time during the Great Depression when people let paint peel, using what little money they had on life's bare essentials. All the idleness allowed the father to have huge blocks of time for intense baseball training with his son, beginning with extended games of catch when the boy reached age four. Jim later said, "I learned how to catch a ball before I learned the alphabet."

Unlike Mutt Mantle, John Piersall was *not* the strong, silent type. Coming out of a rough foster home upbringing, John decided he could best deal with life's hard knocks by screaming at people, particularly the members of his small family. These verbal eruptions drove his wife, Mary, into depression, leading to her having multiple extended stays at Norwich State Hospital starting when Jimmy was in second grade. As the boy moved into adolescence, he tired of his father's verbal attacks on his mother, and one day found the courage to vent his feelings: "Dad, if you'd stop hollering at her, Mom would be all right!" Jim's words fell on deaf ears, and only prompted John's trying to justify his rough edges because of his own unhappy upbringing.

Mary's mental illness became more intelligible to Jim when a nun at his parochial school, who had been a friend of his mother's for years, explained his mom's condition with prophetic words that foreshadowed the boy's future state of mind: "She has a fear she can't express, and it has made her sick."

From the beginning, the Piersall father-son relationship was tense. Jim described it in detail in his book, *Fear Strikes Out* (Little, Brown, 1955; republished by University of Nebraska Press, 1999), co-authored with sportswriter Al Hirshberg:

> There were times when I loved my father and times when whatever emotion I felt for him was anything but love. I respected him, but I was afraid of him. He was stocky and had the strength of a bull. When he was angry, he terrified me, kicking me with heavy shoes that tapered towards a point at the toe. When my dad was really angry, his sharp eyes would bore through me, his face and bald head would redden and he would bellow at me in a voice that made the windows rattle and the pantry dishes jump. I could hear his deep raucous voice in my sleep, and would do anything to avoid his anger. I lived in fear of his wrath.

Like the Mantle family, the task of training a boy to develop skills sufficient to play at the major league level was serious business with the Piersalls. At age five, when he went with his father to watch his first real baseball game at Waterbury's amateur league ballpark, Jim started to squirm, and his father barked, "Quiet down and watch the ballgame. That's the only way you'll learn. You need to learn baseball backwards and forwards." When Jimmy a few years later gushed to his dad about how much fun he had making tough catches, John snapped back at him, "I don't want you thinking about fun."

As with Mickey Mantle, Jimmy's extraordinary baseball skills put him head and shoulders above his peers throughout childhood and adolescence. When the talents improved, John's obsession with achieving the big league goal for his son became more pronounced every year. Among the Piersall family rules were that Jim could never take any job that interfered with his baseball training schedule, and he was prohibited from playing football for fear of sustaining an injury. When the boy broke his wrist playing touch football one afternoon, John broke down and sobbed when he saw the cast. Later, when Jimmy dislocated his jaw in a high school basketball game, his dad collapsed with a heart attack.

In Jim's words, as each year of high school brought him closer to the time when he and his dad expected him to sign a contract with a major league team, the heightened expectations caused Jimmy Piersall to become "wound up like a spring never able to uncoil completely. I might run dry physically, but my nerves kept pushing me to do more. All of my blood, my guts, my flesh, and my physical and mentalcapacities were powered indiscriminately into everything, because *everything* seemed too important." That coiled spring became tighter and tighter throughout Jimmy's teenage years, and produced headaches that wouldn't go away.

The headaches couldn't stop Jim Piersall's rise as a ballplayer, at least for a while. Signing with the Boston Red Sox right out of high school, he started his stint in the minor leagues with Scranton in the A Eastern league, where he met a local nursing student, Mary Teevan, who became his wife before year end. Marriage to Mary helped settle Jimmy down a little, but within a year after his wedding, as he approached spring training in 1951, he became more intense than ever, exacerbated by Mary's becoming pregnant with their first child, and Jim's accepting total financial responsibility for his parents because of his mother's depression and his dad's heart condition.

A solution to the entire expanding family's residence issue appeared to be the purchase of a new home in Waterbury that was large enough for all the Piersalls to live in, but Jim's fear of being locked into a mortgage with his dysfunctional parents underfoot became too great. On the eve of moving into the new house, Jim got cold feet, realizing that with all the Piersalls living under one roof, "I would have to listen to the rasping, nagging voice of my father hollering at my mom, telling her what she was doing wrong. If I had to listen to them arguing anymore, I'd be wishing they were dead." So he backed out of the move and sold the home.

Despite the headaches, the pressures, and his heightened intensity, Jim Piersall left Waterbury in the spring and proceeded to have a great 1951 season with Birmingham in the AA Southern Association, hitting .346, proving himself the premier defense outfielder in the Red Sox farm system, and leading his team to victory in the league championship series. When the season ended in triumph, Jim Piersall expected to be a starting outfielder along with Ted Williams and Dom DiMaggio in the Boston Red Sox lineup on Opening Day 1952.

Anticipating the opportunity of finally starting for the Red Sox, and needing a change of scenery away from his dad, Jim spent the winter with Mary and daughter Eileen living in Scranton with his father-in-law, preparing for the coming season. Mary soon became pregnant with their second child, and Jim searched all over town without success for an off season job. Recognizing the responsibility of having another mouth to feed in the next few months with no prospects for making money until spring training, at a time when he had committed himself to fully supporting his parents, Jimmy Piersall's mind began to unravel. Shortly before Christmas 1951, the wheels came off his efforts at holding onto stability when he read in *The Sporting News* that Boston wanted to turn its best defensive outfield prospect into a shortstop, a position Jim had never played before.

The idea of changing positions turned Jimmy inside out. For the rest of the winter, he stopped his daily workouts at the local gym, and spent every day by himself at theaters watching the same movies over and over again. Returning home at night, his desire to be alone continued, and he refused to socialize with old friends. As his final act of troubled behavior, he balked at going to spring training if it meant he had to learn a new position.

At the urging of his wife, dad, and high school coach, Jim Piersall finally agreed to join the Red Sox at their Sarasota grapefruit league headquarters in January 1952. Once he got to spring training and then started the season with Boston, his mental health spiraled out of control, resulting in constant displays of manic behavior over the next six months on and off the field—clowning to the crowds in the outfield, having fistfights with Yankee second baseman Billy Martin and Boston pitcher Maurice McDermott, pep talking constantly to his veteran teammates with exaggerated animation, and sobbing in the dugout when manager Lou Boudreau took him out of the lineup. Though his level of play was acceptable for a rookie, his antics were not, and in early July the Red Sox sent him down to AAA Louisville. The demotion became the final straw. On July 19, 1952, Jimmy Piersall suffered a nervous breakdown and became a patient in the "violent section" of a sanitarium.

At the Westborough State Hospital, after psychiatrists finally unstrapped his strait jacket, Jim received electroshock treatments and

Early in the 1952 season, Jimmy Piersall managed to fake a smile for a publicity photo, shortly before his nervous breakdown.

counseling in hopes of relaxing his overworked emotions and eliminating the fear that for seven years had caused his constant headaches
and increasingly strange conduct.

The counseling sessions at Westborough focused on Jim's relationship with his dad, forcing the young ballplayer to finally step back and

examine their history together in pursuing the big league baseball dream. At first, Jimmy refused to put blame on John for his psychological demise, but his treating physician persisted.

In the 1957 film made of *Fear Strikes Out,* starring Anthony Perkins and Karl Malden, the screenwriters inserted dialog from the counseling sessions not contained in the book. An agitated Jim (played by Perkins) says to his doctor, "I love my dad. If it wasn't for him pushing and driving me as a ballplayer, I wouldn't be where I am today." Then there's a pause, as Perkins looks around the room and realizes that where he is "today" is in a mental institution coming to grips with major depression. In the film's penultimate scene, Jim has progressed enough in counseling to understand his family history and reaches the point where he agrees to see his dad. They finally meet on the mental hospital's tennis court and start reconciling over a game of catch, more than thirty years before Kevin Costner tossed the ball to his estranged (and deceased) dad in *Field of Dreams.*

By 1953, Jimmy Piersall had unwound himself enough to resume his major league career, which lasted into the 1967 season. In those years, he became a productive player making the American League All-Star team in 1954 and 1956, winning Gold Gloves as an outfielder in 1958 and 1961, and finishing with a .272 batting average. His career .997 fielding average as an outfielder is among the best ever compiled at the big league level, supporting the conclusions of Casey Stengel and Ted Williams who both said Jim was the greatest defensive outfielder they ever saw. After retiring as a player, he then spent most of the next three decades as a big league coach.

Thanks to the effects of lithium, Jimmy Piersall has never had another breakdown since 1952, though his antics over the more than fifty years following his Westborough hospitalization reflect the personality of a chronically unstable man—squirting a water pistol into an umpire's face; engaging in war dances in the outfield as a Cleveland Indian after being traded from the Red Sox to distract former teammate Ted Williams; charging into the bleachers in pursuit of a heckling fan; going out to the monuments at Yankee Stadium and "talking" to Babe Ruth; running around the bases backward after hitting his 100th career homer as a New York Met in 1963; wearing a Beatles wig in the outfield throughout an entire game; and becoming an outspoken (and, therefore, short-termed) Chicago White Sox broadcaster prone to criti-

After recovering from his nervous breakdown, Jimmy Piersall became an accomplished major league player, making the American League All-Star team in 1954 and 1956, and winning Gold Gloves as an outfielder in 1958 and 1961.

cizing his employer's team.

Today, he lives in Chicago and winters in Arizona with his third wife, still makes radio appearances, and spends his leisure time fishing, finding a semblance of peace in solitude. Commenting on the pride he takes in being alone he had said, "I have not made an awful lot of friends in my lifetime, but my dad told me that if you have too many friends, you become a follower."

———————

In the mid-seventies, former American Poet Laureate Donald Hall waxed eloquent in his essay, "Fathers Playing Catch with Sons," weaving throughout its thirty-nine pages the words that track his title.

"My father and I played catch as I grew up. Like so much else between fathers and sons, playing catch was tender and tense at the same time. He wanted to play with me. He wanted me to be good. He seemed to *demand* that I be good.

"Baseball is fathers and sons playing catch, lazy and murderous, wild and uncontrolled, the profound archaic song of birth, growth, age, and death. The diamond encloses what we are.

"Baseball is fathers and sons playing catch, the long arc of the years between.

"Baseball is continuous, like nothing else among American things, an endless game of repeated summers, joining the long generations of all the fathers and all the sons."

The Mantles and Piersalls played father-son catch for the better part of twenty years. Theirs was not tender or lazy, but tense, murderous and controlled. The game became too important, the sole basis by which a son could please his dad, and could only do that by ignoring everything else in life except pushing himself beyond normal limits to a major league level of excellence.

Throughout the game that consumed their lives, there was birth, growth, age, and death, in a long continuous arc that joined these fathers and sons, yet at least partially destroyed them, because it produced too much intensity, too many hard looks, and too few words of love and encouragement.

Early in his book, *Fear Strikes Out,* Jim Piersall wrote a sentence that speaks volumes to fathers and sons, regardless of whether they play baseball. "There is no better therapy than understanding." Through electroshock, medication, and psychiatrists, Jimmy began to find understanding in his relationship with his dad in 1952 at the age of twenty-two. At the Betty Ford Center, disconnected from the crutch and clutches of alcohol, a sixty-two year old Mickey Mantle finally achieved peace with Mutt in 1994, more than forty years after his father's death.

———

These stories of two families demonstrate to the melancholy man in the bar's dark corner and to everyone else that baseball can bring generations together and it can tear them apart. Its impact is unpredictable, and even when they play it well, a man playing the game with his boy does not provide a quick fix for long term harmony, regardless of whether they live in Commerce, Oklahoma, or Waterbury, Connecticut, or anywhere in between.

LIFE

Brazen Empire of Crime, PART II **HOW THE MOB MUSCLES INTO YOUR DAILY LIFE**

The Frenzied Pennant Race

Carl Yastrzemski, Boston's slugger, singles against Chicago

SEPTEMBER 8 · 1967 · 35¢

Carl Yastrzemski made New England's Impossible Dream come true in his Triple Crown season of 1967.

CHAPTER TWO

YAZ AND THE IMPOSSIBLE DREAM
Remembering Baseball at its Best

Growing up, every Boomer baseball fan had a favorite big league ballplayer. Yankee fans had Mickey Mantle and Roger Maris, Detroit had Al Kaline, Pittsburgh had Roberto Clemente, the Giants had Willie Mays, and the Braves had Hank Aaron. For those who grew up in New England and those having "Boston" as a last name, that favorite ballplayer was Carl Yastrzemski. Thank goodness, we rarely had to spell his last name, and could get by using "Yaz," nickname for the man who lifted our beloved franchise up onto his very medium-sized shoulders, and transformed the Boston Red Sox into winners.

In 1989, my desire to write about baseball history popped out from some deep place inside my subconscious when my wife, Claire, and I traveled to Cooperstown, New York, with our friends Peter and Liz Haveles for the induction of Carl Yastrzemski into the National Baseball Hall of Fame. Yaz had been my ballplaying hero since childhood when, in the summer of 1960, his Topps rookie card was among the first I ever collected in my rookie season as a fan. That card is still on display today in my law office.

My traveling buddy, Peter Haveles (a friend who had once been a worthy high school debate opponent), grew up in Brookline, Massachusetts, which by birthright necessitated his becoming a passionate Red Sox fan. Given all that Carl Yastrzemski had done to change the Bosox fortunes for the good, beginning with the 1967 Impossible Dream season, Peter and I made a pact while college dormitory roommates in Austin during the summer of 1974 that when Yaz got into the Baseball Hall of Fame (regardless of what year that might be), we would be there to see him enter into Cooperstown, not knowing his induction year would coincide with the Hall of Fame's

NATIONAL BASEBALL HALL OF FAME LIBRARY, COOPERSTOWN, NEW YORK

At Yaz's 1989 Hall of Fame induction, Commissioner Bart Giamatti savored the glorious 1967 season with the words, "I remember it well."

celebration of its first half-century as well as Yastrzemski's own fiftieth birthday.

Going to Cooperstown changed my life. Before the July 1989 Induction Weekend, I had never written anything for publication about baseball. Since leaving the village nineteen years ago, as my work schedule as a lawyer has permitted, I have written about the game on a regular basis.

At the induction ceremony, Yastrzemski's speech matched the way he always played the game—no subtlety and straight from the gut—and confirmed the wisdom behind our decision to honor our college commitment, and stop our busy lives that summer to travel across the country for Yaz's big day at the Hall. Carl communicated what we already knew as to why he had been our favorite player throughout his career.

> Why am I here in Cooperstown? I was never blessed with superb physical strength. I had to work twice as long and twice as hard as many of my peers....
>
> I stand before you today and can tell you honestly that every day I put on that Red Sox uniform I gave 100 percent of myself. I treated it with dignity and respect in deference to our fans, and my high regard for my teammates, coaches, and management. Anything less would not have been worthy of me, anything more would not have been possible ... The race doesn't always belong to the swift ... It belongs rather to those who run the race, stay the course, and fight the good fight.

In the year following his entry into the Hall of Fame, in a more expanded format, Yaz acknowledged his extreme dedication to the game in his autobiography, *Yaz: Baseball, the Wall, and Me* (Doubleday, 1990) (co-authored by Gerald Eskinazi). Throughout the book, he admitted with brutal honesty, "I got the most out of my ability through just hard work, hard work, hard work ... I was so intent on my next at-bat, my next play, my next throw, that the fun of what I had just done never lingered more than minutes or hours.... I could never leave the game at the ballpark. I had to take it home with me. Even when I was eating with my family, even though I was talking to them, I wasn't really talking to them. I was thinking about the game coming up ... I was just so intense. That's why I never enjoyed it."

ESPN commentator Tim Kurkjian has often said, "Baseball is a hard game played by hard men." No one ever played it harder than Carl Yastrzemski. It was Yaz's 23-year, hard-nosed intensity, total commitment marathon that inspired Peter Haveles and me to pay tribute (along with our long-suffering wives and tens of thousands of Red Sox fans) in July

1989 when our favorite player, from the time we were in first grade until the time we were both well into our careers as practicing lawyers—who had permanently lifted up our favorite team on his very normal-sized shoulders—finally received his plaque at Cooperstown.

Thirteen years after that trip to Cooperstown, in 2002, I had the privilege of writing the segment on Yaz for *The Scribner Encyclopedia of American Lives: Sports Figures.* Upon receiving the assignment, I took responsibility for describing in essay form exactly what it was that made Carl Yastrzemski so special for people like Peter Haveles and me and every red-blooded Baby Boomer baseball fan of the Boston Red Sox. Here is that essay, which I have enlarged in scope for purposes of this book.

Born on August 22, 1939, Carl Michael Yastrzemski grew up on a 70-acre potato farm in a Polish-dominated community near Bridgehampton, New York, where from the time he could first remember, he aspired to become a big league baseball player. His father, Carl Sr., had been an outstanding player, good enough to draw the attention of Dodger and Cardinal scouts, but in the Great Depression passed on the insecurity of pursuing a baseball career so he could start his family with his wife, Hedwig, and make a living in the potato fields.

As a boy, Carl played baseball for his hometown team in the early days of Little League,[1] but his real competition came from being the youngest member of his father's semipro Bridgehampton White Eagles (Carl Sr. played shortstop, with his son, Carl, at second base, and the rest of the team's roster made up of uncles and cousins), who gained regional recognition for their winning record and aggressive style of play. To insure success in the midst of competing against full-blown adults, young Carl prided himself on practicing baseball every day of the year, swinging a lead bat at a ball hanging in the family barn during winter months (which he displayed decades later in a national television commercial for Miller beer).

Such a daily commitment to baseball throughout his childhood and adolescence set the stage for high school heroics. As a star pitcher and shortstop at Bridgehampton High School, Carl hit .650 his senior year

[1] Entering the Hall of Fame in 1989, Yaz became the first former Little Leaguer to be inducted into Cooperstown.

NATIONAL BASEBALL HALL OF FAME LIBRARY, COOPERSTOWN, NEW YORK

Struggling at the start of his first season, Yaz got into a groove in July 1961 after a pep talk from Ted Williams.

(including an amazing streak of 15 consecutive hits), led his team to its second consecutive county championship, and attracted the attention of big league scouts. When teams failed to meet Carl Sr.'s demand of a $100,000 bonus for his son, Carl entered the University of Notre Dame in 1957 on a combined baseball and basketball[2] scholarship.

After Carl's freshman year at South Bend, the Boston Red Sox capitulated to his dad's terms, making the eighteen-year-old phenom a genuine bonus baby, as he signed in the summer of 1958 for $108,000, a guaranteed two-year minor league contract, and an agreement that the team would fund the balance of his college education costs.

Despite his modest size (5'11", 160 lbs. when he signed),[3] Yastrzemski's minor league performance measured up to Boston's high

---

2 Carl averaged 34 points a game in his senior year at Bridgehampton High.

3 In his autobiography, Yaz notes, "My size has always been my obsession....When Red Sox general manager Joe Cronin heard the team had signed the big bonus contract with me, he came over to see what he had bought. The first thing Cronin said—and I could never forget it—was 'We're paying this kind of money for this guy?' I guess he expected somebody six-two and 210 pounds to walk in."

expectations, hitting .377 and becoming the Carolina League's Most Valuable Player for Class A Raleigh in 1959, and then .339 for AAA Minneapolis in 1960 where Carl changed positions from second base to left field and proceeded to lead the league with 18 outfield assists, as the Red Sox groomed him to patrol the Green Monster and replace the recently retired Ted Williams for the start of the 1961 season.

Early comparisons with the legendary Williams (whose rookie year of 1939 coincided with the year Yaz was born) proved troubling to Boston's rookie outfielder as he struggled throughout the first half of this first season. A weekend meeting in July with baseball's Splendid Splinter arranged by Red Sox owner Tom Yawkey at Carl's request (where Ted Williams instilled confidence in the young player, "You look good swinging. Think of the count. Be aggressive. Don't let anyone ever change your swing."), caused the twenty-one-year-old Yastrzemski to regain his confidence, hit over .300 the last two months of the '61 season, and finish with 80 RBIs and a respectable .266 average. In the final game of Boston's 1961 schedule, playing left field for the Red Sox, Yaz witnessed Roger Maris break Babe Ruth's single season home run record by driving his 61st home run of the season over Yankee Stadium's rightfield fence off Bosox righthander Tracy Stallard.[4]

From 1962 to 1966, Carl proved to be a solid but unspectacular player on some truly dismal Red Sox teams,[5] leading the American League in doubles three times, making three All-Star teams, winning his first AL batting title (.321) in 1963, but never hitting more than 20 homers. When each season ended, Yaz worked toward fulfilling the promise made to his father of becoming the first member of the Yastrzemski family ever to earn a college degree. Finally, in the spring of 1966, the young ballplayer received his bachelor of science degree from Merrimack College in Andover, Massachusetts, but then under-performed that summer after his graduation, hitting only .278 after never hitting less than .289 in his prior four seasons.

With no college classes to fill his time after the '66 season, and recognizing he lacked the strength and stamina to withstand the rigors of 162 games each summer, Yastrzemski committed himself during that

4 Maris hit his 61st homer on October 1, 1961. That day, as a big-time Maris fan, the author celebrated a joyous eighth birthday.

5 In the 10-team American League during those five seasons, Boston finished in 9th place twice, 8th place twice, and 7th place once.

off season to a rigorous winter conditioning program (90 minutes/day, six days/week, of sprinting, lifting weights, climbing ropes, doing chin-ups, and jumping rope) under former Hungarian Olympics coach Gene Berde who ran the health club at the Colonial Country Club in Wakefield, Massachusetts.

By the time spring training started in February 1967, Carl felt such confidence in his newly developed strength, quickness, and endurance that he abandoned the gap hitter batting style of his first six big league seasons and dedicated himself to becoming a pull hitter with an authentic power stroke, believing he might finally have the capacity to become as productive a hitter as the great Ted Williams. His confidence surge that spring was such that Yaz confided to Red Sox third base coach Ed Popowski he thought he had a shot at a Triple Crown—not nearly the preposterous boast it now seems in light of Frank Robinson's having won the American League Triple Crown the year before in 1966.

After receiving a tip in May from Red Sox hitting coach Bobby Doerr to hold his hands higher all the way up to his left ear, Yaz almost single-handedly made the difference in changing Boston's fortunes, keeping the Cinderella team in the pennant race from April to October through his sensational offensive and defensive play—outrunning line drives to make diving catches, playing balls hit off the Green Monster like Horowitz once played a Steinway, throwing out runners at home with his cannon-arm, driving in crucial runs in tight games, stealing a base when needed, encouraging his teammates with batting tips and clubhouse pranks—Yaz did it *all* in 1967.

In the process of performing baseball miracles on a daily basis, Yaz became a national celebrity, making the September 8, 1967, cover of *Life* magazine and the October 2, 1967, cover of *Newsweek*. His game-winning plays proved so consistently inspirational that they prompted Boston radio broadcaster Jess Cain to sing "Carl (pronounced "Kahl" with a Boston brogue) Yastrzemski, Carl Yastrzemski" on his show every morning from mid-summer till season's end to the tune of Handel's *Hallelujah Chorus*.

As the 1967 American League pennant race went down to the wire, and the Twins, Tigers, White Sox, and Red Sox stayed within three games of each other all the way to the end, 15 lead changes took place in the season's final 27 games. During that span, Carl Yastrzemski hit .417 with 26 RBIs, and scored 24 runs. At the wire in the final 12 games,

AP IMAGES

"Who is more heroic than Yastrzemski? He seems to have stepped out of the pages of adolescent fiction." — sportswriter Bill Reynolds.

Yaz went 23 for 44, and drove in 16 runs. Orioles third baseman Brooks Robinson marveled at Yaz's powerful finish as the season progressed: "He seems to get stronger every week."

With Boston needing to win its last two games of the season against Minnesota to stay in the hunt for the pennant, Carl Yastrzemski led the Bosox to victories in both afternoon do-or-die contests at Fenway Park, going 7 for 8 (including hits in his final 6 at-bats of the season), finally clinching the pennant on the evening of October 1, 1967, when California beat Detroit 8-5, knocking the Tigers out of a potential first place tie with Boston in the league's final game of the season.[6]

The overachieving Red Sox then took the star-laden St. Louis Cardinals to seven games in the 1967 World Series as Yastrzemski hit .400 with 10 hits, 3 HRs and 5 RBIs. In the Fall Classic, however, Boston had no answer for either Bob Gibson (who pitched and won 3 complete games, giving up a total of 3 runs), or Lou Brock (who stole 7 bases and hit .414) as the Cards ultimately prevailed to win the Series. Even in defeat, however, Yaz's star continued to shine. *Sports Illustrated* described it: "In the last game of the Series, with the Sox hopelessly behind, Yastrzemski came up in the ninth and singled sharply. The crowd in Boston stood and roared its acclaim because, more than anyone else, Carl Yastrzemski still believed in the dream."

After the 1967 season ended, with his Triple Crown final numbers ending up at .326, 44 HRs,[7] and 121 RBIs, honors poured in for the Red Sox hero, including American League Most Valuable Player, *Sports Illustrated's* Sportsman of the Year, and Hickock Belt winner (given annually to the world's greatest professional athlete). Red Sox manager Dick Williams later said of Yastrzemski's Triple Crown season, "In my fifty-odd years in baseball, I never saw another player have the kind of year Yaz had for me in 1967. Running, throwing, hitting, hitting with power ... he did it all."

Journalists waxed eloquent about his performance. In its October 2, 1967, Yastrzemski cover story, *Newsweek* ended the article reporting on the reward Yaz gave sports fans that summer: "They have witnessed the drama of an athlete under incessant pressure, responding with the

---

6 October 1, 1967, was the author's deliriously ecstatic 14th birthday.

7 Teammate George Scott later commented on the timeliness of Yastrzemski's home runs in 1967: "Yaz hit 44 homers that year and 43 of them meant something big for the team. Every time we needed a big play, the man stepped up and got it done."

finest within him." Naming Yaz its 1967 Sportsman of the Year, *Sports Illustrated* explained the reason for its choice: "Nobody in sport in 1967 played any game with greater overall excellence, verve, and dedication than Carl Yastrzemski, no one excited the imagination more, and no one carried out the dramatic promise that is inherent in every com- petitive sport more completely."

Yaz never had a blow-the-doors-off MVP season again after '67. Teammate Rico Petrocelli explained why in his recent book, *Tales from the Impossible Dream Red Sox* (Sports Publishing, 2007): "After 1967, teams stopped pitching to Yaz. They'd just walk him because after Tony C went down with his eye injury, we never had a real big threat to bat behind him."

For the balance of his career from 1968 to 1983, Carl Yastrzemski maintained a steady pace of greatness—winning the American League batting title (his third) in 1968; losing the batting title by .0003 to Alex Johnson in 1970; being a key member of the Red Sox 1975 pennant winning team[8] (with Yaz hitting .455 in that year's ALCS, and then .310 in the Series, giving him a career .369 batting average in post-season play); being named to 18 All-Star teams; winning 7 Gold Gloves while leading AL outfielders in assists 7 times;[9] leading the league in on-base-percentage 5 times (for those with the *Moneyball* statistical bent); setting a league record for career games played (3308) due to his amazing durability, going on the disabled list exactly one time (for one month) in his career, and averaging 144 games per year over the course of 23 seasons; and ending his career as the first American League player to have achieved both of the two premier offensive career milestones—3000 hits and 400 home runs. For these achievements, Carl Yastrzemski was a first-ballot selection for the National Baseball Hall of Fame in 1989, receiving 94% support from the Baseball Writers of America, the sixth highest total ever received at that time.

For almost a quarter century, Yaz proved that a normal-sized person (5'11", whose weight ranged from 160 to 182 over the course of 23 years) could become an elite baseball player through hard work, intensity, and

8 The '75 Bosox lost to Cincinnati's Big Red Machine in the seven game World Series, best remembered for its Game Six, arguably the greatest baseball game ever played, that ended with Carlton Fisk's 12th inning home run hitting Fenway's leftfield foul pole.

9 In his autobiography, Yaz said he would have won more outfield assists titles, but opposing teams simply stopped running on his deadly throwing arm.

sheer determination, endearing himself to an entire generation of Baby Boomer New Englanders as the game's ultimate working man hero. *Boston Globe* sportswriter Peter Gammons put the final touch on Carl Yastrzemski's storied career concluding a column after his final game, "He was never Ted, only Yaz; never celluloid, only calloused flesh."

Today, Boston fans can still boast that over the course of forty-four years (1939-1983), they had the privilege of watching back-to-back baseball legends play the game at its highest level—with Ted Williams as the last major league player to hit .400 in a season, and Carl Yastrzemski as the last guy to win the Triple Crown. Though Williams is undoubtedly the greatest hitter in Bosox history (and arguably in baseball history), Yaz is clearly the greatest all-around player the Red Sox have ever had.

As portrayed in the foregoing essay, Yaz became a superstar once and forever by leading the Boston Red Sox to the American League pennant in 1967, removing them that season from the pits of the AL's second division, and causing them all at once to become one of baseball's elite teams. The '67 season caused attendance at Fenway Park to soar—more than doubling from 811,172 in '66 to 1,727,832 in '67, essentially staying at that attendance level for awhile, and then annually blowing past the 2,000,000 per season mark in recent years. As to the extent of the surge in '67, a mere 8,324 fans showed up for 1967's Opening Day in Boston, and by season's end, Fenway was selling out every game to 35,000+ fans, while turning away disappointed multitudes.

In the eyes of baseball aficionados with a sense of history, the year 1967 became the time when New England (at last) could embrace a team that in the prior 16 seasons had never gotten closer to winning a pennant than being 11 games out, but kick-started itself into becoming a perennial first division team (that thereafter maintained a winning record for 16 consecutive seasons) by defying the 100-1 odds set by Las Vegas bookies before the '67 season started, coming back from its 72-90 ninth place finish in 1966, and becoming the first Red Sox team to win the American League pennant since 1946. With the momentum that began in 1967, the Bosox proceeded to challenge for the AL flag again in 1972, 1977, and 1982; lost a one game playoff to the Yankees in 1978,[10] and then again won the pennant in 1975. Twenty years later in an interview with Red

10 In the game immortalized by Bucky Dent's pop fly home run over Yaz's head and the Green Monster on October 1, 1978—the author's totally despondent twenty-fifth birthday.

Sox broadcaster Ken Coleman, Carl Yastremski accurately reflected, "1967 not only turned on the fans, it turned the whole Red Sox organization around. We became winners instead of losers. We expected to go out and win, instead of lose. Our thinking changed."

Boston Globe columnist Bob Ryan agreed with Yaz. At the Boston Baseball Writers Dinner in January 2006, he advised the crowd, "Everything the Red Sox are today, all the sellouts, stems from 1967. That team can never be honored enough. Nineteen-sixty-seven is the great dividing line in Red Sox history."

Dan Shaughnessy of the *Globe* even exempted the '67 team from being victims of the Curse of the Bambino, in his book by that title (Dutton 1990):

> The Red Sox have blown many pennant races, lost the only two playoff games in American League history, dropped an American League Championship Series in four straight, and lost the seventh game of the World Series four times since Ruth was sold to the Yankees seventy years ago. In all these disappointments, only the 1967 team is immune from criticism, ridicule, and regret. They are spared the second-guessers and the harsh historians who have scrutinized and plagued all other Sox teams since 1918. Nobody held the ball, nobody tripped rounding third base, nobody threw an ill-timed wild pitch, nobody made a hideous and regrettable hunch, nobody let a ground ball slip between his legs and into history.
>
> It was okay for the 1967 Red Sox to lose the seventh game of the World Series because they'd already performed the great service of bringing a moribund franchise back to life and registering millions of new members to the party of the long-suffering.

In the last twenty years, several books have been devoted to describing a single year in baseball, most notably David Halberstam's two bestsellers about 1949 and 1964, Robert Creamer's profile of 1941, Red Barber's "catbird seat" view of 1947, Cait Murphy's superb recent account of the "Crazy '08" season, and (last but hopefully not least) a volume by a Texan who assessed the events of *1939: Baseball's Tipping Point.*[11]

For Baby Boomers with any kind of Boston connection, however, no single season can ever compare with 1967, when the Red Sox transformed the residents of the northeast into the Men and Women of La Mancha, causing them to sing and then live the Impossible Dream. A quarter century after the fact, in 1992, Providence sportswriter Bill Reynolds wrote a fabulous book dedicated to that most critical year in Bosox history, *Lost Summer: The '67 Red Sox and the Impossible Dream* (Warner Books, 1992). I had the pleasure of reviewing it for *Elysian Fields Quarterly*, and turned the review into my own personal walk down Memory Lane. For purposes of this book (as with the Scribner Sports Encyclopedia essay), I have substantially expanded the piece.

———————

At the July 1989 Hall of Fame induction ceremonies, Commissioner Bart Giamatti concluded his introduction of Carl Yastrzemski by describing his leadership of the 1967 Impossible Dream Boston Red Sox, then turned to Yaz, smiled, and said quietly, "I remember it well."

In Danielle Weil's coffee table book of photographs, *Baseball: The Perfect Game* (Rizzoli, 1992), David Halberstam's introduction traces the role baseball has played throughout his life—childhood in the Bronx with his father listening to games on the radio, going to Yankee Stadium, and cheering for Joe DiMaggio; cub reporter in the Congo, keeping track through telex of Mantle's and Maris' pursuit of Ruth's single season home run record; established writer sitting with Phil Rizzuto in the press box of the House That Ruth Built; and finally passing the baseball torch to his then eight-year-old daughter. Halberstam observes that in 1967, at the age of thirty-two, with his heart and mind filled with Vietnam melancholia, "the only thing that cheers me is the stunning personal exhibition that Yaz is making as he leads the Red Sox to the pennant ... Yaz reminds me that there are things about America I still love and that all of this depression, this terribly sad war, will someday pass."

11 *1939: Baseball's Tipping Point* (Bright Sky Press, 2005), by Talmage "Mr. Red Sox" Boston.

For that unfortunate soul not tuned into 1967 American League baseball, and, thus, not having that summer's pennant race permanently etched into his psyche, sportswriter Bill Reynolds of the *Providence Journal-Bulletin* has written an account which preserves for all time the reawakening of baseball in New England throughout that Impossible Dream season, marked by Dick Williams' no-nonsense leadership, Jim Lonborg's inside pitching dominance,[12] Tony Conigliaro's fastball-in-the-face tragedy, and Yaz's Triple Crown. Reynolds' book brings the story back to life for anyone seeking either to refresh his or her memory of that glorious time or to learn why people of Giamatti's and Halbertstam's intellectual horsepower have remembered it so well with such fondness for so long.

Throughout *Lost Summer*, Reynolds puts the baseball season into 1967's societal context—the Vietnam War and its resulting domestic upheaval; the slow progress made in the Civil Rights movement; the widening of the drug culture; and the movies, television shows, and songs of the time. He recognizes that "sports is one of the last arenas unaffected by all this change"—and maybe that's what made the year's American League pennant race so special in that era—giving the American people something to cheer about when nothing else worked to lift us up at that difficult time in our history.

Bill Reynolds also puts 1967 into its baseball context—no free agency, low salaries,[13] no DH, no league championship series, no cable television, and the most expensive ticket at Fenway Park costs $3.75. Above all, "It's still a time when we know very little about our sports heroes other than what they do on the field." In a very real baseball sense, at least, those were the good ol' days.

Reynolds' prologue establishes him as a Hall of Fame baseball fan. Explaining the origin of the book, exactly a quarter century before its publication, his childhood love for the game reawakened as a college junior when, on the afternoon of April 14, 1967, he accidentally found himself listening to the radio when the Red Sox' Billy Rohr (in his first major league game) pitched an almost-no-

---

12 Reynolds reports that Lonnie put a notch on the back of his glove for every batter he hit with a pitch. By the end of the '67 season, his 19 notches led the American League.

13 The total payroll for the '67 Red Sox team was $800,000, with Yastrzemski's $58,000 the highest salary.

hitter at Yankee Stadium against Whitey Ford.[14] With that single dramatic game, the author's enthusiasm for Boston Red Sox baseball ignited, which he can now explain in its full symbolic glory.

> By the end of the year, Rohr will be long gone from the Red Sox; the highlight of his career will be this afternoon in Yankee Stadium. But in a sense, this early-season game played before a sparse crowd in Yankee Stadium on this cold, raw April afternoon, comes to resemble that season that will forever be known as the "Impossible Dream," the season that becomes, as someone once put it, the time everyone forgot about the human race and worried about the pennant race. It is a complete surprise; it's an incredible, memorable performance by a player who isn't supposed to be able to deliver it; and, in the end, it just misses being perfect.

After the landmark game, re-energized Red Sox fan Reynolds finds himself comparing where he is as a student in his early twenties to where Tony C is as a major league star in his early twenties, and how with his Bosox passions now flowing freely, he can feel Conigliaro's success has "somehow become my success," admitting to the reader what is known but rarely acknowledged, "No one ever said being a fan makes any sense."

Because 1967 made Boston Red Sox fans believe in Impossible Dream heroes, the author thankfully preserves them as such. Manager Dick Williams led his team in a manner that was tough but fair, coupled with a timely sense of humor. Ultimate Cy Young Award Winner Jim Lonborg and Tony C (until August 18) have career seasons in the midst of fulfilling their Army Reserve obligations, while five other Red Sox players serve in the Reserves that summer as well. Quiet midseason acquisition Jerry Adair (who is part Cherokee Indian) plays better than he ever did at Baltimore and keeps coming through at crunch time offensively and defensively. Owner Tom Yawkey comes out of his

---

14 With two outs in the bottom of the ninth inning, Elston Howard singled to right field for the Yanks' only hit of the game. Four months later, Howard would get traded to the Red Sox and become their catcher in the pennant race's most crucial games.

twenty-year seclusion to rejoin the team in the locker room and on the road. Rico Petrocelli loses his insecurities and becomes an All-Star. George Scott and Joe Foy survive Williams' constant baiting and the battle of the waistline bulge by producing their best seasons, and along with rookie centerfielder Reggie Smith, reliever John Wyatt, and catcher Elston Howard (who joined the team in August), prove that New England can finally and fully embrace African-American ballplayers, eight years following Pumpsie Green's entry into the Red Sox lineup in 1959, which allowed Boston to become the last major league baseball team to integrate.

Above all other Red Sox, Yaz establishes himself as the undisputed leader and best all-around player, as artfully explained by gifted author Bill Reynolds:

> Who is more heroic than Yastrzemski? He seems to have stepped out of the pages of adolescent fiction. He gets the big hit. He makes the big play in the field. He says the right things afterward. In this age of youthful rebellion, he is a clean-cut athlete, a throwback to a simpler era. And when we appear to be losing in Vietnam, when for the first time there are doubts about the country's ability to get things done, Yaz always delivers. He's become a traditional hero in every sense of the word, has become almost mythic. Like all mythic figures he only seems to exist on the field. We know little about his life off the field. We know little about his innermost thoughts. We don't know what he thinks about hippies, or "Sgt. Pepper's Lonely Hearts Club Band," or the war, or riots in the cities, or any of the things that confuse the rest of us. He seems to come alive only on the field, this place where he continues to do heroic things.

With a dynamic team of young stalwarts (Yaz, Tony C, Petrocelli, Scott, Foy, Mike Andrews, and Reggie Smith), veterans acquired at mid-season who stabilized the chemistry (Adair, Elston Howard, pitcher Gary Bell, and outfielder Ken Harrelson), an ace (Lonborg), and a solid

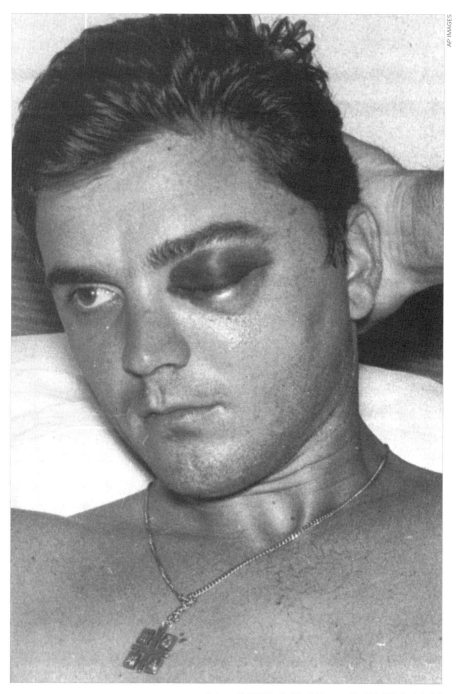

On August 18, 1967, Tony Conigliaro's left eye got hit with Jack Hamilton's fastball.
The injury derailed Tony C's career, but did not end Boston's pennant run.

closer (Wyatt), who all responded to skipper Dick Williams' whip, and after being in fifth place, six games out of first place, at the All-Star break, the team exploded during the second half of the '67 season (in his 1990 memoirs Yaz described the second half of the '67 season as his "personal crusade … when I finally had a reason to go all out, all the time.") with a .617 winning percentage, winning 50 of their final 81 games, including 10 in a row in late July, and 7 in a row in late August. Detroit, Chicago, and Minnesota, however, would simply not go away. On September 7, 1967, the four teams were essentially tied for first place, separated collectively by a winning percentage of .000867 (the difference in being 78-61 and 79-62), and were still separated by only 1½ games on September 28. Going into the season's final day, only Chicago had been eliminated from the chance to win the pennant.

After Boston wins the American League pennant in a photo finish captured in the end by Red Sox ace Jim Lonborg being carried off the field by hundreds of maniacal Red Sox fans after beating the Twins in the season's finale, the year ends with Game Seven of the World Series, when a rested Bob Gibson beats a wearied Lonborg (pitching on only two days rest), and Yaz tells Lonnie in the aftermath, "You can't always put your heart in your arm." With that Fall Classic's negative outcome, alas, in 1967 the Impossible Dream proved to be Impossible.

Bill Reynolds' epilogue confirms that the Impossible Dream ended in 1967. Tony Conigliaro's loss of eyesight (from being beaned on August 18, 1967) ultimately became permanent, leading him into a downward physical spiral and early death. Lonborg broke his leg after the World Series and never regained his Cy Young level of command. Only late-season acquisition Ken Harrelson ever duplicated even for one season his '67 achievements. Elston Howard (another mid-season pick-up), Jerry Adair, Joe Foy, and Don McMahon all died young, in addition to Tony C. George Scott still waits for a baseball job that does not come.

On the back of *Lost Summer*'s dust jacket is an evaluation from noted historian Doris Kearns Goodwin, an articulate and passionate baseball fan if there ever was one: "A TREASURE … Written with such grace and humanity that it reads like a novel."[15]

15 After Reynolds' book's release in 1992, Ms. Kearns Goodwin would become one of the leading commentators in 1994 for Ken Burns' *Baseball* documentary that ran on PBS, and later write her own classic baseball book, *Wait Till Next Year* (Simon & Schuster, 1998).

In 1967, Jim Lonborg won the Cy Young Award and 2 games in the World Series before falling to Lou Brock, Bob Gibson and the Cards in Game Seven.

Ms. Kearns Goodwin's sentiments about Bill Reynolds' account of the 1967 season match my own. Despite growing up in Texas, but having "Boston" as my last name, I have been a Red Sox fan ever since I can remember. The first newspaper I ever read was a September 1960 issue of the *Houston Post* bearing a wirephoto of Ted Williams in the sports section, promoting my family's last name across the front of his Red Sox "away" uniform. Then and there a decision was made by a six-year-old baseball fan. From that day forward, this Boston boy would always root for the Bosox.

In 1967, approaching the age of fourteen, my family lived in Corpus Christi, Texas, a city of 250,000 people that not only had no major league baseball team—it had no minor league team.[16]

Life and *Sports Illustrated* magazines, Associated Press daily newspaper accounts appearing in the *Corpus Christi Caller-Times*, and weekend network television brought to life that unforgettable season to those of us geographically separated from major league ballparks.

For years, until it faded badly, the (matted and framed) September 8, 1967, *Life* magazine cover of Carl Yastrzemski hung on my law office

16 Thankfully, for the cultural enrichment of South Texas, Nolan Ryan finally brought minor league baseball back to Corpus Christi in 2005, with the arrival of the Corpus Christi Hooks, his AA franchise in the Texas League.

wall, with Yaz running to first base bearing the look of an almost crazed yet totally focused man, legging out one more base hit in order to lift up the Red Sox to one more come-from-behind, bite-off-all-your-fingernails victory. *Life* appropriately entitled its cover story "The Frenzied Pennant Race."

NBC television brought into our home that final Bosox series with Minnesota on September 30 and October 1, where the seemingly out-manned Sox had to win both games from the Killebrew-Allison-Oliva-Kaat Twins, or else be denied the opportunity of playing in the World Series. In those two dramatic victories, Yaz just kept on making the big hits, going 7 for 8, and simply refusing to let the Impossible Dream die.

Just like Commissioner Giamatti, "I remember it well," and Bill Reynolds' book cements those magnificent memories for all time.

The closest I ever got to Carl Yastrzemski in person was at the 1989 induction ceremony in Cooperstown where my lawn chair rested about forty yards away from the podium where he spoke. Later that year, knowing of my fascination for Yaz, a friend in Connecticut sent me the video about Yaz's career that was produced with his cooperation and sold throughout New England. One comment from the Hall of Famer stayed with me from his on-camera interview. When asked what he missed most about baseball after his playing days ended, Yaz answered with certainty, "I miss the head-to-head competition between pitcher and batter. There's nothing in life I've found that can measure up to the thrill of that competition." Maybe that's why he ended his memoirs published in 1990 with an account of his last game at Fenway Park in 1983—as if nothing important had happened in his life since his final ballgame.[17]

Since his induction into the National Baseball Hall of Fame, Yaz has maintained a low profile existence—making occasional appearances at card shows and Red Sox fantasy camps, returning rarely to Cooperstown for the induction of others, and mainly staying out of the

[17] His prologue described his Hall of Fame induction, but there is no epilogue to his autobiography.

limelight by concentrating on fishing in his Florida retirement.

Regardless of where he is now personally, long after his baseball career ended, at least for us Baby Boomers who have consistently (and sometimes religiously) cheered for the Bosox over the last several decades, Carl Yastrzemski stands at the top of Red Sox mountain. It was Yaz who delivered the Impossible Dream in 1967, and pushed himself and our beloved Red Sox to a new level of excellence for more than two decades, playing hardball on the field and inside his head at its highest physical and emotional level, fully utilizing his talents and blue collar passions to do his best for his team every single game. A baseball player at the major league level simply cannot perform any better than that.

POSTCRIPT

After the Red Sox lost seven-game World Series in 1967, 1975, and 1986, lost a single game playoff to the Bucky Dent Yankees that kept them out of the '78 Series, and then blew a lead on a Pedro Martinez meltdown in the ninth inning of the final ALCS game (again to the hated Yankees) that kept them out of the 2003 Series, the Curse of the Bambino had become a real live seemingly permanent King Kong-like gorilla on the team's back.

Then along came 2004, when David Ortiz and his Red Sox team-mates finally succeeded in shooting that monkey dead. Like many long-suffering Bosox fans, I *had* to express my feelings in response to this miracle that most diehard Boston fans believed could not possibly happen in anyone's lifetime, and did so for my neighborhood news-paper on November 4, 2004, in a column entitled, "The Worm Has Turned":

Imagine being eighty-six years old, and having nothing great to show for your life. On a few occasions through the years, bad luck seemed to depart, and your fingertips faintly touched the brass ring. But as soon as contact was made, a big monkey came out of the sky, jumped on your back, and in an instant, caused the ring to slip away, allowing someone else to grab it and receive the concomitant riches.

If the reader can visualize that scenario, then he or she must be a Boston Red Sox fan. The greatest Bosox fan in history, former Yale

President and Baseball Commissioner Bart Giamatti, died suddenly from a Pete Rose induced heart attack in 1989. He had seen his team win the American League pennant in 1946, 1967, 1975, and 1986; had seen them extend each of those World Series to the climactic seventh game; and had then seen the Red Sox lose all four Game Sevens.

He had also known them to play one-game playoffs against the Cleveland Indians in 1948 and then the New York Yankees in 1978, after the teams finished the regular season tied and World Series glory was on the lip of the cup. His Red Sox had also lost both of those crucial games, when surprise Bosox starting pitcher Denny Galehouse got hammered by the Tribe in '48 and then Yankee slap singles hitter Bucky Dent lofted a pop fly to left field in the eighth inning of the '78 playoff that somehow sailed over Carl Yastrzemski's head and Fenway Park's Green Monster for the game-winning homer.

Such a lifetime of baseball frustration caused Bart Giamatti to wax eloquent about his beloved bridesmaid ball club. "The Red Sox are an affliction. But even more, the team annually reenacts the fall of humankind. They, more than anybody or anything in our culture, every year re-create the ancient story of admiration, aspiration and expulsion, coherence declining into exile, the story that seems to be a basic story about our human declination." After Boston lost the '86 World Series, Giamatti commented, "Mutability had turned the seasons and translated hope to memory once again."

Then along came the 2004 baseball season, followed by the Division Series, League Championship Series, and World Series. It all ended October 26, with Baseball Commissioner Bud Selig presenting a large trophy to "the 2004 World Champion Boston Red Sox!"

For those of us with graying hair, who have cheered for and had our hopes dashed by this maddeningly cursed team for half a century, Selig's words seemed like a dream come true, an impossible dream that, in our hearts, we knew would never happen. The monkey would always jump on the team's back at crunch time, and the brass ring would always elude our grasp.

Ron Darling, a great major league pitcher in the eighties, grew up in Worcester, Massachusetts, and, therefore, was raised as a rabid Red Sox fan. In 1986, however, Darling found himself as a New York Mets pitcher, facing the Bosox in the World Series, and, of course, beating them in seven games. When the Series ended, a reporter, aware of the

AP IMAGES

October 26, 2004: The Curse of the Bambino dies, and at last there is joy in Mudville for Red Sox Nation.

pitcher's upbringing, asked him how he would have felt if Boston had won the Fall Classic.

Darling, a Yale University graduate, paused and then answered, "If the Boston Red Sox ever win the World Series, it will change the way New England looks at life."

The Red Sox, after eighty-six years of futility, have now won the World Series. The fates have exorcised the Curse of the Bambino. There is joy in Mudville. Hope abounds. Seize the day.

Emancipation Conversation, with Abraham Lincoln on the wall looking over the shoulders of Jackie Robinson and Branch Rickey.

CHAPTER THREE

JACKIE ROBINSON AND BRANCH RICKEY
The Elegant Dance

Jackie Robinson's major league career lasted from 1947 to 1956, meaning most Baby Boomers never actually got to see him play, though we've seen newsreel footage of his daring exploits on the diamond hundreds of times. Despite that unfortunate timing, we have lived our lives hearing the story time and again of how the Great Jackie and Brooklyn Dodgers President Branch Rickey produced, in George Will's words, "the opening salvo in the American Civil Rights Movement."

n 1972, twenty-five years after blazing the trail for minority athletes in the professional team ranks, Jackie Robinson died at the age of fifty-three. The death of his son, Jackie Jr., in a car wreck the year before had broken his heart; diabetes had taken his sight; poor circulation caused doctors to prescribe amputation for his barely shuffling legs; and advanced heart disease and chronic lung disease finally stopped his system. Baseball's guinea pig in Branch Rickey's "Noble Experiment" got old before his time, and his passing confirmed the adage, "Only the good die young."

In life, there is stress in handling day-to-day issues, there is major stress when tragedy strikes, and then there is Jackie Robinson stress when one man carries fifteen million people's hopes on his shoulders.

No one knows why Jackie

Jackie Robinson at the 1972 World Series, exactly nine days before his death.

Robinson's magnificent body degenerated as fast as it did. Maybe compressing the drama of ten lifetimes into one did it. Maybe the extreme heat passing through his unique wiring, which allowed him to withstand constant abuse without ever losing his vital human spark, finally melted down. Maybe advancing civil rights every day for over thirty years in the fields of athletics, the military, business, and politics meant rolling too heavy a rock up too steep a mountain too many times for even "the black Jim Thorpe" to endure.

No one knows what caused Jackie Robinson's rapid physical decline. More notably, no one knows how he was able to do what he did when he was healthy. We just know that in his brief lifetime, he became the most important athlete in history, opening the door for future generations of African-Americans, Latin Americans, and Asians to enjoy the fruits of competing on a level playing field, not just in baseball, but in all professional team sports.

On his tombstone are words from his final autobiography: "A life is not important except in the impact it has on others." Truer words were never spoken. In the end, after all the exhaustive rock rolling, aided by baseball's "Mahatma" Branch Rickey, Jackie Robinson stood at the top of the mountain as the man who made the National Pastime national, and opened the World Series to the world. How Robinson and Rickey did what they did became the most important sports story in the Baby Boomer era.

To understand what Jackie Robinson did for baseball, beginning with his first encounter with Branch Rickey in 1945, requires an understanding of at least an overview of his life before then; that is, what events prepared the game's trailblazer for the road ahead by the time he reached the trail's starting point?

His story began January 13, 1919, when Mallie and Jerry Robinson welcomed their fifth child and fourth son into the world in the hamlet of Cairo, Georgia. Mallie named the baby Jack Roosevelt Robinson in honor of Theodore Roosevelt who had died just a few weeks before, viewed by many African-Americans as their greatest white ally in the national political arena since Abraham Lincoln. Like his namesake,

Teddy Roosevelt achieved success in many fields, had legions of supporters and detractors, and died before reaching old age.

In childhood, Jackie Robinson's mettle was tested early on. Soon after Jackie's birth, father Jerry, a sharecropper, abandoned the family, causing Mallie to move her children across the country to Pasadena, California, where she blazed a trail for the Robinsons on Pepper Street, becoming the first African-Americans to live in the neighborhood. In no time, without provocation, bigots started hurling a steady stream of rocks and racial epithets at the family home. Eight-year-old Jackie Robinson decided he'd had enough, and responded to the attacks by throwing his own rocks and verbal zingers back at the local racist troublemakers, proving at a young age that asserting his civil rights was embedded in his DNA.

While Mallie worked long days as a maid in the Los Angeles area, her unsupervised youngest son soon drifted toward juvenile delinquency, but his propensity for misconduct came to a halt when neighbor Carl Anderson, founder of the first African-American Boy Scout troop in Pasadena, came into the boy's life as his first mentor, taking Jackie under his wing and advising him to disconnect from the Pepper Street Gang if he had aspirations to advance in life. Heeding Anderson's counsel, Jackie started focusing on athletics, left the gang behind, and was soon starring in every sport he played.

Entering Pasadena's John Muir Technical High School in 1935, and weighing 135 pounds, Jackie led the football, basketball, baseball, and track teams with his unique combination of speed, guile, strength, and hand-eye coordination. His confidence in his athletic potential surely grew in 1936 upon brother Mack's winning a silver medal at the Berlin Olympics, finishing a close second in the 200-meter dash to the great Jesse Owens.

After graduating from Muir, Jackie stayed home and pursued higher education at nearby tuition-free Pasadena Junior College where, as on Pepper Street, he again encountered hostility because of his color. Much of the football team at PJC had just left the Oklahoma Dust Bowl during the Great Depression, where they had never had a black teammate before moving to California, and vocalized their desire to keep it that way. Jackie soon emerged as the team's best player, and sensing the bad blood, threatened to transfer to another school if the hostility continued. In a foreshadowing of the 1947 Brooklyn Dodgers' delayed appreciation of Jackie, the Okies quickly changed their attitude, knowing that having Robinson in the lineup enhanced their chances to win games. As the threatened conflict over integration passed before the season's first game, and Jackie reached out to establish better chemistry with his new white teammates (as he would later do with the Dodgers), PJC's squad soon jelled on and off the gridiron.

In his final year of junior college, Jackie was the football team's biggest star in an undefeated season; set the national junior college broad jump record (25' 6½"); led his basketball team in scoring; and hit .417 for the baseball team. His dominant skills in every sporting endeavor soon drew the attention of those major colleges that had already integrated their athletic programs.

Jackie Robinson admitted in a later autobiography that while at PJC, he lost his shyness and, as on Pepper Street, started retaliating whenever and wherever slurs arose, even when the voice of racism came from a policeman. As Jackie got crossways with the Pasadena police force, new mentor Rev. Karl Downs, pastor of the nearby Scott United Methodist Church, entered Robinson's life, calmed the star athlete's outspokenness, deepened his faith, and even got Jackie to teach Sunday school, causing all confrontations with local authorities to stop.

Developing his body into a 175 pound, rock-hard athletic machine at PJC, Jackie Robinson was ready for a national stage, and found it on the UCLA playing fields beginning in 1939. To the extent he needed any additional motivation to concentrate on succeeding as an athlete, his brother Frank Robinson's death in a motorcycle accident during the summer of 1939 caused Jackie to push himself harder in the Bruins' contests as a means of coping with the grief over losing his brother and biggest fan.

Robinson's two years at UCLA were marked by continued athletic success, as he became the first athlete in the school's history to letter in four sports, earning himself the moniker "the black Jim Thorpe" by veteran West Coast sportswriter Vincent X. Flaherty. If the 1940 Olympics had not been canceled because World War II had started on the European front, Robinson likely would have competed for the gold medal in both the broad jump and the decathlon.

As important as providing an opportunity for athletic achievements, UCLA also opened the door to Jackie's finding and successfully wooing the love of his life, Rachel Isum, a beautiful and quietly brilliant

Jackie Robinson— NCAA broad jump champion in 1940.

nursing student, who ultimately became his wife.

Similar to what had occurred on Pepper Street and at Pasadena Junior College, prejudice reared its ugly head at UCLA when Jackie led the Pacific Coast Conference in basketball scoring during both his seasons as a Bruin, yet failed to be named first, second, or even third team All-Conference.

On March 3, 1941, within four months of graduating, Jackie Robinson shocked his family and friends by quitting UCLA. He had never enjoyed the classroom, and at a time when there were precious few black professionals, Jackie saw his only career opportunity to be in the coaching ranks, for which no degree was required. After leaving UCLA, Robinson spent the rest of 1941 working at a National Youth Administration camp in California, and then played semi-pro football in Hawaii until receiving his draft notice shortly after the attack on Pearl Harbor.

Growing up in Pasadena and competing on integrated collegiate athletic teams had certainly helped prepare Jackie Robinson to blaze

NATIONAL BASEBALL HALL OF FAME LIBRARY, COOPERSTOWN, NEW YORK

United States Army Lieutenant Jackie Robinson

baseball's equal opportunity trail, but the hottest crucible for his historic future came from serving in the United States Army during World War II. There, as before, Jackie stood his ground and refused to tolerate bigotry, ever fearless in facing the consequences of his courage.

In the Army, every military unit fielded sports teams, and their *esprit de corps* rose and fell with their won-loss record. At Fort Riley, Kansas, however, where Jackie did his basic training, military leadership maintained strict segregation throughout the post, including on the baseball team. Robinson learned of the discriminatory policy, but decided to stare it in the face and try out for the team. Surprising no one, the officer/ baseball coach refused to give Robinson the chance to compete on his diamond, and the young private reluctantly accepted his fate, knowing he would soon have the chance to get even.[1]

Fort Riley football was different from baseball. With the college game already integrated at an ever increasing number of schools before the war, the Army allowed black soldiers to play for their post football teams. As expected, the head coach invited Pacific Coast Conference star running back Jackie Robinson to play for his team, but to his amazement and that of everyone else at Fort Riley, Jackie refused. If the commanding officers wouldn't allow him to participate in Army baseball, then by golly he sure wouldn't risk his valuable athletic body

---

1 Future Brooklyn Dodger teammate Pete Reiser was present on the day Jackie Robinson learned that he would not be permitted to play on the post's baseball team, and said Jackie's reaction to the news gave the appearance of someone who "swallowed his scream," as detailed in Scott Simon's book, *Jackie Robinson and the Integration of Baseball*, (John Wiley & Sons, 2002).

and make their day by helping them win football games.

More important than the racism in the Army post's athletic program, the "gentlemen's agreement" policy in place at the outset of World War II was that black soldiers who had joined the American military services should not be eligible to become officers, similar to the "gentlemen's agreement" baseball owners had maintained throughout the twentieth century prohibiting African-Americans from playing for their teams.

Establishing himself as a model soldier and expert marksman during basic training, Jackie Robinson easily qualified as being worthy of consideration for the Army's Officer Candidate School (OCS), but as with the baseball team, the army brass initially rejected him. Never one to accept racism without challenge (beginning with his childhood days on Pepper Street), Jackie conceived a plan to move up into the officer ranks by collaborating with his new friend at the post, reigning heavyweight champion Joe Louis, already an American hero before the war by first knocking out German Max Schmeling (Hitler's favorite athlete) and then donating the gate receipts from another fight to the Navy Relief Society.

Together, Robinson and boxing's Brown Bomber obtained the assistance of Louis' friend in the War Department, who strong-armed the "gentlemen's agreement" and succeeded in getting Robinson and a few other qualified African-American soldiers into OCS in January 1943. After successfully finishing his officer training, Second Lieutenant Jackie Robinson was transferred to Fort Hood, Texas, to lead a platoon in tank warfare, where he steadily progressed as an officer until the fateful night of July 6, 1944.

That evening, at approximately 11:00 p.m., Jackie boarded a Fort Hood bus and sat on one of the middle rows beside the light-skinned African-American wife of another officer in his tank battalion. The driver apparently believed Robinson was sitting next to a Caucasian female, and ordered Robinson to move to the back of the bus, which Jackie knew was a violation of a new Army regulation that prohibited segregation on military vehicles. Asserting his rights, and setting the stage eleven years later for Rosa Parks in Montgomery, Alabama, Robinson refused to change his seat, prompting a heated argument with the driver who called Army Police to remove Jackie from the bus for interrogation by a team of officers upon their arrival at Fort Hood's terminal. The questioning produced a disputed account as to how Robinson interacted with his superiors in the aftermath of the bus incident, and caused Army leaders to prosecute him *not* for refusing to move to the back of the bus (since Jackie was clearly within his rights to maintain his seat position under the new regulation), but for the way he acted with disrespect and exhibited willful disobedience to a superior officer during the interrogation that followed his leaving the bus.

In the next four weeks, the story of the circumstances regarding the Army's decision to court-martial former UCLA athletic superstar Jackie Robinson received national attention. At Lieutenant Robinson's direction, word of the improper prosecution arising out of his justified insistence that the Army comply with its own regulations was communicated to the major African-American newspapers, government leaders in Washington, D.C., and the NAACP.

The actual trial of Jackie Robinson lasted over four hours on the afternoon of August 2, 1944. Nine men heard the case, with Jackie needing the votes of six for acquittal. Through the support of three high-ranking officers who served as character witnesses, and Jackie's own testimony explaining his justified outrage over being called a "nigger" by a captain that night, the trial produced a unanimous verdict of "Not Guilty" on all charges. By November, understandably tired of the Army's racism, Jackie Robinson pursued an immediate discharge and succeeded in being "honorably relieved from active duty"(something less than a full-blown honorable discharge) by the Army.[2]

In his final days in the service, Robinson met Ted Alexander, a soldier who had played with the Kansas City Monarchs baseball team in the Negro League before the war and planned to rejoin them after leaving the Army. The $400 a month paid top black ballplayers was well above what Jackie had made playing semi-pro football before the war, the risk of injury in baseball seemed less than in football, and the Monarchs were the league's most financially stable organization. Though baseball had never been Jackie's best sport, playing for the Monarchs seemed his best option upon re-entering civilian life, and would hopefully generate sufficient income to (at last) persuade Rachel he had the wherewithal to support her as his wife.

2 Scott Simon in *Jackie Robinson and the Integration of Baseball* (Wiley, 2002) provided this concise summation of Robinson's military experience: "Robinson, for his part, had experienced only that part of the American military that defended segregation, not the part that battled for freedom."

In recent years, the history of Negro League baseball has been well chronicled in books and documentary films. Off the field, teams traversed the country in undependable buses and found themselves in venues where few restaurateurs and innkeepers allowed black ballplayers to use restrooms and obtain lodging and meals. On the diamond, much like the Harlem Globetrotters in basketball, games played in Negro League baseball focused as much on entertainment as on hard-nosed competition. As far as the strength of teams' financial footing, it was largely touch-and-go, with most Negro League owners being heavily involved in gambling operations.

In that context, Jackie Robinson joined the Kansas City Monarchs and became their starting shortstop and one of their leading hitters in the spring of 1945, five years after playing his last competitive baseball game as a junior at UCLA. His honeymoon with the team didn't last long, however, as his fierce competitive drive clashed with teammates' laid-back and often comedic style. Furthermore, given the vagabond lifestyle, Jackie could see no reason to believe that playing in the Negro Leagues offered any real future, as no one in any big league team's front office appeared a likely candidate to break baseball's color line during his lifetime, particularly after he received only a sham of a tryout with the Boston Red Sox in April 1945 at the behest of crusading African-American journalist Wendell Smith, which ended abruptly just like Robinson's audition for the Fort Riley Post baseball team.[3]

It takes two to tango, and it took two to integrate professional baseball. In the summer of 1945, in the aftermath of confronting racism on Pepper Street, at college, and in the Army, twenty-six year old Jackie Robinson was ready to begin baseball's integration tango. Unfortunately, despite his extensive life-experience preparation and sizable athletic talent, the dance hall's door was locked, and only the top executive for a major league team had the key. Brooklyn Dodgers President Branch Rickey met Jackie Robinson at the door, and in a style evoking synchronized images of Fred Astaire and Ginger Rogers on

---

3 The Red Sox would become the last major league ball club to integrate when Pumpsie Green finally played for the team in 1959. Wall Street Journal reporter and baseball writer Jonathan Eig observed in his book, *Opening Day: The Story of Jackie Robinson's First Season* (Simon & Schuster, 2007), just as Scott Simon did in his 2002 book on Robinson, that since 1946, the Bosox's baseball fortunes may have been harmed more by the curse of not signing Jackie Robinson than the curse of trading "The Bambino," Babe Ruth. Always "one player away," Boston lost Game Seven in the '46, '67, '75, and '86 World Series.

their best day, together they unlocked and opened the door, and advanced the American Civil Rights Movement by combining their strengths in a smooth and elegant dance that lasted five years until Rickey left the Dodgers after the 1950 season.

Jackie Robinson as a Kansas City Monarch in the spring of 1945—not a pleasant experience.

The man who joined forces with Jackie Robinson in August 1945 was sixty-three years old at the time. Between 1905 and 1925, Branch Rickey had played and managed baseball at the major league level without distinction (as a back-up catcher appearing in 120 games over 4 seasons, he hit .239; and managed teams for 10 seasons in St. Louis for the Browns and Cards, compiled a .473 winning percentage, and never finished higher than third place). In that twenty year period, he also (i) earned a Bachelor of Arts degree from Ohio Wesleyan University and a Doctor of Jurisprudence from the University of Michigan, and coached baseball at both schools; (ii) married and had six children; (iii) survived serious bouts of tuberculosis and pneumonia; (iv) served as a major in the U.S. Army's Chemical Warfare Service in France during World War I in the same unit as Christy Mathewson and Ty Cobb; and (v) became the St. Louis Cardinals' team president before the start of the 1917 season and would remain the head of the Cards' front office not just through 1925 but on through the following 17 seasons before joining the Dodgers after the 1942 season.

Throughout his life, Branch Rickey created an indelible image of himself in the American psyche as a man possessing (and possessed with) a unique combination of devout faith, innovative business acumen, and an overbearing personality entirely bereft of self-doubt.[4] This pious freight train of a "ferocious gentleman" heightened the effect of his unforgettable character by punctuating his high-powered conversations with the rising movement of his bushy eyebrows and the thrusting of the ever-present thick cigar held in his left hand.[5]

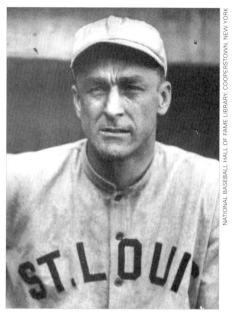

Branch Rickey as a catcher for the St. Louis Browns in 1906.

While leading the Cardinals organization in the decades that preceded World War II, Branch Rickey pioneered the development of the team's massive minor league system (which other teams would soon attempt to emulate) and made them winners. In his final 22 seasons as team president between 1921 and 1942, the Redbirds had winning records in 19 of them; played in 6 World Series and won 4 of them; and finished in second place 5 times—meaning Rickey's Cards finished in first or second place 11 out of those 22 seasons. Only the New York Giants matched St. Louis' record of success in the National League during that time span.

Branch Rickey left the Cardinals' front office after the team's successful trouncing of the Yankees in the five game 1942 World Series because his contract expired, and St. Louis' Chairman of the Board Sam Breadon refused to renew it. The agreement had provided Rickey with an annual salary of $50,000 in its final five years during the end of the Great Depression, and Breadon decided the compensation was excessive.

4 Branch Rickey became one of the founders of the Fellowship of Christian Athletes in the early 1950's.

5 Rickey's most recent biographer, Lee Lowenfish, entitled his book *Branch Rickey: Baseball's Ferocious Gentleman* (University of Nebraska Press, 2007), in the context of his subject's stated desire to always have a baseball team made up of "ferocious gentlemen."

Rickey's success in building and maintaining St. Louis as a perennial contender for the National League pennant made him a hot commodity in baseball's executive market for those teams seeking to achieve the Cardinals' level of success. The Brooklyn Dodgers found themselves in need of new leadership after the 1942 season with the departure of president and general manager Larry MacPhail. Known as "The Roaring Redhead," MacPhail had moved the Dodgers' fortunes forward in 1939 by naming Leo Durocher manager. In his first season at the helm, feisty Leo "the Lip" transformed the seventh-place Brooklyn team of 1938 (with a record of 69-80) into a third place (84-69) ballclub, and then kept the upward momentum going, leading them to second place (88-65) in '40, first place (100-54) in '41, and finishing a strong second with a 104-50 record in '42, two games back of Rickey's powerhouse Cards.[6]

When Branch Rickey took over the Dodgers at the start of the 1943 season, Leo's troops had become decimated by many of them being called into active duty during World War II. The team of substitutes fell to third place in 1943, dropped to seventh in '44, and then started regaining their pre-war momentum when veterans returned to the ballfields in mid-season '45. Brooklyn bounced back to third place in 1945, and then finished in a dead heat with St. Louis in '46, with the Cards prevailing in a three-game playoff to capture the flag.

With Mr. Rickey leading Brooklyn's front office, he immediately expanded the team's miniscule 5-team farm system (compared to St. Louis' having entries in 44 leagues) up to 27 teams within 6 years. To stock these teams with talent, Rickey changed Brooklyn's approach to scouting young players, implementing a series of tryout camps all over the country, beginning in July 1943, that resulted in the team's signing the likes of Gil Hodges, Duke Snider, Carl Erskine, George Shuba, and Ralph Branca.

More important from a historical standpoint than the multiplied minor league growth, Branch Rickey commenced a secret plan in 1943 aimed at terminating the "gentlemen's agreement" in place among major league owners for over a half century that prevented teams from signing African-American players to their rosters. Having witnessed

6 The '41 Dodgers lost to the Yankees in the World Series on catcher Mickey Owens' infamous ninth inning dropped third strike in Game Four that allowed batter Tommy Henrich to advance to first, opening the door for a four-run rally that dashed the Dodgers' hopes of prevailing over the Bronx Bombers in the Fall Classic.

dozens of games between major league All-Star barnstorming teams and Negro Leaguers every year in the off-season, Mr. Rickey knew of several black players who clearly had the talent to compete and excel at the big league level, and who were available to join his team since none plied their trade under the burden of binding contracts.[7] Contending teams in the competitively tight National League (unlike the American League where it was the Yankees and the Seven Dwarfs) were typically "one player away" from a flag, and a Negro League star could easily become that "one player" to bring home the pennant once the color barrier broke.

Before Brooklyn Dodger President Branch Rickey could integrate the game, however, he knew the following events had to occur:

- World War II had to take place and then had to end. As for the need for it to take place, historian Jules Tygiel explained why in his masterwork, *Baseball's Great Experiment: Jackie Robinson and his Legacy* (Oxford University Press, 1983), "World War II, more than any other event, caused Americans to re-evaluate their racial attitudes. Many historians view the war as a watershed in the struggle for civil rights. The conflict against Nazi racism exposed the contradictions of racial practice in the United States." The war also had to end. Nothing as significant as mixing races could start until baseball resumed its pre-war social status quo. The country was too disrupted by the war effort for something else to get injected into American society likely to shake the national mindset to its very core.

- Commissioner of Baseball Kenesaw Mountain Landis, a notorious racist who had been the dictator presiding over the game since 1921, had to die. He finally obliged with his passing on November 25, 1944, at the age of seventy-eight. Landis then had to be succeeded by someone more enlightened than he on the subject of civil rights. On April 24, 1945, major league owners selected "Happy" Chandler, a former governor and U.S. Senator from Kentucky, to become the game's second commissioner. After being confirmed, Chandler

---

7 Rickey's eye for talent was second to none. Author Jonathan Eig in his book, *Opening Day*, quotes legendary sportswriter Jim Murray for the proposition, "Branch Rickey could recognize a great player from the window of a moving train."

immediately proved himself open to integration.

- The media had to embrace the idea. Clearly, those newspapers with largely African-American readership favored integration. Many white sportswriters also endorsed the need for baseball to open its doors, particularly in the context of thousands of black American soldiers giving their lives for the Allied cause during World War II. As for the other key media component of the time besides newspapers, Mr. Rickey lined up the top radio sportscaster in baseball, Brooklyn's own Red Barber, to accept the idea. Though Barber, a Southerner, had misgivings at the outset when Rickey told him of his plan in 1943, upon reflection, as a committed Christian, he came around to recognizing that segregation and the denial of equal opportunity to the races was simply not fair, and therefore, not right.

- The first African-American to play baseball in the major leagues during the twentieth century had to be located, evaluated, and tested for having the necessary skill set both as a ballplayer and as a man strong enough to withstand the torrent of abuse that would surely fall upon the racial trailblazer.

As of August 28, 1945, all five precedent conditions necessary for big league baseball to integrate became satisfied with the surrender of Japan to end World War II exactly two weeks before, and Branch Rickey's deciding upon Jackie Robinson as the guinea pig for his Noble Experiment.

In Mr. Rickey's eyes, what was it about Jackie Robinson that made him the best African-American candidate to sign a baseball contract with the Dodgers organization in August 1945? Brooklyn's president studied reports on all the leading black ballplayers aspiring to take center stage, evaluated their athletic talent and character, i.e., their strengths and their weaknesses, and saw Robinson as the clear choice for several reasons—

- He didn't smoke, drink, or chase women. His mother, his mentor, Rev. Karl Downs, and his longtime fiancée, Rachel, all had the highest moral standards, and Jackie Robinson never considered

Racial integration in professional baseball could begin only upon the death of Commissioner Kenesaw Mountain Landis and his being replaced by an enlightened soul like "Happy" Chandler.

disappointing those three most important people in his life. Mr. Rickey knew that the ballplayer he chose as the game's trailblazer would be highly scrutinized by the media and everyone else, and wanted his man to have to answer only for his baseball skills and not his lifestyle.

- He had a college education, spoke well, and was battle-tested in interracial athletic competition. At both Pasadena Junior College and UCLA, Robinson had played with white teammates, including some who didn't want to be his teammates, and managed to get along with them over the course of a season. Surely, that's how it would be with the Brooklyn Dodgers, who like every other big league team, had their fair share of Southern players with racial prejudice embedded in their consciousness.

- He had a ferocious personality that he kept under control most of the time. Mr. Rickey knew all about Jackie's military experience, including the Fort Hood bus incident and court-martial trial. The Dodgers president concluded that Robinson's passionate attitude and his expectation of being treated with respect by all would be essential personal characteristics in a partner in order for the Noble Experiment to conclude with the desired result. A passive, passionless man willing to go with the anticipated race-baiting flow would perish or quit the team while living in the boiling social pressure-cooker where this century's first African-American ballplayer would surely be called upon to perform.

- He was an outstanding ballplayer. Clearly, baseball was not Robinson's best sport, but he had played it well at UCLA, and after a long layoff, had proven he could still play it well with the Kansas City Monarchs and at the Boston Red Sox tryout in April (the reports of which Rickey received from African-American journalist Wendell Smith who was on the scene). To the extent there were any doubts about Robinson's baseball abilities, Rickey had no intention of starting Jackie's career with the Dodgers at the major league level—Robinson would be given at least a full year in the high minors to demonstrate whether he had the skills necessary to succeed in the National League.

- He had a deep religious faith. Had Branch Rickey not been a baseball executive, he likely would have become a minister. As a player, he had refused to play games on Sunday, and his readiness to inject his Christian beliefs into conversation was a lifetime tendency. From Mr. Rickey's perspective, in order to succeed, the player who broke the color barrier would have to keep his mind and heart centered on a higher power, and Rickey wanted to have confidence that whoever he teamed with would be on the same Biblical page as he when the inevitable crunch-time encounters arose. Jackie Robinson passed the faith test in flying colors. Under the longtime mentorship of Rev. Downs, the ballplayer spoke openly of his prayer life and trust in God.

- He was a position player and not a pitcher. Given that an important part of successful pitching at the big league level has always required the ability to throw inside, which often has resulted in bean balls (which often has provoked fights, brawls, and retaliation), Mr. Rickey decided he wanted the trailblazer to be a position player whose daily activities did not involve throwing a hard baseball under batters' chins.

Branch Rickey did not embark on the task of integrating professional baseball in an information vacuum. First, he digested the sociological analysis of Gunnar Myrdal in his 1944 book, *An American Dilemma: The Negro Problem and Modern Democracy*, followed by Columbia University history professor Frank Tannenbaum's book, *Slave and Citizen*, and then comparative religion professor Dr. Edmund Raymond Soper's book, *Racism*, which contained the prophetic sentence Rickey quoted often: "Of all the ills to which humanity finds itself heir today, there is none more virulent with so many facets, and involves so many world issues, as that of race."

Mr. Rickey believed that the social scientists' theories of how best to achieve successful integration could be realized in the baseball diamond test tube of his Noble Experiment by prudent and patient planning. In particular, as Jay Jennings pointed out in a 2007 *New York Times* book review, Myrdal's strategy for achieving effective integration surely resonated: "If Negro workers are introduced a few at a time, if they are carefully picked, if the leaders of the white workers are taken into confidence and if the reasons for the action are explained, then the trouble can be minimized, and the new policy may eventually become successful."

———————

On the enchanted morning of August 28, 1945, having completed his research as to which candidate was most likely to succeed in executing the most complicated and challenging tango ever attempted by a human being in the twentieth century, Branch Rickey invited Jackie Robinson to step up and dance for the Brooklyn Dodgers. Before the dance began, however, they would first have to meet.

The dialog in the first meeting between Robinson and Rickey is arguably the most important conversation of the twentieth century. In fact, it can accurately be called the "Emancipation Conversation." There in Mr. Rickey's office on Montague Street in downtown Brooklyn, for a period of almost three hours, the Caucasian team president did most of the talking, while testing the mettle of the quiet African-American man in his presence. The high points of the historic conversation were corroborated by the consistent recountings of the two participants, as well as by Dodgers scout Clyde Sukeforth, who had brought Robinson to New York for Mr. Rickey, and during the meeting played the proverbial role of silent fly on the wall.

After shaking hands and eyeballing each other for a few moments,[8] Rickey initiated the discussion by verifying that Jackie Robinson possessed the personal essentials of having the loving support of a good woman, clean living habits, and a strong faith. With that confirmed, it was time to get down to business.

Though Jackie Robinson entered Mr. Rickey's office believing (because of what Clyde Sukeforth had told him) he had been summoned to New York to see if he wanted to play for the Brooklyn Brown Dodgers in a proposed new Negro League, the team president advised the twenty-six-year-old ballplayer at the outset of their meeting that what the Dodgers really wanted was for him to become big league

---

8 Clyde Sukeforth later gave his impression of the meeting's opening stare-down: "They were trying to get inside each other. The air was electric in there. They just stared and stared at each other. Oh, what a pair, those two!"

baseball's racial trailblazer, first at AAA Montreal in the International League, and then with the parent club.

To satisfy himself that Robinson was up to the defined task, Mr. Rickey then began using the tool of aggressive role playing, pulling no punches by unloading fully loaded epithets, so that the young man with whom Rickey planned to make history understood the fact that success would only come if Jackie Robinson had sufficient "guts *not* to fight back" against the certain taunts, threats, and attacks that would be coming his way.

In persuading Jackie Robinson of the necessity to "turn the other cheek" in order for successful integration to be achieved, Rickey reached into his desk drawer and pulled out a copy of Italian priest Giovanni Papini's recent book, *The Life of Christ*, and read aloud the author's tight statement on nonresistance:

> There are three answers which men can make to conflict with another man: revenge, flight, turning the other cheek. The first is the barbarous principle of retaliation ... Flight is no better than retaliation. The man who takes flight invites pursuit ... His weakness becomes the accomplice of the ferocity of others ... Turning the other cheek means not receiving the second blow. It means cutting the chain of the inevitable wrongs at the first link. Your adversary is ready for anything but this ... Every man has an obscure respect for courage in others, especially if it is moral courage, the rarest and most difficult sort of bravery ... It makes the very brute understand that this man is more than a man ... Man is a fighting animal; but with no resistance offered, the pleasure disappears; there is no zest left, and yet the results of nonresistance, even if they are not always perfect, are certainly superior to those of resistance or flight ... To answer blows with blows, evil deeds with evil deeds, is to meet the attacker on his own ground, to proclaim oneself as low as he ... Only he who has conquered himself can conquer his enemies.

After finishing the passage, Mr. Rickey gave Papini's book to his disciple as a gift and then required Jackie Robinson to confirm he would utilize both cheeks in responding to the future vicious acts of racism that would surely be aimed at him. The Dodgers president then signed his new infielder to a contract ($3,500 signing bonus and $600 per month for the upcoming '46 first season), and ordered the ballplayer to maintain the confidentiality of their little secret, save and except for being authorized to tell his fiancée and family about the road ahead.

In trying to imagine Jackie Robinson's state of mind as he left Branch Rickey's office at noon on August 28, 1945, the following assumptions can be made:

- He knew that under the terms of the contract he had just signed with the Dodgers, he now had sufficient economic security and he and Rachel, engaged for over four years, could tie the knot (which, in fact, happened on February 10, 1946);

- He knew he was clearly being given the opportunity by Mr. Rickey to become a hero to all African-Americans, if he could succeed on the field in the coming seasons;

- Despite a lifetime of setbacks in dealing with white Americans, he believed he could trust Branch Rickey to follow through on the plan they had discussed, deciding that the Dodgers' top executive was sincere in both his faith and his desire to win the National League pennant;[9]

- Most unsettling, he knew he had given his word to his new boss not only to play his best baseball in the all-white major leagues, but also had given his word he would avoid any retaliation against racists on and off the field. After hearing Papini's words consistent with his own understanding of Scripture, Jackie Robinson knew what the Bible and Mr. Rickey called him to do; knew his own personal history in responding to bigotry; and certainly must have had doubts about his ability to control his temper in the tough

---

9 Surely, during their meeting, Robinson must have taken comfort in two items framed and hanging on Mr. Rickey's Wall—a Mathew Brady photograph of "the Great Emancipator" Abraham Lincoln, and a quotation scripted in calligraphy from Scottish philosopher William Drummond, "He who will not reason is a bigot; he who cannot reason is a fool; and he that dares not reason is a slave."

days ahead. Of course, he would try to turn the other cheek to his enemies, but could he or any other African-American ballplayer possibly succeed in maintaining a super-human level of self-control for a period of years?

Having these thoughts about his situation, in the context of possessing extraordinary self-confidence in his own abilities, and knowing the personalities and talents of the other top Negro League players, Jackie Robinson surely knew that Branch Rickey had picked the best candidate to dance with on August 28, 1945. Without a doubt, he knew that only one man in the world possessed the total package of talents capable of achieving success in this high stakes drama—the man Jackie Robinson saw every time he looked in the mirror.

And how did Branch Rickey feel about his dance partner after their first conversation? In his only book, *The American Diamond* (Simon & Schuster, 1965), Mr. Rickey answered the question: "With the endorsement of Brooklyn scouts Wid Matthews, George Sisler, and Clyde Sukeforth, I knew Robinson could play at the major league level. At the beginning of our first meeting, however, he had more and deeper racial resentment than was hoped for or expected. After we spent time reading Papini's book together, Jackie Robinson, a Christian by inheritance and practice, became fully convinced that the Papini doctrine of turning the other cheek to racism was necessary and acceptable. He understood that the success of Negro employment in baseball depended very largely on himself ... It took an *intelligent* man to understand the challenge—it took a man of *great moral courage* to accept it and make the commitment to see it through. I believed Jackie Robinson had both essential traits."

After two months of internal strategizing as the '45 season and World Series came to an end, and in response to pressure for baseball integration applied by New York City Mayor Fiorello LaGuardia, Branch Rickey let the world learn of his Noble Experiment at a press conference held in Montreal on October 23, 1945. Surprisingly, Mr. Rickey himself did not attend the event, entrusting the announcement to the man in charge of minor league operations for the Dodgers front office, a fellow by the name of Branch Rickey Jr., who was joined at the event by Montreal Royals team president Hector Racine, and by Jackie Robinson. The Royals' newest player confidently stepped to the microphone and announced to the world, "I can't begin to tell you how happy I am that I am the first member of my race in organized baseball. I can only say I'll do my very best to come through *in every manner.*" Clearly, by Jackie's choosing those words, the main lesson from the August 28 meeting with Mr. Rickey had sunk in, as he recognized that his upcoming task would involve a whole lot more than playing baseball.

As expected, the reaction to the October 23 press conference was mixed. Clearly, the media, the game's top executives, and the fraternity of major league ballplayers all had bigots within their ranks who spoke up in outrage over Branch Rickey's audacity. These three echelons involved with the National Pastime also had some enlightened souls who expressed their delight over the prospect of having the "gentlemen's agreement" terminated at last, and believed that Jackie Robinson would be the first of many black ballplayers coming into the professional game's highest levels. All the integration proponents knew, however, that Jack Roosevelt Robinson had to succeed in order for other opportunities to follow.

Four months later, the Brooklyn Dodgers began their spring training regimen near Daytona Beach in Sanford, Florida, on March 1, 1946. To the dismay of Branch Rickey, his most important ballplayer failed to arrive on time. When Jackie Robinson called his new boss on March 2 and explained the difficulties he and his new bride, Rachel, had encountered in their cross-country odyssey traveling from West to East Coast, Mr. Rickey accepted the fact that no aspect of his Experiment would be easy. Between New Orleans and Daytona Beach, the Robinsons endured the indignities of being (i) bumped off a commercial airplane in favor of white passengers, (ii) forced to stay in an unsanitary blacks-only hotel, and (iii) ordered to sit at the back of the bus which carried them to Florida. For the newlyweds, turning the other cheek had immediately become a 24/7, full-time existence.

Jackie Robinson's 1946 experience as a member of the Montreal Royals proved to be a perfect first step transition into the Noble Experiment. Mr. Rickey hired African-American journalists Wendell Smith and Billy Rowe of the *Pittsburgh Courier* and Negro League pitcher John Wright to join Robinson and prevent him from feeling isolated during spring training. Though Royals manager Clay Hopper, a Mississippian, began the year with an ignorant attitude, remarking to Mr. Rickey before the season started that he didn't regard Negroes as

In Jackie Robinson's first game as a Montreal Royal, he went 4 for 5, scored 4 times, and hit a home run. This was an omen of things to come in 1946, when he won the International League's batting title and Most Valuable Player award.

human beings, it didn't take long for Jackie's magic on the field and charisma and courage off the diamond to awaken Hopper's sensitivities and respect.

Of course, throughout the first spring training in the Dodgers organization, the trailblazer and his bride felt the pain of discrimination, ranging from their Florida housing accommodations (the Royals' team hotel refused to accept African-American guests) to Rachel's having to watch her husband play from seats in the segregated part of the grandstand, to having some spring training games cancelled because certain Florida cities refused to allow blacks and whites to play on the same field. Despite Jackie's suffering a batting slump and battling a sore throwing arm in the midst of this spring turmoil, Branch Rickey held fast as his new player's biggest public and private cheerleader, staying supremely confident that when the bell rang on Opening Day 1946, the infielder would remove all doubts about his baseball abilities.

And so it came to pass. On April 18, 1946, minor league baseball became integrated once and for all, as Jackie Robinson went 4 for 5, scored 4 runs, stole 2 bases, caused 2 balks with his daring baserunning, and hit a home run in leading Montreal to a 14-1 victory over the Jersey City Giants. That game set the tone for the entire season. Jackie led the Royals to the International League championship, and won the league's Most Valuable Player Award, hitting .349 to win the batting title, scoring 113 runs, stealing 40 bases, having the League's highest fielding percentage for a second baseman, and causing so much positive excitement that Montreal broke its single-season, home-and-away attendance records. Robinson simply could not have played better baseball during the '46 season in either his own or Mr. Rickey's wildest fantasies. While Jackie dominated the International League, Brooklyn manager Leo Durocher begged Mr. Rickey to move Robinson up to the parent club for the final weeks of the pennant race against the Cardinals, but the boss refused, knowing that making such a controversial move at the season's crunch time had too much risk for all concerned.

In the turn-the-other-cheek department over the course of the 1946 season, relying on Rachel's steady temperament, Robinson survived a multitude of tests from a wide variety of sources—a stream of epithets from Baltimore and Louisville grandstands; an opposing ballplayer's taunting him in Syracuse for being the "cousin of a black cat," while he waited to bat on the on-deck circle; pitchers' bean balls; and base runners' spikes-high slides. In his book, *Baseball's Great Experiment*, Jules Tygiel revealed that the stress of being professional baseball's trailblazer in 1946 resulted in Robinson's having to endure not only sleepless nights, but also almost caused him to suffer a nervous breakdown.

In the midst of such social, athletic, and personal turmoil, Jackie Robinson also dealt with the anxiety and excitement of becoming a father, giving comfort to Rachel up to and following the arrival of Jackie Jr. on November 18, 1946.

Knowing that his disciple-dance partner would clearly be playing for Brooklyn in the coming season, Mr. Rickey made plans to avoid another spring training debacle in Florida by announcing that the Dodgers and Montreal Royals would have their 1947 spring training operations in Cuba and Panama. For the preseason preparation, Rickey supplied Jackie with some much needed company (in the absence of Rachel, since no players' wives were allowed to join the team in spring training) in the form of three other African-American players—Roy Campanella, Don Newcombe, and Roy Partlow.

Ever confident in his actions as an amateur social scientist, Branch Rickey decided that his best chance to avoid mayhem in moving toward his inevitable decision to integrate the Dodgers would require a gradual ice-breaking approach to mixing the races together. In that regard, when training camp opened, he refused to announce his ultimate intention to promote Robinson to the parent club before Opening Day and also sequestered his four black ballplayers in a run-down hotel away from where their future white teammates stayed at Havana's ritzy Hotel Nacional (for the Dodger players) and the new National Military Academy dormitory (for the Royals). Mr. Rickey calmed Jackie's anger over the differential housing by advising him the arrangements lessened the likelihood of any disruptive incidents.

From a baseball standpoint, to get infielder Jackie Robinson into the '47 Dodgers starting lineup would require him to learn a new position, given that Pee Wee Reese had a lock on shortstop, as did Eddie Stanky at second base, and Jackie seemed to lack the big throwing arm required of a major league third baseman.[10]

10 Eventually, in 1953, with the arrival of second baseman Jim "Junior" Gilliam on the Dodgers team, in order to keep Jackie's bat in the lineup, they moved him to the outfield and then third base.

The moment of truth when baseball's playing field finally became level occurred when the Dodgers and Royals played their first spring training games in Panama. Robinson commenced the spring season with a bang, getting five base hits in his first two games, and doing a surprisingly solid job of fielding his new position at first base.

Off the field, however, things didn't go smoothly. Dodgers pitchers Hugh Casey and Kirby Higbe, outfielders Dixie Walker and Carl Furillo, and catcher backup Bobby Bragan all opposed the idea of having Jackie Robinson as a teammate and made no secret of their feelings. The prospective player revolt was quelled by manager Leo Durocher in an emergency middle-of-the-night team meeting in the kitchen of an old army barracks near their hotel with all his ballplayers, reminding them that *he* made the decisions as to who would be playing for the Dodgers and *he* would play whoever gave Brooklyn the best chance to win games and the pennant, regardless of a player's race. Durocher's directive was then followed by Mr. Rickey's meeting in his hotel suite one-on-one with each of the five complainants, advising them he would arrange to trade whoever felt uncomfortable participating in his Noble Experiment, with only Kirby Higbe and Dixie Walker taking their boss up on the offer.[11]

As spring training ended in early April with the Dodgers and Royals returning to Brooklyn for the preseason's final two games, two changes in the team's chemistry rocked their world. First, on April 9, Commissioner of Baseball "Happy" Chandler announced his decision to suspend Leo Durocher from having any participation with major league baseball for one year in light of his past "accumulation of unpleasant incidents ... and publicity–producing affairs" claimed to be "detrimental to baseball" arising from Leo's longtime associations with gamblers.

On the next day after Durocher's suspension, Mr. Rickey had his assistant, Arthur Mann, pass a cryptic note to the media covering the exhibition game at Ebbets Field, containing two typed sentences— "The Brooklyn Dodgers today purchased the contract of Jackie Roosevelt Robinson from the Montreal Royals. He will report immediately."—with the press release ending with the signature of Branch Rickey.

Five days later, the game of baseball and the United States of America changed for the better. On April 15, 1947, at Ebbets Field in front of 27,000 fans, the Dodgers opened the season against the Boston

---

11 Both would be traded to Pittsburgh—Higbe in mid-season of 1947, and Walker swapped after the '47 season.

Braves and the entire country focused on Brooklyn's first baseman who that day earned his permanent nickname, "The Trailblazer," by becoming the first African-American to play at the major league level since 1884.

Jackie Robinson's hitless performance on Opening Day 1947 against Braves ace Johnny Sain[12] disappointed many (and, sadly, pleased many), but by the end of the season, he had established his worthiness as a big league player, hitting .297, scoring 125 runs in 151 games, and sparking the Dodgers to first place in the National League, all of which caused him to be named Rookie of the Year.

In 2007, sixty years after Jackie Robinson broke baseball's color barrier, *Wall Street Journal* reporter Jonathan Eig released his superb book, *Opening Day: The Story of Jackie Robinson's First Season* (Simon & Schuster, 2007). In it, the author details the highlights and lowlights of the first big league year of the Rickey-Robinson Noble Experiment. Most notably, during that historic season, the following occurred:

- Ever the social scientist, Mr. Rickey took it upon himself before the start of the season to organize a meeting of the top African-American community leaders in New York, and told them in no uncertain terms that the success of integration in baseball absolutely depended on their communicating to their respective black networks that their response to his Noble Experiment had to be subdued. Any unbridled celebration and/or displays or arrogance over the successful play of black ballplayers could well ignite a bigoted backlash among white ballplayers and fans.

- Despite going hitless on Opening Day, Jackie got off to a fast start, and was hitting .429 after the season's first week.

- In the season's first months, he weathered a torrent of verbal abuse led by opposing manager Ben Chapman in a game with the Phillieson April 22, and a threatened boycott against playing on the same field with a black player by the Cardinals in early May.

- Robinson's standing up to bigotry by turning the other cheek soon led to a profound level of respect shown him by his Dodgers teammates, the media covering their games, and fans of all races.

12 To his everlasting credit, Sain resisted the encouragement from bigots all over the country, and refused to throw at Robinson's head.

- Jackie played an aggressive style of baseball not seen before in major league ballparks, particularly while running the base paths—deliberately getting into run-downs and then escaping to dash for an additional base, stealing home, and taking the extra base on his hits when noone expected it.[13] In Eig's marvelously concise description, "He was electricity. He made things go ... playing the game with equal parts speed and guts." Branch Rickey made a similar comment in his book, *The American Diamond*: "No one who has ever played the game could put mind and muscle together quicker and with better judgment than Robinson."

- Other teams soon followed the Dodgers' integration lead. On July 5, Larry Doby broke the American League's color barrier, pinch-hitting for the Cleveland Indians, at the start of his 13-year Hall of Fame career. Later in July, the St. Louis Browns joined the baseball integration party by signing Willard Brown and Harry Thompson, and in August, the Dodgers added pitcher Dan Bankhead to their roster.

- Negro League attendance began to drop, an obvious reaction to African-American fans' clear desire to witness the Noble Experiment.

- In a dash to first base on August 20, Enos "Country" Slaughter deliberately stomped on the back of Jackie's right foot, and in the face of such a vicious physical attack, the Dodgers' first baseman amazingly shook it off, stayed in the game, and didn't retaliate.

- The Dodgers lost to the Yankees in the seven game World Series, the first Fall Classic ever to be televised, and for the first time, many Americans got to see Jackie Robinson play his unique style of aggressive baseball. When the Series ended, every Brooklyn Dodger ballplayer made a point of shaking hands with and congratulating Jackie on his outstanding season.

---

13 In his book, *Jackie Robinson and the Integration of Baseball*, Scott Simon puts Jackie's special talent in perspective: "Every detail in the design of baseball tilts against a player stealing home ... A runner who dares to steal home gambles that he can run down the third baseline quicker than a pitcher can speed the ball to exactly the same spot. The move astonishes because it seems to make as much sense as jumping off the Golden Gate Bridge—if you're safe, it's an accident. Such is the play that became the signature of Jackie Robinson's career."

In the 1948 season, Robinson maintained his turn-the-other-cheek pace and produced another solid season, essentially matching his '47 hitting numbers, while moving to second base (after the Dodgers traded Eddie Stanky) where he formed a tight double play partnership with Pee Wee Reese. Leo Durocher rejoined the team at the start of the year as manager, but by mid-season, he and Mr. Rickey got cross-ways, resulting in the Dodgers and Giants executing a bizarre "trade" of managers on July 16, with Durocher becoming the new skipper for the New York Giants, while Giant manager Mel Ott moved over to lead the Dodgers, only to be fired instantly, and replaced by Brooklyn's 1947 interim manager, Burt Shotten. Despite all these developments in 1948, the Dodgers slipped to third place, $7\frac{1}{2}$ games behind the famous "Spahn-and-Sain-and-pray-for-rain" pennant-winning Boston Braves, though good things for the team appeared on the horizon. Over the

April 15, 1947: The Noble Experiment begins with Jackie Robinson as the Brooklyn Dodgers' starting first baseman.

course of the '48 season, the Dodgers added first baseman Gil Hodges, third baseman Billy Cox, center fielder Duke Snider, and catcher Roy Campanella to their starting lineup, who would all remain Brooklyn stalwarts for years to come.

By 1949, Branch Rickey saw that circumstances involving his Noble Experiment had truly changed. As more and more African-American players entered and excelled at the major league level, going into the third season of integration, even the most unregenerate racists had to acknowledge that the "experiment" had ended, and blacks were here to stay as a fixture in big league baseball in perpetuity. The Dodgers' boss

"He was electricity. He made things go ... playing the game with equal parts speed and guts." Jonathan Eig

told Jackie Robinson it was now acceptable (as of Opening Day) to relieve himself of his nonresistance mindset, turn on all of his extra-ordinary competitive juices, and be himself for the 1949 season. The Great Jackie did just that and unleashed himself on the National League, winning the batting title (hitting .342), producing a career-high 122 RBI's, scoring 124 runs, and being named the league's Most Valuable Player.

Baseball fans saw for the remainder of Jackie Robinson's career from 1949 to 1956 what was already well known by UCLA's athletic opponents (where Robinson played multiple sports from 1939 to 1941) and the Kansas City Monarchs' Negro League foes (where Robinson played in 1945)—Jackie Robinson was the most ferocious competitor in the game. In the final eight years of his big league career, Robinson challenged umpires, ran over opposing players in the baseline, and played the game like no other ballplayer, within the rules, but in a constant mode of attack. To see the man be himself and explode in those eight years put into perspective the effort behind his super-human level of self-control during the 1946 to 1948 years of the Noble Experiment, when with the help of his God, his mentor, Mr. Rickey, and his wife, Rachel, the fiercely competitive Jackie Robinson clearly achieved what had seemed impossible when he left Branch Rickey's office after their first meeting in August 1945.

As mentioned previously in this chapter, the most racially antagonistic National League team in 1947 had been the Philadelphia Phillies. In fact, in a game against Philly early that season, while waiting to bat in the on-deck circle, as Jackie Robinson received a steady stream of epithets from the opposing bench, he admitted (in his auto-biography) that he almost lost his self-control, coming within seconds of jumping into the Phillies' dugout and attacking them with his "despised black fists."

As baseball's trailblazer considered full-scale retaliation while preparing to hit in that April 1947 game against the Phillies, he reflected on all the sacrifices Branch Rickey had made on his behalf, and decided to return the Dodgers president's favor, choosing not to respond to his opponents' taunts, and thereby allow himself to keep playing that night without incident in a game where he ultimately scored the game's winning run.

Three and a half years later on October 1, 1950, those same Phillies took the Dodgers down to the last game of the season, with the National League pennant hanging in the balance. Philadelphia won the game in the tenth inning on Dick Sisler's home run, putting them into the World Series.

According to Hall of Fame pitcher Robin Roberts, the Phillies' biggest star on that team, as he and his teammates celebrated winning the pennant in their champagne-soaked locker room, a visitor entered without fanfare to offer his congratulations. Jackie Robinson extended his hand to the new National League champions, seemingly oblivious to the hate-mongering from three years before.

Knowing the details of his life, and the elegant dance he executed with Branch Rickey from 1945 to 1950, moves the Great Jackie to the top of the mountain as an authentic American hero in the mindset of Baby Boomers and everyone else who knows his story. Not only did the man turn the other cheek to his belligerent antagonists, he also took the next (and equally difficult) step. To the delight of Mr. Rickey in what proved to be their final game together with the Dodgers, Jackie Robinson completed the hate-love cycle against the Philadelphia Phillies in the autumn of 1950 by putting aside his opponents' wretched past misconduct, and elevating himself to that higher level of emotional intelligence where forgiveness and reconciliation actually occur.

"To succeed at the major league level, you have to be single-minded with total concentration." — Nolan Ryan

CHAPTER FOUR

NOLAN RYAN
Baby Boomer Symbol of the Game

In his first published article written on the subject of baseball, Bart Giamatti made the observation, "Among all men who play baseball, there is, very occasionally, a man of such qualities of heart, mind, and body that he transcends even the great and glorious game." For Baby Boomers, particularly those who reside in Texas, Giamatti's statement hit the mark in describing Nolan Ryan, the greatest power pitcher in baseball history.

It started in 1953, the way baseball is supposed to start—with a father giving his six-year-old son a glove and playing catch with him in their front yard. From there, the boy decided on his own that he loved playing the game, and the local action moved to a nearby vacant lot, where neighborhood kids built a diamond, and Robert Ryan refined his skills as a catcher by having little brother Nolan pitch to him. Little League Baseball had only recently come to Alvin, Texas, and soon provided the official start to Nolan Ryan's career at Schroeder Field, where he became an "All-Star" player.

Starting in the second grade, besides his passion for baseball, Nolan Ryan became fortified by working on his father's newspaper route. Between the ages of 8 and 18, he spent every morning with his dad between 1 and 4 AM delivering the *Houston Post* to 1,500 homes in the Alvin area. Rolling newspapers into tight cylinders and delivering them to residents before the sun rose gave the emerging pitcher a work ethic, sense of personal responsibility, and maturity that would lead to his becoming a team leader in high school and a professional player immediately thereafter.

By the time he reached junior high, Nolan Ryan had the arm strength to stand on the goal line of a football field and throw a softball over

95

100 yards—30 yards farther than any other boy in the area. In the ninth grade, Ryan became even more focused on baseball after abandoning his short-lived football career in the aftermath of a head-on collision with future NFL great Norm Bulaich that produced a dazed and embarrassed Alvin cornerback and a La Marque Junior High touchdown.

In 1963, as a sophomore, Nolan Ryan pitched for the Alvin High School varsity baseball team, and then started attracting major league scouts his junior year by averaging 2 strikeouts per inning, including 21 in a nine-inning game against LaPorte.

In the days before radar guns, scouts could appreciate the velocity of Ryan's fastball because of Alvin's close proximity to Houston where the Colt 45's had just joined the National League in 1962. New York Mets scout Red Murff remembered the first game he saw Ryan pitch: "The night before, I had seen the two fastest pitchers in the National League at that time, Jim Maloney and Turk Farrell. Nolan Ryan was already faster than both of them by far."

The arrival of major league baseball in Houston helped Nolan Ryan another way, giving him the opportunity to observe first-hand the pitching performances of his baseball hero, Sandy Koufax, whose strikeout and no-hit records the Alvin teenager would later break. While watching Koufax, Ryan became so mesmerized, he would not speak to Ruth, his then girlfriend, who later became his wife.

During his senior year, Nolan Ryan dominated Gulf Coast baseball, posting a 19-3 record, and pitching the Alvin Yellow Jackets into the Texas high school state finals in Austin. During that 32-game season in the spring of 1965, Ryan pitched in 27 games, starting 20, and finished the year with 12 complete games, 211 strikeouts and only 61 walks.

Alvin head coach Jim Watson and the other players on the '65 team described Ryan's senior year performance with the same term. He was the team's "wheel horse"—the horse closest to the wagon that pulls the heaviest share of the load—and his statistics proved it. On March 25, 1965, Ryan pitched a seven-inning complete game shutout. The next day, in a doubleheader, Ryan appeared as a reliever in the opener and pitched 3 innings, giving up 1 run and striking out 5. In the nightcap, he started the game, pitched 5 innings, gave up 1 hit, and struck out 10 in a 9-2 victory. On April 1 and 3, in a space of 48 hours, Ryan pitched back-to-back complete game victories. In the post-season, he got better.

To reach the state playoffs, Ryan pitched a no-hitter against Brenham on June 10, striking out 12. Five days later, in the state semifinals, he threw a two-hit shutout against Snyder, striking out 9.

The stories behind Nolan Ryan's senior year triumphs exceeded his statistics. In the first inning of a March 20 game against Deer Park, after he cracked the batting helmet of the leadoff hitter, and then hit and broke the next batter's arm, the third hitter decided he had seen enough, and refused to enter the batter's box until his coach finally shamed him into an at-bat that produced the season's quickest three-pitch strikeout. In the June 10 regional playoff against Brenham, Ryan's inside fastballs caused opposing hitters' bats to break with such frequency that fans complained, genuinely believing his pitches had razor blades attached to them.

Nolan Ryan's high school heat sawed off more than bats. As the 1965 season progressed, Alvin catcher Jerry Spinks observed a tear that soon developed into a sizeable hole in his mitt, caused by the force of Ryan's fastball hitting his glove, the sound of which Red Murff compared to a "muffled rifle shot." The bullet-holed mitt produced a side effect—Spinks' underwhelming batting average during his senior year—which the young catcher could easily justify: "No matter how much padding I put in my glove, as each game wore on, I had fewer fingers on my left hand capable of gripping a bat."

The only blemish on Nolan Ryan's senior year proved to be costly. New York Mets scouting director Bing Devine finally responded to Red Murff's pleas by making an unexpected appearance to see Ryan pitch against Channelview on May 20, 1965. Murff's top prospect reluctantly took the mound that afternoon, less than a day after Coach Watson had death-marched the Yellow Jacket team through endless windsprints over a perceived lack of concentration in practice. With his strength depleted, Ryan simply could not perform with distinction in front of his most important audience, causing his stock to plunge on the eve of the baseball draft.

THE MET YEARS

In the spring of 1965, at the insistence of scout Red Murff, the New York Mets selected 18-year-old Nolan Ryan as the 295th player in

As a New York Met from 1968 to 1971, Nolan Ryan received little instruction.
"We tell him to throw as hard as he can for as long as he can." – Mets pitching coach Rube Walker

baseball's first major league amateur draft. Ryan left Alvin that summer, making the first airplane trip of his life, on the way to Marion, Virginia, where he began his professional career in the Appalachian League. From 1965 to 1967, per Murff's prediction, Nolan Ryan's fastball overpowered minor league hitters just as it had Texas high school players. In 291 innings, he struck out 445 batters, an average of 14 every 9 innings.

Aside from his staggering power numbers, Ryan demonstrated unusual maturity during his brief minor league career. In 1967, he suffered an arm injury. Though the team doctor recommended surgery, Nolan Ryan refused, preferring to rehabilitate the arm on his own. The 20-year-old pitcher already knew enough to know that no one should cut prematurely on what Red Murff had already described in his Mets scouting report as "the BEST arm I ever saw ANYWHERE in my life!"

By 1968, the Mets could no longer hold Nolan Ryan down on the farm. In spring training, his fastball earned him a spot in the starting rotation. In Ryan's first start of the year against Houston on April 14, 1968, the young right-hander got his first major league win by holding the Astros hitless for the first 5 innings, and then leaving the game because of a blister on his pitching hand after 6 $\frac{2}{3}$ shutout innings.

Following his strong debut, in the first six weeks of the 1968 season, Ryan pitched a shutout for 7 innings against the Philadelphia Phillies, threw his first major league complete game with a win over the World Champion St. Louis Cardinals, and hurled a four-hitter while striking out 14 Cincinnati Reds.

The national news media took immediate notice of the rookie sensation, highlighted by *Life* magazine's feature on him in its May 1968 issue. The National League's best hitters already rated Ryan ahead of Sandy Koufax in the speed of his fastball, and 1967 MVP Orlando Cepeda observed, "Nolan Ryan is the best young pitcher I've ever seen in the major leagues."

Injuries, finger blisters, and a continuing military obligation prevented Ryan from maintaining his dominant pace for the remainder of 1968 and most of 1969. The '69 season ended on a happy note, however, as he got the win in clinching Game 3 of the first NLCS with seven innings of relief. He followed that with what would prove to be the only World Series appearance of his career, helping the Amazin' "Ya Gotta Believe" Mets win a Cinderella championship over the heavily-favored Baltimore Orioles by saving Game 3 with 2 $\frac{1}{3}$ innings of shutout relief pitching. The first batter he faced, Paul Blair, blasted a drive to right-center with the bases loaded that turned into Tommie Agee's second remarkable catch of the game.

By the time Ryan completed the 1971 season in New York, he had fulfilled his early career goal of pitching long enough in the majors to earn a pension, but he had not fulfilled the many predictions of greatness, due largely to inconsistent control. After four years with the Mets, his career record stood at 29-38, and he had struck out almost a batter an inning for over 500 innings, but had also averaged 6 walks per game.

Three factors hindered Nolan Ryan's development in New York. First, his Army Reserve commitment disrupted each season, sometimes causing him to go more than a week between starts. Manager Gil Hodges exacerbated the situation by refusing to adjust his pitching rotation to accommodate Ryan's schedule.

Second, despite throwing the National League's hardest fastball, Nolan Ryan got no special treatment from Hodges because he was simply not among the most effective pitchers on the young Mets staff. Tom Seaver, Jerry Koosman and Gary Gentry were already complete pitchers with good control and a more versatile repertoire of pitches. Seaver and Gentry, coming from top college programs, had benefited from sound college coaching. Ryan, on the other hand, received no significant pitching help before reaching the major leagues at age 19.

Finally, Nolan Ryan received no meaningful instruction from the Mets coaching staff. Pitching coach Rube Walker described his simple (unsuccessful) strategy for working with Ryan: "We tell him to throw as hard as he can for as long as he can." This combination of circumstances appeared to be leading toward a dead end to a once promising baseball career. The young pitcher told his wife, Ruth, after the close of the 1971 season that if the Mets failed to trade him over the winter, he would quit the game.

On December 10, 1971, in what would prove to be one of the most lopsided deals in baseball history, the New York Mets traded Nolan Ryan and three marginal players to the California Angels for former All-Star infielder Jim Fregosi. The trade allowed baseball's most awesome thrower to grow into a consistently dominating pitcher.

THE ANGEL YEARS

From 1972 to 1979, Nolan Ryan spent the most productive years of his career with the California Angels. In Anaheim, all obstacles went away that had prevented his achieving greatness in New York. With his Army Reserve duty completed, Ryan could develop a better rhythm by getting to pitch every four days. He eliminated the blister problem on his pitching hand by using a surgeon's scalpel to remove scar tissue and calluses on his fingers before every start.

More important, Nolan Ryan got his first exposure to a coach who could actually teach him how to be a complete pitcher. Angels pitching coach Tom Morgan broke down and overhauled Ryan's delivery, taught him how to throw a sharp breaking curveball, and provided the moral support that the young right-hander had never received with the Mets.

During his 8 years with the Angels, Nolan Ryan threw 4 no-hitters, struck out 383 batters in one season to break Sandy Koufax's major league, single-season record, established the world record for a timed fastball at 100.9 miles per hour, led the league in strikeouts 7 times, won more than 20 games twice and 19 games two other times, and averaged 7 $\frac{1}{3}$ innings per start with an ERA slightly above 3.00 in his 288 California starts.

Surprisingly, Ryan never won the Cy Young Award as an Angel, though a strong argument can be made for his entitlement to it in the 1972, 1973, 1974 and 1977 seasons. What prevented him from having the sensational won-loss record in any one year necessary to win baseball's most prestigious pitching award was the Angels' complete inability to score runs. In Ryan's first five years with the Angels, they finished last in the American League in runs scored four times and next to last the other year. Billy Martin said of those California teams, "They could take batting practice in a hotel lobby and never break anything."

Ryan once described the difficulty of pitching for the weak-hitting Angels: "I feel like I have to pitch a shutout every night or lose. If I throw one bad pitch, I'll be beaten." Ryan's first year with the Angels proved the point. Six different times in 1972 he pitched games allowing two runs or fewer and still lost because California could not score a single run.

Though award voters failed to recognize Nolan Ryan's greatness, hitters knew which pitcher they least wanted to face. When Ryan's night to pitch arrived, the opposing team's starters often came down with a disease known as "Ryanitis," a one-day malady that prevented them from playing. One victim of the epidemic commented, "A good night against Nolan Ryan is going 0 for 4 and you don't get hit in the head." Oakland catcher Dave Duncan put it this way: "Ryan doesn't just get you out. He embarrasses you."

Nolan Ryan's confidence grew to the point that he would advise league MVPs Dick Allen and Reggie Jackson that in his next start

As a California Angel from 1972 to 1979, Ryan received little run support. "I feel like I have to pitch a shutout every night or lose. If I throw one bad pitch, I'll be beaten."

against them, he would only throw fastballs, daring them to match his power. Neither managed a hit in those confrontations.

Jackson gave his own unique account of facing Ryan: "I love to bat against Nolan Ryan and I hate to bat against Nolan Ryan. It's like ice cream. You may love it, but you don't want it shoveled down your throat by the gallon. I've never been afraid at the plate, but Mr. Ryan makes me uncomfortable. He's the only pitcher who's ever made me consider wearing a helmet with an ear flap."

After a lackluster 1978 season, Ryan roared back in 1979, posting a record of 12-7 in the first half of the year, leading to his being named the American's starting pitcher in the All-Star Game. In early August, however, he strained a muscle near his right elbow, causing him to finish that year with an underwhelming 16-14 record.

When the disappointing 1979 season ended, the Angels decided to abandon their top star, as California general manager Buzzie Bavasi justified his decision by saying, "Nolan Ryan can be replaced by two 8-7 pitchers." As the Mets had done eight years before, California chose to let its strongest right arm go, figuring his effectiveness as a power pitcher at the age of 32 had to be in its final stages. Bad decision. History proves that when he left the Angels, Nolan Ryan had not yet reached the halfway point in his career.

THE ASTRO YEARS

In the early years of free agency, Nolan Ryan fulfilled a lifelong dream in November 1979 by signing to pitch for his hometown team, the Houston Astros. Many years before, he had remarked, "I'd buy my own bus ticket to get to Houston if I could pitch for the Astros." New owner John McMullen provided his new pitcher with a lot more than a bus ticket, signing Ryan to a three-year contract that allowed him to become the first athlete on a professional sports team to be paid one million dollars a year.

Initially, the biggest part of the Nolan Ryan media story in Houston was the money. In his first two years with the Astros, he made more than he had in his 12 seasons with the Mets and Angels combined. As more major league stars became millionaires in baseball's lucrative free agent market during the early 1980's, attention finally focused on the mound performance of the game's premier power pitcher.

Nolan Ryan's nine years in Houston became a time for achieving career milestones. On July 4, 1980, Ryan recorded career strikeout number 3,000. On September 26, 1981, he held the Dodgers hitless, thereby establishing the major league record with his fifth no-hitter. On April 27, 1983, Ryan broke Walter Johnson's career strikeout record of 3,508, which had stood since 1927. In 1987, he became the only pitcher in major league history to lead his league in both strikeouts and ERA and not receive the still elusive Cy Young Award. In 1987 and then again in 1988, Ryan became the oldest pitcher ever to lead his

As a Houston Astro from 1980 to 1988, Ryan started breaking career records for strikeouts and no-hitters.
"At the age of 41, Nolan Ryan is the top power pitcher in the league. No one throws as consistently hard as he does." — Pete Rose

league in strikeouts.

More important than the records in Houston, Nolan Ryan came into his own as a complete pitcher. Though he put up amazing numbers as an Angel, Ryan was every bit as effective during his nine years with the Astros. His Houston ERA was almost identical to what it had been in California and his strikeout-to-walk ratio was much higher. His increased control culminated in his winning the 1987 National League Control Pitcher of the Year Award, in recognition of having the league's lowest ERA, giving up the fewest hits, and recording the most strikeouts and the fewest walks for every nine innings of work.

At Houston, pitching into his 40's, Nolan Ryan lost essentially no velocity on his fastball and still had the big breaking curve he had learned from Tom Morgan in California. In addition, as an Astro he added to his repertoire a more effective changeup taught him by former Cincinnati pitcher Joe Nuxhall, and later put a circle change into the mix learned from scout Red Murff.

Unlike the hapless Angels, the Astros were a first division team in the Ryan years, getting into post-season play (though never into the World Series) in 1980, 1981 and 1986. The most dramatic game in his playoff career came in Game 5 of the 1986 National League Championship Series, when he pitched 9 innings against the Mets' Dwight Gooden, gave up 2 hits and 1 run, struck out 12, and did it all with a sore elbow and stress fracture in his right foot.

As Ryan had conquered the American League's best hitters in the 1970's, he did the same to the top National League stars in the 1980's. Two time MVP Dale Murphy commented on Ryan's dominance, saying, "He is the only pitcher you start thinking about two days before you face him." Going into Ryan's final season in Houston, Pete Rose made a stronger statement: "At the age of 41, Nolan Ryan is the top power pitcher in the league. You can talk about Dwight Gooden, you can talk about Mike Scott, you can talk about whoever you want, but none of them throw as consistently hard as Ryan does."

What kept Nolan Ryan smoking pitches into his forties with the Astros was a training regimen developed by Gene Coleman, Houston's strength and conditioning advisor. Adhering to Dr. Coleman's weight-lifting, running, exercise and stationary bicycling program, Nolan Ryan maintained the body of a man 20 years younger.

After the 1988 season, Houston owner John McMullen ignored the facts that Nolan Ryan had come within two outs of throwing a no-hitter that year and had also led the league in strikeouts the previous two years, and decided a pay cut was in order for his theoretically aging pitcher.

Knowing his value, Ryan proceeded to leave his hometown team for greener Arlington pastures where the Texas Rangers ownership welcomed him with open arms and a sizeable raise. Veteran Houston sportswriter Mickey Herskowitz accurately expressed the city's sorrow after Ryan left the Astros: "In Houston, the fans had mixed feelings about Nolan. Some miss him every day of their lives, and some just miss him every fifth day."

THE RANGER YEARS

After spending a career being ultimately rejected by the Mets, Angels and Astros, Nolan Ryan finally found a team that wanted to embrace him on a permanent basis. The Texas Rangers had always been a floundering organization, playing in an expanded minor league

As a Texas Ranger, Ryan flashed a rare smile on the field at the end of his seventh no-hitter.

ball park, and never participating in post-season play.

With the signing of Ryan on December 7, 1988, the Rangers gained something they had never had before—national credibility. Texas general manager Tom Grieve put in perspective the signing of Nolan Ryan: "To get a player of his caliber, all those statistics, and the kind of guy he is, well, you don't want to get up on a podium and start bubbling over, but that's how we felt."

Motivated by the challenge of continuing to succeed on a power level with younger competition, Nolan Ryan proceeded to have three full-blown years of greatness with Texas from 1989 to 1991. In those years, he compiled a record of 41-25 with a 3.20 ERA, struck out more batters than anyone else in the American League, had a strikeout-to-walk ratio of better than 3 to 1, and pitched through the fifth inning in 54 of his 59 starts.

As a Ranger, Nolan Ryan's continuing to rack up milestones overshadowed his contributions every fifth day in the rotation. On August 22, 1989, he achieved career strikeout number 5,000. On June 11, 1990, Ryan pitched his sixth no-hitter. On July 31, 1990, he won his 300th game in the major leagues. On May 1, 1991, Ryan shut down Toronto, the league's best hitting team, to record his seventh no-hitter.

As Ryan soared to new heights, so did Arlington's attendance. In his first season as a Ranger, the team drew over two million fans for the first time in franchise history. When he pitched, average attendance was 8,000 more than on other nights. Texas continued to top the two million mark every year after 1989, making the ownership's decision to build The Ballpark in Arlington an easy one; the construction commenced in 1991.

Fans knew that every time Nolan Ryan took the mound, it might be a no-hitter. In his first three years with the Rangers, on top of the 2 no-hitters, Ryan also pitched 6 one-hitters, 8 two-hitters, and 12 three-hitters.

What kept Ryan throwing in the mid-90's as he aged into his mid-40's was his relentless dedication to fitness. His daily off-season workouts lasted up to five hours. During the season, on nights he pitched, Ryan stationary bicycled for at least 45 minutes after the game. Between starts, baseball's bionic man spent over two hours every day lifting weights, running, and biking. Ranger pitching coach Tom House said of his star pupil, "He's still throwing hard because he does what it takes to prepare himself. He's like the mailman. Nothing keeps him from making his rounds in the weight room."

Ryan completed his final season as a Ranger in 1993 hampered by injuries to his knee, rib cage, and elbow. Pitching in between stays on the disabled list, Nolan Ryan gave Texas fans one final lasting memory. On August 4, 1993, in the third inning of a game against Chicago, Ryan's fastball hit Robin Ventura in the arm. The young White Sox slugger stormed the mound and tried to attack a man 20 years his senior. Ryan had been in this situation once before when Dave Winfield charged him at Houston. In that incident, Ryan followed his coaches' instructions and simply ducked Winfield's punches, and coiled up to protect his pitching arm.

Rejecting the Winfield defensive strategy that had bothered him for 13 years, Ryan responded to Ventura's attack with force of his own—putting the Chicago third baseman into a headlock, and punching the top of his head, making the batter pay for his aggressive tactics. Ryan said later that night, "All you can do is react. You don't have time to figure your options." After the fight, the umpires ejected Ventura and allowed Ryan to stay in the game. Unfazed by the altercation, he lasted 7 innings, allowing 3 hits, and retiring 12 of the last 13 men he faced to get the victory.

The end came on September 22, 1993, at Seattle. In his last career start, while throwing a fastball in the first inning, Nolan Ryan tore the ulnar collateral ligament in his right elbow. Later that night in the clubhouse, Ryan described his final game: "I heard the ligament pop like a rubber band. There's no way I'll ever be able to throw again. My body is telling me it's time to move on and do something else."

The Ranger years established that Nolan Ryan was more than a major league superstar. In Texas, he became a baseball legend whose final career records are so far ahead of his nearest rivals that when the great power pitchers of all time are discussed, there is simply Nolan Ryan … and there is everyone else. In the words of 1993 World Series hero Joe Carter, "There's always one guy who defies the odds. In baseball, Nolan Ryan is that guy."

August 4, 1993: When Robin Ventura charged the mound, he found himself being pounded in a hammerlock. Ryan explained his actions, "All you can do is react. You don't have time to figure your options."

STAYING CONNECTED TO THE GAME

To the surprise of no one, Nolan Ryan became a first-ballot inductee into the National Baseball Hall of Fame and was joined in Cooperstown on July 25, 1999, by George Brett, Robin Yount, and Orlando Cepeda. Their respective fan clubs generated the biggest attendance for a NBHOF induction ceremony the village had ever witnessed until July 29, 2007, when Cal Ripken and Tony Gwynn became initiated into the game's most hollowed fraternity.

To the surprise of many, in his acceptance speech, Ryan paid tribute to Marvin Miller, leader of the Players Union in its early years, who caused player salaries to increase exponentially by getting arbitration, free agency, and a strong pension plan into the compensation mix, allowing the ballplayers of Ryan's era to obtain lifetime financial security before their playing days ended.

Missing the thrill of pitching competitive baseball, Nolan Ryan kept finding ways to stay active in the game after walking off a major league mound the last time in September 1993. While sons Reid and Reese pitched in college in the mid-nineties for TCU, their dad served as the Horned Frogs' volunteer pitching coach and donned a uniform for the games.

After the boys graduated, Nolan Ryan joined with longtime colleague Don Sanders to form Ryan-Sanders Baseball, and purchased the Jackson Generals, the Houston Astros' AA farm team then competing in the Texas League. Not surprisingly, Ryan-Sanders decided the team needed to be moved from Mississippi to the best possible location in Texas, and with the help of CEO Reid Ryan and CFO Reese Ryan, the baseball enterprise started its search.

Knowing North Texas already had the Rangers, the Gulf Coast had the Astros, Ryan-Sanders could see that the best location for a minor league baseball team with a ready-made critical mass of potential ticket buyers was in Central Texas. Nolan Ryan approached Austin about bringing his minor league ballclub there, but city leaders rejected his proposal, not wanting competition with Texas Longhorns baseball. Then Ryan had another idea. Knowing what was happening north of Austin, he called the mayor of Round Rock to explore the possibility of locating his Jackson team there. The mayor instantly thought of an available piece of land with frontage on Highway 79 that for years had been used only as a cornfield, and invited Ryan to come take a look. A few weeks later, the deal was made, and the city of Round Rock held a groundbreaking ceremony. There, in the middle of the field, after walking over a path cut through rows of stalks, Nolan Ryan smiled, and giving his best Kevin Costner imitation, announced to the crowd, "If we build it, they will come."

Ryan-Sanders built what became the Dell Diamond in time for Opening Day of the 2000 Texas League season, and the people came. Over the Round Rock Express' first 4 seasons, they shattered all league attendance records, and their success motivated the Ryan-Sanders ownership group to purchase the AAA Edmonton Trappers in the Pacific Coast League, move the Edmonton franchise to Round Rock in time for the 2005 season (where it became the Astros' AAA team), and transfer the AA franchise from Round Rock to Corpus Christi (where it's the Astros' AA team). The Corpus Christi Hooks have maintained a

Round Rock pace of record-breaking Texas League attendance in their first three seasons, averaging a higher level of game ticket sales than the team's new Whataburger Field has seats, due to a grassy berm in left field that attracts hundreds of fans every game.

The same level of success Nolan Ryan enjoyed over his 27-year career as a major league pitcher is now in the process of being matched by his Texas baseball business, with the Round Rock and Corpus Christi franchises attracting over 6 million fans in a space of only 7 years. Most recently, in February 2008, Ryan was named president of the Texas Rangers, becoming the first Hall of Fame player to be the top executive at a major league franchise since Christy Mathewson. For the Ryan family, regardless of their endeavors, the combination of their work ethic, acumen, and integrity has ensured that failure is not an option.

THE PITCHING RECORDS

In baseball, there are two marks of permanence—induction into the National Baseball Hall of Fame and the record book. In Cooperstown, a member's plaque is etched in bronze. Because of the game's evolution since the 1970's toward the quicker use of relief pitchers and the abandonment of having starting pitchers work on only three days' rest, in baseball's record book, Nolan Ryan's 53 career records are carved in stone.

Strikeouts. With the exception of Roger Clemens' having twice struck out 20 batters in one game, all the important major league strikeout records belong to Nolan Ryan—most strikeouts in a season; most strikeouts in a career; most years to record 100 strikeouts; most years to record 200 strikeouts; most years to record 300 strikeouts; most games striking out 10 or more batters; most games striking out 15 or more batters; most strikeouts per 9 innings over a season; and most strikeouts per 9 innings over a career.

As a major league pitcher, Nolan Ryan struck out 5,714 batters. Baseball's next best strikeout artist, which may be either Roger Clemens or Randy Johnson, has almost 4,700, and both of them gave every indication of being close to the end of their careers in 2007. To understand the significance of the strikeout record, if there existed the same margin between the best and the second best in baseball's other major individual statistical categories, a batter would have to hit 916 career home runs to establish a Ryan level of percentage superiority over Hank Aaron's 755 homers (or Barry Bonds' steroid-clouded 762 homers as of the end of the 2007 season), and would have to get 5,162 career base hits to achieve the same distance from Pete Rose's 4,256 hits.

No-Hitters and Low-Hitters. Nolan Ryan pitched 7 no-hitters in his career. Baseball's next best no-hit pitcher, Sandy Koufax, got 4. Coupled with his 12 one-hitters, Ryan pitched 19 career low-hitters, while baseball's second best low-hit pitcher, Bob Feller, had 15. As with his strikeouts, Ryan's distance from the rest of the low-hit pitching pack was sizeable.

In 1972, Nolan Ryan set the single-season record for giving up the fewest hits per nine innings. Not surprisingly, upon his retirement, he also had the career record for per game hitting infrequency. In baseball, pitching a six-hitter is something special. Nolan Ryan did it almost every time he took the mound.

Durability. Pitching effectively in the major leagues between the ages of 21 and 46 produces a stream of career records—most years to do this, most games to do that, oldest pitcher to do this, largest time span to achieve that. Nolan Ryan power pitched for over a quarter of a century by simply maximizing this short-term performance. With California in his late 20's, Ryan told reporters he anticipated having perhaps another four or five years of power pitching ahead of him. With Houston in his mid-to-late 30's, he said the same thing. Despite his expectations of having a normal career length, his arm and body simply refused to slow down, due to his extraordinary daily conditioning and preparation. While finishing his career in Arlington, Ryan explained his durability: "I never thought about playing in four decades. I don't think in decades. I go day by day."

Achieving major league records comes at a price. The night Nolan Ryan broke Sandy Koufax's single-season strikeout record, he withstood severe leg cramps requiring almost constant massages that allowed him to fan his 383rd victim in the 11th inning of his last start in 1973. The night Ryan broke Walter Johnson's career strikeout record, the Astros' trainer drained a blister on his right hand to allow him to continue. The night Ryan pitched his sixth no-hitter, he did it with constant pain in his lower back (later discovered to be a stress fracture),

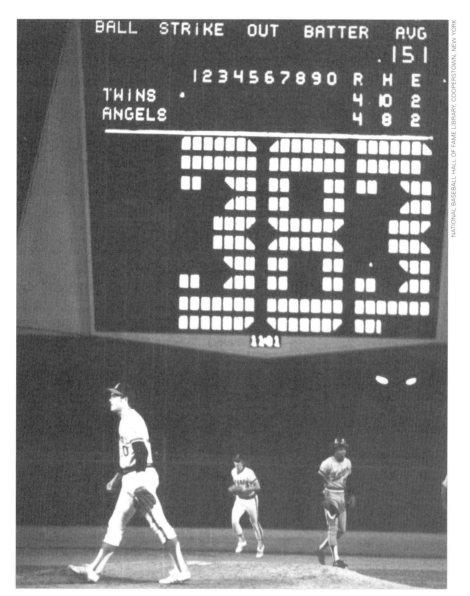

Nolan Ryan battled severe leg cramps to pitch eleven innings in his final start of 1973, in order to break Sandy Koufax's single season strikeout record.

the significance of which he tried to minimize after the game: "It wasn't all that bad. It only hurt when I threw the ball." Ryan then pitched his seventh no-hitter with a sore Achilles tendon, constant back pain, and a cracked-skinned, bloody right middle finger, all of which went with the territory of power pitching into his mid-40's.

Records are objective. Awards are subjective. Through 26 years of greatness, Nolan Ryan never received the Cy Young Award, though a strong statistical argument supports his entitlement to it in 5 different seasons. That didn't bother him. He told a reporter early in his career, "To tell the truth, the Cy Young has never been one of my goals. My goals are simply to be consistent and keep the respect of my fellow players." Because he achieved that subjective career goal of maintaining both his pitching consistency and the respect of other players over the course of 26 full major league seasons, the record book for major league pitchers is in large part Nolan Ryan's biography.

THE METHODS

Major league pitchers do not perform for 26 seasons, complete 5,387 innings, and strike out 5,714 batters by being merely traditional in attempting to master their craft. Nolan Ryan realized early on that to fulfill his sizeable potential required constant innovation and discipline in every aspect of his game.

During Ryan's brief minor league career, he learned to appreciate the fragility of a pitcher's arm. In 1967, his military reserve duties kept him away from baseball until the middle of the season. Ryan finally rushed into the Jacksonville Suns' starting rotation in June and temporarily overachieved, striking out 17 of the 20 batters he faced in his first start. While warming up before the next game, he heard something pop in his arm, which turned out to be a torn ligament in his right elbow. The 20-year-old pitcher then stood up to the team doctor, refused to submit himself to the recommended surgery, and healed the arm through rest and rehabilitation.

In 1968, as a fully recovered rookie phenom with the Mets, Nolan Ryan's power delivery combined with the friction of the ball's seams against his fingers to produce severe blisters on the middle finger of his right hand. The blisters produced diminished effectiveness as each game progressed. Using the first innovative technique in his career, Ryan started soaking his finger in pickle brine to toughen the skin, a tactic which had been used by boxers for years to toughen their hands. When the pickle brine proved only marginally successful, he switched to olive brine, which worked slightly better. Finally, Ryan solved his blister problem by using a surgeon's scalpel to shave off the excess skin and scar tissue on the fingers of his pitching hand before the start of each game, a process *Sports Illustrated* compared to "peeling grapes, causing the baseball clutched in his right hand to feel as smooth as a bullet."

Inclined initially as a young pitcher toward the use of homespun remedies, Ryan tried treating a sore right elbow in his first year as an Angel by rubbing rattlesnake oil onto the joint. What proved to be more successful than the snake oil, however, was the weight conditioning program he started in California to build up his arm and entire body. Before 1972, baseball's "experts" had concluded that weight training made a player too muscle-bound, causing him to lose the smooth movement necessary for arm speed in a pitcher and bat speed in a hitter. Nolan Ryan became the first big league pitcher to enhance his performance through the use of weights, the approach to which he described in his autobiography: "It's weight *conditioning*, not weight lifting. I was not trying to see how much weight I could lift. I was trying to lift the right weights in the right way."

The successful but unsupervised use of weights in California was followed by Ryan's total conditioning program in Houston under the direction of Dr. Eugene Coleman, the Astros' strength instructor, who had learned his profession training astronauts at NASA. Following Dr. Coleman's suggestions, Ryan's exercise workouts now had a specific purpose, from Nautilus training, to jogging underwater in a swimming pool, to maintaining a running and bicycling program. Ryan explained his emerging obsession with conditioning in a 1988 interview: "I never want to walk off the field feeling I got beat because the other guy was in better shape than I was."

In addition to using the most sophisticated conditioning techniques, Nolan Ryan stayed effective longer than any pitcher in history by constantly studying and then incorporating new mound techniques. Pitching excellence requires a mastery of fundamentals— pushing off the rubber with maximum force; keeping the body low, thereby producing more strength to support the arm; and releasing the ball at precisely the same millisecond in each delivery. Ryan's perfected fundamentals allowed the implementation of new pitches, changed speeds, and improved control.

What also enabled Nolan Ryan to break so many baseball records was the application of old-fashioned common sense to his daily regimen. He never risked wearing out his arm by pitching in winter ball. The off-season physical activities Ryan pursued did not include bowling, volleyball, skiing, or any other sport which might likely result in a hand or leg injury. Adding to his prudent exercise decisions, he maintained a calm lifestyle sustained by a balanced moderate diet, no smoking, and no excessive drinking, celebrating his no-hitters drinking orange juice instead of the traditional champagne.

The science behind the artistry of Nolan Ryan involved the full utilization of his body and mind, knowing when to accept instruction and when to follow his own instincts. Veteran *Newsweek* sportswriter Pete Axthelm summarized the total commitment to pitching which drove Ryan's unprecedented career: "Other pitchers are satisfied in getting a win after a routine outing. Nolan Ryan spent over two decades using everything he had to be Picasso."

THE PERFECT POWER PITCHER

In the words of Hall of Famer Sandy Koufax, "Pitching is the art of instilling fear by making a man flinch." No pitcher in history has ever instilled more fear causing more batters to flinch than Nolan Ryan. Former American League outfielder Tom Grieve gave the hitter's perspective on an encounter with Ryan: "He was the only pitcher I ever faced where it entered my mind that it might be dangerous to bat against him. He threw the ball so hard you had to be on your guard."

How hard? Ryan's 100.9 mile per hour heat gave a batter exactly .409 of a second to react compared with his having .454 of a second to respond to an above average major league 90.9 mph fastball.

The Body. To throw a baseball harder than anyone else in the game every year for 26 years requires, first of all, a special physique that stays healthy on a consistent basis. Above the waist, maximum arm speed comes when the shoulder, elbow, and snapped wrist move together in perfect synchronized coordination. Below the waist, to push off the rubber with the greatest possible thrust, the pitcher must have legs strong enough to generate total body momentum. Driving the arms and

With his body, mind, lifestyle, and conditioning program, Nolan Ryan became baseball's perfect power pitcher for more than a quarter of a century.

legs must be a heart which knows no restraint, allowing the pitcher to throw as hard as he can for an average of 150 pitched over a nine-inning game.

Nolan Ryan had the requisite physical tools. Long arms, supple wrists, huge hands, a thick chest, massive thighs, all held together with quality connective body tissue provided the essential framework for throwing fastballs with textbook mechanics and perfect pitching rhythm. Ryan's body stayed strong for the duration of his major league pitching career because of the rigorously sustained conditioning program he followed every month of the year. Beyond the body, the coordination, and the conditioning, Ryan's heart became so absorbed with throwing his hardest that each fastball climaxed with an urgent grunt which echoed throughout the ballpark.

The Mind. The second element of the power pitcher is the attitude. He must have the hard stare revealing the killer instinct necessary to put away a batter. Nolan Ryan acknowledged he has two personalities. "I'm a totally different person on the mound. I don't even look the same. The casual country gentleman I try to be when I'm away from baseball wouldn't get anybody out in the big leagues. To succeed at the major league level you have to be single-minded with total concentration. You also have to be tough enough to go after the hitters, take every advantage you can to work on their weak spots, and beat them. There's nothing 'nice guy' about it."

Ryan's teammates witnessed his tenacity. Former Houston relief Joe Sambito observed in his teammate that when he got the ball and took the mound, you could see him change. He had that look about him that said, "nobody is going to beat me." Texas catcher John Russell saw the same thing in catching Ryan's sixth no-hitter. "I've never seen a more determined look in a pitcher's eyes in my life."

The Game Plan. The final element of power pitching comes with executing strategy that keeps hitters both afraid and off balance. To incite fear in a batter, the pitcher must have velocity, coupled with an acceptable level of wildness. Veteran catcher John Roseboro, who caught Koufax in his prime and then coached Ryan during the Angel years, described the advantage of a power pitcher with less than perfect control: "Wildness works to his advantage. The hitters don't know where he's going to throw the ball and won't dig in unless they're imbeciles."

Nolan Ryan never seemed troubled by his bases on balls totals, saying, "It doesn't matter how many you walk as long as they don't score."

Keeping hitters out of sync so that they don't just wait on the fastball requires having command over a repertoire of other quality pitches. Ryan expanded his pitching menu throughout his career, mastering the sharp breaking curveball at California, and then the changeup with Houston. Pete Rose described Ryan's curveball as "one of the best secrets in the game. When it was working, you never could hit the fastball." Former Astro Phil Garner said of Ryan, "The thing that took him from being an awesome fastball thrower to a pitcher was the changeup. With that pitch, the batter had to protect for the off-speed stuff, and if he was looking for a change, Nolan would blow him away with the fastball."

Combining his physical tools, menacing attitude, and versatile repertoire, at the height of his baseball career, Nolan Ryan became what *Sports Illustrated* described in a 1975 cover story as "the supreme fastball pitcher, baseball's noblest creation, who brings down thunder from the skies. He does not throw a ball. He throws lightning, smoke, flames, heat, blue darters, dark ones, high hard ones, hummers and aspirin tablets. In baseball vernacular, he does not throw at all. He brings it."

SYMBOL OF THE GAME

From the time he received his first glove in 1953 until his seemingly indestructible arm finally gave out in Seattle at the end of the 1993 season, Nolan Ryan and baseball fulfilled each other. The temperament and talents of the man matched the nature and challenges of the game, resulting in a Hall of Fame career.

The game of baseball is about individual achievement amidst the play of a team. A player's personal success is enhanced or diminished by his team's overall performance. Nolan Ryan's experience in the major leagues confirms this reality of the game. His individual achievements are unique, but with the exception of the 1969 New York Mets, the accomplishments of his teams were often ordinary. Ryan's final statistical record shows the results when an overwhelming talent is placed with a frequently underwhelming team—the greatest strikeout and no-hit pitcher of all time had an unspectacular lifetime winning percentage because of receiving consistently poor run support. The game when he recorded his five-thousandth strikeout on August

22, 1989, epitomized his career. As with so many other performances throughout his 26 big league seasons, that night Nolan Ryan pitched well enough to give his team the chance to win, yet achieved only mixed statistical success. Although he pitched a 5 hit complete game and struck out 13 while giving up only 1 earned run, the Rangers failed to score in a tight 2-0 loss. Ever the team player, in the clubhouse after the game, Ryan's disappointment over the loss outweighed any elation from his personal achievement.

The game of baseball requires the capacity to block out all distractions, allowing a player's temperament to stay at an even keel. Throughout his career, Nolan Ryan was the master of baseball's mental game. A batter's aggressiveness, a fielder's error, an umpire's missed call, a crowd's standing ovation—nothing interrupted the line of constant concentration between pitcher and catcher. When Bo Jackson hit a bouncer up the middle that split Ryan's lip in the first inning of a game in 1990, which would later that night require eight stitches to close the gash, he pitched into the eighth inning, and gave up a total of only three hits, while blood kept steadily flowing onto his uniform.

The game of baseball demands ferocity. A pitcher must have the fire to dominate and destroy the opposing lineup's nine hitters. Veteran Houston sportswriter Mickey Herskowitz saw the sixty-foot-six-inch confrontation in epic terms: "The essence of the game of baseball is the will of the solitary man to take on the many." Over a quarter of a century, more than 16,000 batters returned to their dugout knowing they had been put away by baseball's toughest competitor—the man with the hard stare, the swagger around the mound, the dangerous inside heat, and the violent grunt.

The game of baseball compels players on a team to get along with each other over the course of an extended hard season. Nolan Ryan relished the daily camaraderie in being a part of a team. Former Houston General Manager Al Rosen had the opportunity to observe the effect of Ryan on his team over an extended period of time. "Nolan Ryan was like Joe DiMaggio—not a holler guy but a quiet leader. The players responded because there was a sense of majesty about him." Ryan's teammates, in fact, responded to his leadership with the ultimate tribute. Ten of them named their sons after him.

Finally, the game of baseball is about coming home. Nolan Ryan pitched the last game Bart Giamatti ever saw ten days before the commissioner's sudden death. This final connection between baseball's greatest power pitcher and the game's most eloquent spokesman seems natural because it was Giamatti who once articulated the metaphor that Nolan Ryan embodied: "Baseball is about going home, and how hard it is to get there, and how driven is our need. It tells us how good home is. Its wisdom says you can go home again, but you cannot stay. The journey must always start once more until there is an end to all journeying." Nolan Ryan's remarkable journey through life has always carried him back to Texas where he is safe ... safe at home.

Nolan Ryan once said of life, "The secret is knowing that there's no secret." His accomplishments as a baseball player and a person flow from simple unmysterious virtues: natural talent, hard work, integrity, self-discipline, common sense, humility, loyalty to a supportive family and friends, and respect for all people.

It is one thing to have an awareness of virtue. It is another to live it. Since childhood, Nolan Ryan has practiced the same straightforward approach to life that comes from having a clear understanding of himself. "I know who I am. I'm a country kid from Texas with the ability to throw a ball and the dedication to keep myself in shape. I'm just a man. I'm no better than anybody else, even if I have an unusual and marketable talent. My basic philosophy of life came from my parents: Treat others the way you want to be treated, with honesty and respect."

The pitching numbers go beyond "great." They are "unique." No one before Nolan Ryan had ever struck out over 5,700 batters, thrown 7 no-hitters, or power-pitched for 26 major league seasons. Beyond the seemingly unbreakable records, however, his proudest professional achievement defies quantification. "I'll always be able to look in the mirror and know that the guy looking back gave the game, the fans, and his ball club everything he had to give for as long as he could."

To honor the man whom this writer regards as the Baby Boomer Symbol of the Game, in 1999, my family and friends decided to join the multitudes attending Nolan Ryan's induction ceremony at the National Baseball Hall of Fame. Our trip set off internal fireworks of the uplifting variety, and my assessment of that experience appeared in the August 15, 1999, issue of the *Dallas Morning News.* Bob Moos, then the editor of that newspaper's Op-Ed section, accurately chose for its title— "Cooperstown Helps Us Satisfy a Deep Need."

In 1999, Nolan Ryan earned his ticket into the National Baseball Hall of Fame along with Orlando Cepeda, Robin Yount, and George Brett.

Cooperstown, New York, population 2,400 and home of the National Baseball Hall of Fame and Museum, is one of the most remote locations in the eastern United States. It is nowhere near a major highway, with the closest airport in Albany some seventy-five miles away.

The village served as the boyhood residence of Abner Doubleday, once thought to be the creator of our National Pastime, whose failure to invent baseball was not fully appreciated until after the Hall of Fame was up and running. Regardless of the historical error, for the past sixty years, Cooperstown has been the home of one of the most successful museums in America with more than 400,000 baseball fans each year going through its turnstiles.

On Sunday, July 25, 1999, over 50,000 people from all over the world by-passed the nearby frenzied Woodstock music festival (organized in the context of its being the thirtieth anniversary of the original Woodstock festival) and instead chose to bake in the sun for two hours in an unfrenzied environment on a local green field for the Hall of Fame's annual induction ceremony. The crowd proved to be the largest ever to honor those most skilled users of bat, ball, and glove who officially become immortalized upon receiving their plaques, which hang in the local shrine.

Baby Boomers composed the substantial majority of the perspiration-soaked audience. Rapidly balding and graying children of the fifties and sixties can now (thankfully) resist many things perceived as essential in years past. Some have even outgrown toys. This crowd of 50,000, however, could not resist and had not outgrown one of life's vital needs, which exists for all true boys and girls of summer, regardless of how many birthdays have passed—the need to honor heroes.

Those who traveled over 1,500 miles from Texas came to pay tribute to one singularly sensational hero. The little kid inside the audience's collective psyche, which keeps a fan young at heart at least some of the time, stood and applauded Lynn Nolan Ryan Jr., the man known to Texas Rangers fans as "Big Tex."

The big right-handed pitcher's records are unparalleled, but never mind the 5,714 strikeouts, the 7 no-hitters, or the 324 wins. The most enduring memory of Texas Ranger fans who witnessed the Ryan Express during his five glorious years in Arlington from 1989 to 1993 was not a statistic but a sound. Every time the forty-something power pitcher delivered his heat, the Rangers' first and foremost franchise player threw the ball with such total passion that a bellowing grunt could be heard throughout the ballpark. When it was his day to pitch, Ol' Nolan gave it all he had.

A commercial from two decades ago comes to mind as we reflect on our desire to travel across the country and be in the same green field with Nolan Ryan when he receives baseball's greatest award. Portly John Houseman, best remembered as Professor Kingsfield in the movie *The Paper Chase*, purred to the camera with Shakespearean flair about how an investment firm made its profits. Yes, in the presence of fifty thousand persons, the slow-talking man at the Cooperstown podium garnered the everlasting respect of the assembled multitude the old fashioned way. He earned it.

Baseball's poet laureate, Commissioner Bart Giamatti, whom Roger Angell of *The New Yorker* magazine described as "a lifetime .400 talker."

CHAPTER FIVE

BART GIAMATTI
Baseball's Lyricist

Baseball's scope is so vast it creates opportunities even for those lacking the skills to play the game well. Though he could not walk the walk, Bart Giamatti talked baseball's talk better than anyone in postwar America, helping Baby Boomers and everyone else understand once and for all exactly what it is about the game that wraps itself around our lives.

There's a well-traveled joke about baseball: Why is it the favorite sport of intellectuals? Punchline: Because the game moves so slowly they can understand it.

While intellectuals on the order of George Will, Stephen Jay Gould, David Halberstam, Doris Kearns Goodwin, and Scott Simon have written and spoken at length on their respective love affairs with the game, the consensus among baseball aficionado luminaries since World War II is that the most eloquent voice ever to address the many facets of baseball was Angelo Bartlett "Bart" Giamatti, National League President from 1986 through the spring of 1989, and then Commissioner of Baseball for five months before suffering a fatal heart attack at the age of 51.

When Commissioner Giamatti died suddenly on Friday, September 1, 1989, exactly one week after reaching a final settlement of the issues related to Pete Rose's sordid gambling activities, many fans, including this writer, who had grown to admire his passion, intelligence, integrity, and command of the English language during his short stint on the national baseball stage, felt we had lost the one person in the world who had succeeded at articulating all the nuances of this game that holds us so tightly in its clutches.

Having just seen Giamatti preside over the Baseball Hall of Fame's 1989 induction ceremony that brought first ballot inductees Carl

Yastrzemski and Johnny Bench into the Hall (along with Veterans Committee selections Red Schoendienst and umpire Al Barlick), and then shortly thereafter having received a ball autographed by the Commissioner, courtesy of Sara Brown (wife of American League President Bobby Brown), I had been so moved by the entirety of that Cooperstown experience (see Chapter 6) that I commenced writing for publication about baseball upon leaving New York on my flight back to Texas. When word of Giamatti's death hit the wire services that fateful Friday, the pen in my hand took off onto the blank page in hopes that a written response to the tragedy would lessen my grief. This reflection on his passing became my first essay ever to appear in print, making it into the Sports Section of the now defunct *Dallas Times Herald*. Alas, every writer has to start somewhere, so here was my tribute to Bart Giamatti, a man who became my hero by providing the words that perfectly meshed with the music of the game on the field.

Heroes. Most children have heroes. Unfortunately, too often these days they are athletes with drug problems or actors with babies born out of wedlock. To many, an adult with a hero suggests arrested development. So be it. I am 35 years old, a trial lawyer, a husband and father, a baseball fan, and I had a hero who just died last Friday. His name was A. Bartlett Giamatti.

I never met Commissioner Giamatti, and that's fine. Heroes are better appreciated at a distance. In his four years as a baseball executive, the national media communicated to the masses that it was possible for one person's life to stand for the propositions that—

A person can achieve top-of-the-mountain success in more than one field;

A person can maintain both a consuming passion for his interests and a healthy life balance;

A person embroiled in the hurly burly of the arena can still articulate thoughts with precision and imagination;

> A moral person at work and play, with family, friends
> and foes, can stay centered in his integrity.

From my perspective, this combination of qualities made Bart
Giamatti a hero, defined by *Webster's* as "a person admired for both
his achievements and noble qualities." How many successful people
lack eloquence? How many passionate people lose their balance? How
many elite intellectuals live in the safe walls of a university, writing
unintelligible books and staying disconnected from society rather
than entering the public arena? How many people live in a mode of
uncompromising integrity on a daily basis?

For mid-life Baby Boomer baseballphiliacs like me, whose family
and friends have sometimes (in fact, many times) rolled their eyes at my
lifelong devotion to the game, I needed a spokesman—someone who
made sense of my telescopic focus on a game. Yet despite extensive education and reflection, my best efforts to find the right words to explain
the reasons behind baseball's hold on me never quite hit the mark.

Then along came Bart Giamatti in 1986. At last, as National League
President and then as Commissioner, here was someone with an
impeccable pedigree (an Ivy League Ph.D. in comparative literature,
who as Yale president turned the ink of that institution's finances from
red to black), who made public statements about the game that read
 like poetry and could be appreciated by all levels of intelligence, even
those (like my parents) who had been in the eyeball rolling business for
decades. Two examples:

> Baseball is not simply an essential part of this country;
> it is a living memory of what the American culture at
> its best works to be. Baseball is about going home, and
> how hard it is to get there, and how driven is our need.
> It tells us how good home is. Its wisdom says that you
> can go home again, but you cannot stay.

> The game is quintessentially American in the way it
> puts the premium on both the individual and the team;
> in the way it encourages enterprise and imagination
> and yet asserts the supreme power of law.

With Bart Giamatti in the national media limelight spouting insights like these in non-stop mode, we baseball fanatics could respond with force (At Last!) to the rolling eyeballs, "You think I'm a kook? Maybe so, but I'm in with real good company."

In the context of Commissioner Giamatti's tragic death, it would definitely dull the pain of the grieving masses if baseball writers and Hall of Fame Veterans Committee members could now direct their attention away from the current national obsession over Pete Rose's chances of ever getting a plaque in Cooperstown and instead turn toward the opportunity to open the Hall's doors to the person who for the last four years has served, and will surely serve in perpetuity, as the premier spokesman and conscience of baseball fans. In furtherance of dissipating the distress over the Commissioner's recent passing, those who choose Hall of Fame inductees should go the extra mile and not wait the obligatory six years to induct Giamatti into the Hall. Just as they honored Roberto Clemente in the year after he gave his life aiding earthquake victims, they should do the same for the man who gave his life to rid the game of Pete Rose's lunacy and thereby preserved the integrity of the National Pastime.[1]

Rest in peace, baseball's poet laureate and noble hero. Thanks to your sacrificial efforts in the summer of 1989, the game has weathered its storm.

Thirteen years after his death, I accepted the assignment of profiling Commissioner Giamatti for *The Scribner Encyclopedia of American Lives: Sports Figures*, and as with my pieces on Carl Yastrzemski and Lou Brock for that same encyclopedia (which also appear in this book), used it as my vehicle for attempting to affirm his legacy to a larger audience. In transferring the profile for Scribner's into the text of this book, I have expanded my write-up substantially and have woven additional research into it from sources not available in 2002.

1 My plea for Hall of Fame induction (communicated by my sending letters with this request to many HOF board members in the fall of 1989) fell on deaf ears. To this day, Giamatti has no plaque in Cooperstown, and on reflection, I agree with this decision, given his short time as an executive in the game. No one has ever gotten into the Hall of Fame who participated less than a half decade on baseball's national stage. In tribute, the Hall of Fame did, however, name its research center after him shortly after his death.

The son of a literature and Italian language professor at Mount Holyoke College, baseball's seventh commissioner, Bart Giamatti, was born on April 4, 1938, and grew up in South Hadley, Massachusetts. He devoted his formative years to maximizing his connection with his father, Professor Val Giamatti, and through that effort, young Bart learned (in no particular order) to love Dante (reciting *The Divine Comedy* to his dad at the breakfast table), the art of conversation, and the Boston Red Sox. As a boy, although devoid of baseball playing skills, Bart felt such a deep passion for the game that his middle school coach in South Hadley made a place for him on the squad as the team's manager, allowing him to demonstrate his organizational skills as a baseball administrator i.e., dugout organizer, for the first time. He also used this position as a means of bonding with the umpires who presided over the school's games, a practice he would follow years later in the national arena. Given that any baseball diamond on game day is intended to be an idyllic "free and ordered space," Bart Giamatti paid special attention early on to those charged with the responsibility of maintaining that order.

Throughout his son's youth, in serving as the most influential person in Bart's life, Val Giamatti also set the unfortunate example of smoking four packs of cigarettes a day, which led to his suffering a massive but non-fatal heart attack at the age of 51. Bart would soon embrace cigarettes with the same lifelong passion as he gave to Dante and the Boston Red Sox, but was not as lucky as his dad, becoming the victim of a fatal smoking-induced heart attack upon reaching the exact same age.

After leaving South Hadley to attend Andover Academy, Bart emerged as a speaker and performer on center stage at the prestigious prep school, thriving there as an accomplished debater, orator, and actor in dramatic productions, while gaining popularity among his classmates through the sheer force of his personality. In the words of James Reston Jr., in his book, *Collision at Home Plate* (Edward Burlingame Books, 1991), given Bart's clear lack of athletic talent in high school, "conversation was his sport," operating at the dormitory dinner table and everywhere else at Andover in a mode of high-gear, mesmerizing communication as if always "on stage."

After finishing high school, Giamatti matriculated at Yale in 1956 where quickly (as at Andover) he became an academic and social star, a close friend of classmate (and future television celebrity) Dick Cavett, and the recipient of a Yale student's highest honor, selected to give the class oration at his 1960 graduation. In that speech, he identified the goal that would stay with him the remainder of his life, encouraging his peers to avoid apathy, and instead be "creative and humane men in society. Let us not seek always a sedative, in one form or another, for what ails us, but let us seek a cure." A self-professed agnostic by the age of 22, Giamatti told his class in the graduation speech that their apathy came from a "void; for what we lack is a myth, a unified body of belief." Thus, in Giamatti's eyes, the power of myth had more capacity to serve as a unified body of belief sufficient to fuel a cure for society's problems than any higher power available from a religious faith.

Upon receiving his Ph.D. from Yale in 1964, where his dissertation addressed the role of "the garden" in Renaissance literature,[2] Giamatti began his teaching career at Princeton for two years, but then returned to New Haven and joined the Yale faculty in 1966. His theatrical presentation style, rapport with his students, and ability to draw parallels between Renaissance literature and contemporary American life soon electrified the campus, leading to his becoming a full professor in 1971. A former student observed that Giamatti "read Dante's original Italian as a maestro reads music—with love."

Before reaching his fortieth birthday, after telling his colleagues, "All I ever wanted to be president of was the American League," Bart Giamatti was named the nineteenth President of Yale University in early 1978. Never bashful about his idealism, on his first day in office, the new boss issued a memo to the entire Yale community, requesting, "Henceforth, as a matter of university policy, evil is abolished and paradise is restored. I trust all of us will do whatever possible to achieve this policy objective."

During his eight years at Yale's helm, Bart Giamatti imposed a balanced budget on the university, made significant inroads in restoring the campus' physical plant, proved to be a major league fundraiser, suffered through an extended labor strike with the university's custodial and maintenance workers, and began to raise his

2 Years later, he would proclaim the baseball field as America's most important "garden."

national baseball profile. His passion for the Boston Red Sox had already asserted itself at Yale when he became president, as he negotiated into his contract a requirement that the school had to install cable television in his residence so he could watch more ballgames featuring his favorite team. Then, to fully advertise his passion, Giamatti often walked around campus wearing his Red Sox cap and jacket.[3] Most importantly, in furtherance of raising his baseball profile, Yale's president started writing for publication about the National Pastime.

Giamatti's first major piece of baseball writing for the national media came in his 1977 article for *Harper's Magazine*, devoted to Giamatti's expression of outrage over the New York Mets trading their star pitcher Tom Seaver (a man capable of "brilliantly blending control and speed, those two capacities for restraint and release that are the indispensable possession of the great artist") to the Cincinnati Reds. The essence of his outrage: The Mets had ignored "a simple, crucial fact: that among all the men who play baseball, there is, very occasionally, a man of such qualities of heart and mind and body that he transcends even the great and glorious game, and that such a man is to be cherished, not sold."

Next, following the *Harper's* Seaver piece, came his classic essay, "The Green Fields of the Mind," published in the *Yale Alumni Magazine* in 1977 shortly after Giamatti was named Yale's president.[4] The piece opens with words no baseball scribe had ever expressed before, yet every fan knows in his subconscious.

> It breaks your heart. It is designed to break your heart.
> The game begins in the spring, when everything else
> begins again, and it blossoms in the summer, filling the

---

3 Giamatti waxed eloquent on the mixed blessing of being a Boston Red Sox fan in the twentieth century after Babe Ruth left the team and the Curse of the Bambino kicked in for over eight decades: "The Red Sox are an affliction. But even more, the Red Sox—even more than the other 26 teams—annually reenact the fall of humankind. They, more than anybody or anything in our culture every year re-create the ancient story of admiration, aspiration and expulsion, coherence, declining into exile, the story that seems to be, indeed to all cultures, a basic story about our human declination."

4 Giamatti originally submitted the essay to the magazine earlier in the year while still a professor, and the editors rejected it. In his Symphony Space performance in New York City with Roger Angell in the summer of 1989, he explained how it finally got published. "Then when, unaccountably, two months later I became president, [pause] the *Yale Alumni Magazine* printed it."

afternoons and evenings, and then as soon as the chill rains come, it stops and leaves you to face the fall alone. You can count on it, rely on it to buffer the passage of time, to keep the memory of sunshine and high skies alive, and then, just when the days are all twilight, when you need it most, it stops. Today, October 2, a Sunday of rain and broken branches and leaf-clogged drains and slick streets, it stopped, and summer was gone.

Keeping his typewriter percolating in those green fields, when major league players went on strike in 1981, Giamatti wrote a *New York Times* editorial blasting everyone involved with stopping the game's music: "O Sovereign Owners and Princely Players, you have been entrusted with the serious work of play, and your season of responsibility has come. Be at it. There is no general sympathy for either of your sides. Nor will there be. The people of America care about baseball, not about your squalid little squabbles."

By 1983, due to his widely circulated writings on the National Pastime, as well as his extraordinary zeal for the game that he communicated whenever an opportunity arose to express it, the lords of baseball had Yale President Bart Giamatti on their short list of candidates to be considered for replacing outgoing Commissioner Bowie Kuhn. Pressured by high-powered Yale alumni to stay put in New Haven, Giamatti withdrew his name from consideration for Commissioner of Baseball, and after a year's search, coming off his highly acclaimed leadership of the 1984 Olympics in Los Angeles resulting in his being named *Time* Magazine's "Man of the Year," Peter Ueberroth was chosen.

Baseball's leaders did not forget Giamatti's flair for the game, however, and again rang his phone in 1986, offering him the position of National League President upon Chub Feeney's retirement from that position. This time, having been worn down by the campus' custodial and maintenance worker strike, which had already caused him to announce his nonnegotiable desire to step down from his leadership of Yale, his answer to baseball quickly came back in the affirmative. At the press conference announcing his selection, Bart Giamatti had no problem justifying his decision to make such a dramatic career change in the context of his academic background. "Men of letters have always gravitated to sports. I've always found baseball the most satisfying and nourishing pursuit outside literature."

From his first day on the job as National League President to his final days as Baseball Commissioner, Giamatti believed he had only one real constituency, the fan. He told Frank Deford for an April 1989 *Sports Illustrated* profile, "The ultimate purpose of the game of baseball is to bring pleasure to the American people." He would later add meat to the bones of this thought in August 1989:

> Baseball is an important, enduring American institution. It must assert and aspire to the highest principles of integrity, of professionalism of performance, of fair play within its rules. It will come as no surprise that like any institution composed of human beings, the institution will not always fulfill its highest aspirations. I know of no earthly institution that does. But this one, because it is so much a part of our history as a people and because it has such a purchase on our national soul, has an obligation to the people for whom it is played—to its fans and well-wishers—to strive for excellence in all things and to promote the highest ideals.

In furtherance of bringing pleasure to the fans and preserving the game's integrity, when Cincinnati Reds skipper Pete Rose pushed umpire Dave Pallone in a game, Giamatti suspended Rose for thirty days and fined him $10,000. When Billy Hatcher of the Astros got caught with a corked bat, and the Dodgers' Jay Howell and the Phillies' Kevin Gross put pine tar on, and sandpaper in, their respective gloves, the National League President imposed the stiffest penalties ever assessed for such acts of cheating.

His written decision in 1987 on Kevin Gross' appeal of his ten-day suspension for sandpapering his glove was a particularly expressive statement of his passion for fair play.

> Cheating is a very serious offense and merits serious discipline. It corrodes the integrity of any game. It undermines the assumption necessary to any game declaring a winner, that the contestants are playing fairly,

i.e., under identical rules and conditions. It destroys public and participant confidence, morale, and goodwill. If participants and spectators alike cannot assume integrity and fairness and proceed from there, the contest cannot in its essence exist. Mr. Gross acted with indifference to these principles, exhibiting a reckless disregard for the reputation and good name of his teammates, club, and league and for the integrity of the game.... The appeal is denied.

When Commissioner Peter Ueberroth decided to step down from his position, there was an understanding among Major League Baseball owners that Bart Giamatti would take his place, and on April 1, 1989, the torch passed and baseball had a new leader. Giamatti recognized the power of the office. "Commissioner is a calling in a structure that has a secular religious calling.[5] You're given *extraordinary powers* and faith, but you should only use them when it's *really warranted.*"

During his five month reign, Giamatti's predominant activity as commissioner, which "really warranted" full use of his "extraordinary powers," became the disposition of allegations regarding Cincinnati Reds manager Pete Rose's having violated baseball's most important rule by betting on baseball games. Throughout the summer of 1989, the dispute was litigated in courts and received constant front page media coverage. Finally, on August 24, 1989, a settlement was reached under the terms of which Rose was banished from the game for life, subject to his ability to petition for reinstatement, but without there being a specific finding by Major League Baseball that he had gambled on the game.

Commissioner Giamatti's public statement to announce the settlement agreement with Rose and, at last, achieve closure of the insidious matter measured up to the historic moment, and ended in no uncertain terms. "The matter of Mr. Rose is now closed. It will be debated and discussed. Let no one think that it did not hurt baseball. That hurt will pass, however, as the great glory of the game asserts itself

---

5 Giamatti's Deputy Commissioner and close friend Fay Vincent, who succeeded Giamatti as Commissioner following his death, in his book, *The Last Commissioner* (Simon & Schuster, 2002), maintains that Bart was an "agnostic, and not a man of faith," such that baseball may well have been the closest thing he had to a religion.

Bart Giamatti pursued his responsibilities as Commissioner of Baseball with a heartfelt passion that proved fatal.

and a resilient institution goes forward. Let it be clear that no individual is superior to the game."

Following that public statement, Giamatti responded in the affirmative to a reporter's question on the subject of whether he personally believed that Pete Rose had bet on baseball. Yes, the carefully worded settlement reached with Rose prohibited the entity Major

League Baseball from ever stating an official finding on the subject, but the agreement did not prohibit the Commissioner from expressing his personal opinion. Of course, in 2004, in his book, *My Prison Without Bars* (Rodale Books, 2004), after fifteen years of adamant denial, Pete Rose finally admitted that Giamatti's "opinion" regarding the hit king's gambling habits was an absolute fact, and that Rose had, in fact, not only bet on games, but actually bet on games involving the Reds while he was their manager.

Exactly one week after concluding the Rose matter, preparing for a Labor Day weekend at his Martha's Vineyard summer home, Bart Giamatti's system shut down on September 1, 1989, and he died of a massive heart attack, survived by his wife, Toni, and children, Marcus, Elena, and Paul.

In the context of the many tributes paid in life and after death to Commissioner Bart Giamatti, the most memorable came from acclaimed baseball writer Roger Angell. In researching an exhaustive article about Giamatti for *The New Yorker* in 1988, the journalist came across his subject's own words in an obscure book, *Exile and Change in Renaissance Literature*, written years ago by the then Yale literature professor to describe a largely forgotten fifteenth century Italian poet named Matteo Boiardo. Angell determined that in summarizing the essence of Boiardo, Bart Giamatti had likely attempted to make a statement about his own self-image.[6] In the aftermath of Giamatti's sudden death, constant republication of the closing excerpt from Angell's *New Yorker* article pronounced the public consensus on the late Commissioner in a manner actually articulated in the decedent's own words.

> His deepest desire is to conserve something of purpose in a world of confusion. He knows that chivalry is an outmoded system, but he wants to keep something of its value, its respect for grace and noble behavior, even

---

6 Angell's insight into the way Giamatti wrote about others as a way of expressing his thoughts about himself presumably inspired James Reston Jr. to do the same in his book, *Collision at Home Plate*. Reston saw Giamatti's writings on Machiavelli in the same way Angell had perceived Bart's writing on Boiardo. Giamatti saw Machiavelli as Giamatti surely viewed himself—"the poet of power—[who was] shrewd, warm, full of sly humor, with an extraordinary capacity for friendship ... and scrupulously honest in his personal dealings and financial affairs."

while he relinquishes its forms and structures. He wants to check the urge to dissolution that time seems inevitably to embody. He does not want to turn back the clock and regain the old world, but he does want to recapture the sense of control of oneself, if nothing else, that marked life under the old system. He wants to be able to praise something other than the giddy headlong rush.

Even after admitting in his book that he bet on big league games, Pete Rose still believes he should be a Hall of Famer.

Almost a decade after Commissioner Giamatti's death, in the foreword to the book edited by Kenneth S. Robson, *A Great and Glorious Game: The Baseball Writings of A. Bartlett Giamatti* (Algonquin Books of Chapel Hill, 1998), David Halberstam raised the bar for expressing exactly what the late lamented Giamatti had meant to the residents of Baseball America:

> Those of us who love sports and want there to be some measure of civility in them are the worse for his death.... His was a voice imbued with the pleasure of the game, yet aware as well of the moral consequences of everything we do in society, and how there are no exemptions from our actions. Whether, given the forces at play in today's society that have worked greatly to lessen the game's attractiveness in the years since his death, Bart Giamatti would have been able to hold the line against the power of modern greed and materialism is doubtful. But at the very least, even if he had failed, one would have heard his voice, and that is no small thing.

Two years after Scribner's published my profile of Giamatti, Pete Rose made a final stab at making a buck (more accurately, five hundred thousand bucks) off his baseball activities by writing his final (at least hopefully his final) memoirs, *My Prison Without Bars* (Rodale Books, 2004), which for the curious can now be purchased on amazon.com for a grand total of one cent per copy. To the extent there were any doubts as to this writer's attitude towards the ultimate disposition of "The Pete Rose Question," I answered them with a column that ran shortly after his book's release.

The American people typically systematize an official means for honoring those who have reached the pinnacle in their chosen professions. For a professional baseball player, that specific means is to be inducted into the National Baseball Hall of Fame in Cooperstown, New York. The imperfect human system of honoring achievement gets turned upside down, however, when someone who has excelled in a field to the point of reaching its pinnacle, then commits serious acts of misconduct capable of destroying that field's very foundation.

The problem surfaced last week with the release of Pete Rose's newest autobiography, *My Prison Without Bars*, in which he publicly admits for the first time that all the allegations with which he was charged in 1989 are, in fact, true, such as the manager of the Cincinnati Reds in 1987-1988, he constantly bet on the outcome of major league baseball games, including his own Reds' games. Rose has confirmed the statements made in 1989 by his gambling accomplices that the then manager of the Reds made the bets from his locker room office, after gathering updated information about the status of certain players from his friends on other teams.

Rose's new book affirms the August 1989 action of Bart Giamatti, who saw his responsibility as Major League Baseball Commissioner to protect "the game's authenticity, honesty, and coherence," and, therefore banned the Cincinnati legend from baseball for life because he had "engaged in a variety of acts which have stained the game."

In this free country of ours, there will always be diehard supporters of celebrities, who will forgive any transgression. Pete Rose is one of those guys who has attracted that kind of supporter, having spent twenty-four major league seasons proving that the "little guy" can become a superstar when on a daily basis he does whatever it takes to win ballgames.

Amazingly, in 2004, there exist fans of Pete Rose who say that his egregious and now admitted acts of misconduct, which clearly compromised the fundamental integrity of America's National Pastime, should be ignored, and thus, in spite of everything done in defiance of the game's most important rule, he should still be elected to the Baseball Hall of Fame because he has finally "come clean." Perhaps even more amazingly, current Baseball Commissioner (and former car dealer) Bud Selig has said he will withhold judgment on his decision whether Pete Rose should be reinstated so as to become eligible for Hall of Fame consideration until after he has read and considered the new book.[7]

Yes, as the Bible and virtually every other religious book notes, we are all sinners and have fallen short of God's glory. Yes, human beings should leave the business of ultimate judgments regarding earthly conduct in the hands of a higher power. However, as human beings, when it comes to the various imperfect human ways we have created to honor our heroes, maybe expressing a human opinion on this subject is appropriate.

Here is mine on the Pete Rose question: The ultimate foundation of baseball that made it the National Pastime is the game's integrity, as reflected in the basic rational proposition that a contest's outcome should only be determined by what transpires on the playing field.

But Mr. Rose says he only bet on the Reds to win. What's so bad about that? Former Baseball Commissioner Fay Vincent answers the question this way: "Rose bet only on select days. A manager who bets on certain days has an inherently corrupt conflict. He might, for instance, save his relievers for the day he plans to bet. He might leave a starter in longer, depending on how much he cares about the outcome. More important, a gambling manager might amass large debts, then be unable to pay off those debts without doing special favors for the bookie."

Per Mr. Vincent's analysis, Pete Rose tried to destroy baseball's foundation of integrity for his own financial personal gain, putting his

---

7 Presumably, Selig read Rose's book and decided to make no changes to Giamatti's 1989 banishment ruling.

own interests above the game's best interests. Because he did this, he should not receive his chosen profession's highest honor, regardless of the extent to which he may have "come clean." Any person who purposely attempts to crack a structure's foundation is unambiguously acting to destroy the structure itself.

Hopefully, Commissioner Bud Selig will see it this way. But if he doesn't, and if Pete Rose's permanent banishment from the game ends, and 75% of the Baseball Writers of America vote for his induction, then the pure and pristine village of Cooperstown, New York, can start marketing itself to the world as the home of baseball's Hall of Shame.

My profile for *The Scribner Encyclopedia of American Lives: Sports Figures*, which appeared earlier in this chapter, put a full-blown positive spin on the life of Bart Giamatti from the perspective of information available in 2002, as synthesized and executed by a writer ever vigilant in search of baseball heroes. Most definitely, the late Commissioner of Baseball had a multitude of virtues that led to his achievements. However, two baseball books published after my turning in the encyclopedia write-up to Scribner's presented a more balanced perspective on the life of a man who clearly had at least some personality deficits, confirming once and for all that upon thorough examination, everyone (even the most noble) has some warts located somewhere in his human package.

Fay Vincent served as Deputy Commissioner under Giamatti and then advanced to the position of Commissioner of Baseball from the time of Giamatti's death until September 1992, when he "resigned" because he knew the owners intended to fire him. Vincent waited ten years after his ouster before having his baseball memoir published, *The Last Commissioner: A Baseball Valentine* (Simon & Schuster, 2002).

In his book, Fay Vincent identifies Bart Giamatti as the special friend with whom he so badly yearned to work, that he took a pay cut from what he was making as a lawyer with a New York firm in order to join his buddy in the Commissioner's office. Despite having his own case of hero worship disease for Bart Giamatti, Vincent does not portray his predecessor through the lens of rose-colored glasses. He notes that, among other things, on occasion, Commissioner Giamatti had the capacity to make a bonehead move. In the battle that led to Pete Rose's banishment from baseball, Vincent details Bart Giamatti's doing a really stupid thing by sending a letter to the federal judge who was about to sentence Rose's bookie, Ron Peters, on a drug charge while Major League Baseball was in the big middle of the Rose investigation. Because Peters had given such favorable testimony, at the urging of John Dowd, a prominent attorney whom Giamatti had named Special Prosecutor in charge of the investigation, Giamatti stated in his letter to the sentencing judge (seeking a less severe punishment for the criminal defendant) that the Commissioner of Baseball believed Peters to be "candid, forthright, and truthful."

This letter to Ron Peters' sentencing judge immediately provided Pete Rose with his best piece of evidence in the Ohio state court lawsuit he brought against Giamatti, aimed at enjoining the investigation, given that it strongly supported Rose's allegation that Commissioner Giamatti, who was supposed to be serving as an impartial arbiter presiding over the ultimate determination of the Rose matter, in fact, was not impartial in his role and had prejudged Peters as credible, even though his anticipated testimony had never faced the fire of cross-examination. When the tactical blunder arising from the letter to Peters' judge became apparent, and Giamatti was blasted for his clear partiality by Rose's lawyers, the media, and everyone else, the Commissioner then exploded at both Vincent and Dowd over dinner, blaming the Deputy Commissioner and the Special Prosecutor for Giamatti's poor decision, even though the letter had never crossed Vincent's desk before it was signed and mailed. Later that evening, after all had gone to their homes, Giamatti settled down and telephoned an apology to his colleague, thereby eliminating Vincent's thoughts of resigning his position in the aftermath of the angry dinner.

Going beyond that specific incident, Fay Vincent shoots a broader arrow into his friend's Achilles heel. Although Vincent relished the opportunity to witness Giamatti at his eloquent best when participating in arguments and debates over esoteric issues involving interpretations ranging from Dante to the balk rule, the real life hardball fight between Major League Baseball and Pete Rose was more of a fight than Giamatti could physically stomach. The daily media assessment critical of his performance crawled up under the Commissioner's skin and ate at his

The stress of the Pete Rose matter made 51-year-old
Bart Giamatti, all of a sudden, look like a very old man.

ego, such that his adverse reaction to the public criticism, combining with his being eighty pounds overweight, smoking non-stop (even while eating his meals), and dissipating in fatigue from insomnia, all acted in unison to shut down his system and stop his heart.

After Giamatti's death in September 1989, and Fay Vincent's being chosen to succeed him, the new Commissioner got cross-wise with baseball's owners in 1990-1991 after he confronted them with the ugly fact that they had clearly colluded amongst themselves in their collective treatment of free agent ballplayers in hopes of breaking the players union. In describing the labor nightmare that faced Major League Baseball when the Deputy Commissioner recognized the strength of the players' allegations regarding the owners' illegal collusion, and consistent with his assessment of Giamatti's "weak stomach" during the Pete Rose war of 1989, in his book, Vincent contrasts his own confrontational style in responding to the players-owners' labor dispute (which accelerated his unpopularity with the owners) with Giamatti's preferred avoidance mode, and then proceeds to broaden his conclusion (well outside of the Pete Rose battle) regarding his predecessor's great flaw as a leader:

> Bart's view as commissioner was that he would not get involved in labor problems. He had endured a very bad go-round with the unions at Yale and it hurt him. I used to remind him that the last Italian who went up on a mountaintop and fiddled while the enterprise burned

is not well regarded by history. (His usual and erudite reply was, "Go f— yourself.")

In short, from Fay Vincent's perspective, when a battle arose that absolutely required Bart Giamatti's participation (be it the Yale custodial worker strike or the investigation of Pete Rose's gambling habits), having no other options, Commissioner Giamatti necessarily jumped into the fray that arose under his area of responsibility and addressed it with full force and the best of intentions, though he allowed the stress associated with such battles to ravage and destroy his body (it had happened at Yale during the strike just as it did during the Rose fight). However, when a potential battle arose that Giamatti could dodge by coming up with a philosophical argument that the issue out of which the dispute arose was arguably outside his authority, then according to Vincent, conflict avoidance became his preferred strategy.

Fay Vincent's assessments of Giamatti were confirmed by author Robert P. Moncrieff in his book, *Bart Giamatti: A Profile* (Yale University Press, 2007). While preparing the biography, in addition to Vincent, Moncrieff interviewed many of his subject's family members (though not his widow and children who refused to be interviewed), boyhood friends, and Yale colleagues. The assessment of Giamatti's complex personality by Moncrieff, driven by the dozens of perspectives revealed during his research on the book published by Yale University Press, reveals a man filled with eloquence and charisma, but who like so many virtuosos, was also filled with "an acute sensitivity to criticism;... an exaggerated need for recognition and approval who badly wanted acceptance from the world around him;... a desire to be intensely private (to the extent that in his house, Giamatti permitted essentially no visitors) despite having many friends;... an inability to handle stress (which he attempted to deal with by over-smoking and over-eating);... a tendency to micromanage while being chronically guilty of failing to consult with his colleagues."

Based on the breadth and depth of his interviews with the many constituencies in the Yale community, Mr. Moncrieff goes so far as to say, "Giamatti's presidency at Yale was fatally flawed by his inability to function well in an environment of turmoil.... He was unable to accept with equanimity the discontinuities between the *real* world as it is, and the *ideal* world as it ought to be."

Along Moncrieff's wavelength, clearly baseball played at the highest professional level has its *ideal* world of perfect geometry and radiant "garden" ballparks, combining with the poetic notion of what it means to go home, the fluid tension between individual performance and teamwork, and the game's many characteristics that serve as sparkling metaphors. On the other hand, however, the game also has its *real* world of Pete Rose's betting, Kevin Gross' cheating, the Mets trading Tom Seaver, and its periodic labor strife. As in essentially every aspect of life, the ideal *and* the real are *both* part of the game. In life and in baseball, imperfections comprise part of the scene in any picture painted that purports to be an accurate rendition of its subject. A baseball executive who goes about his business by dealing with these very problems on the basis that those problems he absolutely must confront are pursued in such a physically reckless way as to destroy his health, and those problems he does not want to confront, he purposely avoids as long as he can come up with a philosophical basis for avoiding them, is clearly not someone who is doing himself or his chosen game and its organization any favors.

Clearly, the perspectives on Giamatti offered by Fay Vincent (based on his personal experience) and Robert Moncrieff (based on his extensive research) in their respective books result in making the late Commissioner more of a human being and less of a saint, which presents baseball fans with the unanswerable question, "Do we really want or need to know everything there is to know about someone we regard as a hero?"

———————

For the Baby Boomer baseballphiliac straining at midlife to find the right words for justifying his fascination with this game, Roger Angell in his famous 1988 *New Yorker* article, which drew the aforementioned Boiardo parallel, may have described best what Giamatti meant to those of us who had waited a lifetime for someone who could articulate some sense of his passion for baseball. Angell called Bart Giamatti "a lifetime .400 talker," in a sport that has never had a lifetime .400 hitter.

In that light, despite acknowledging the existence of Giamatti's deficiencies as a leader, this chapter must now end with the words of this lifetime .400 talker, this lyricist who harmonized his eloquent words into the game's rhythmic music, this Commissioner of Baseball who cared most of all for the fans, by using the words he chose to end his piece, "The Green Fields of the Mind." These closing words are engraved and sit in a prominent place in my law office, and may be the only words I've memorized since childhood. Whenever the need has arisen to explain for the benefit of the rolling eyeballs exactly why my passion for baseball does not diminish with time, my recitation of this closing passage from Bart Giamatti's greatest baseball essay has never failed to bring the rolling eyeballs to a dead stop.

> I am not that grown-up or up-to-date.
> I am a simpler creature tied to primitive patterns
>   and cycles.
> I need to think something lasts forever.
> And it might as well be
> That state of being that is a game.
> It might as well be that,
> In a green field
> In the sun.

The National Baseball Hall of Fame and Museum—the game's Mecca since its opening in 1939.

CHAPTER SIX

COOPERSTOWN AND THE HALL OF FAME
The Magic of Baseball's Home Plate

Baseball in postwar America has had its greatest players and its articulate voices, but it also has had its most special place—Cooperstown, New York—home of the National Baseball Hall of Fame and Museum. In a game of Password, one giving the clue "Cooperstown" to his partner would surely provoke one and only one response—"Baseball." Those Boomers who have traveled to this small village in upstate New York get to create their own personal baseball history stories, which may or may not involve Abner Doubleday, Elihu Phinney, and James Fenimore Cooper.

———————

P rofessional athletes often speak of the turning point in their careers when great plays begin to outnumber mistakes. That time arrives when, in the athlete's words, "the game starts to slow down." All at once, to the skilled eyes of the batter (or the quarterback, or the point guard), he can raise his perspective above the action on the field, understand his opponent's moves as if they were in slow motion, and then enter a comfort zone where he can consistently make great plays in big money games with the same effortless ease he had in childhood.

As in sports, life improves when it elevates above the hurly-burly and slows down, allowing full appreciation of the moment, as evidenced by the way things work in Cooperstown, New York, population 2,400, home of the National Baseball Hall of Fame and Museum. The tenth chapter of my earlier book, *1939: Baseball's Tipping Point*, was entitled "The Doubleday Myth: How Cooperstown Got the Hall of Fame," and explained the history of how organized baseball happened to settle on Cooperstown as its permanent geographic home plate in 1939.

This chapter in this book is *not* about the historical connection between baseball and Cooperstown. No. Since Bart Giamatti is not around to do it, this chapter represents its author's vain attempt, based on my own personal experience, to articulate the magic of a remote village in upstate New York and its seventy-year-old baseball history institution, which motivates hundreds of thousands of people every year to take a break from busy-ness, travel there, slow down life's pace for a few days, and allow memory, imagination, and positive energy to lift off the ground and surge as easily as they once did in childhood.

As with most stories and journeys, this saga begins at the beginning. Like many Baby Boomers of the male variety, from first grade all the way through high school, my reading preferences entailed a steady diet of history books and magazines devoted to baseball. Many of the materials landing in my lap profiled star ballplayers who had retired and been inducted into the Baseball Hall of Fame or else were in the prime of their careers and were already expressing hopes of receiving a plaque in Cooperstown somewhere down the line. Those few books and encyclopedias in the school library that addressed the subject of baseball's origins dutifully preserved myth as history and claimed Cooperstown as the probable center of the action when the Grand Ol' Game began before the Civil War. The desire to learn about baseball's supposed place of beginning extended to my reading James Fenimore Cooper's thick novels to know more about the area around Cooperstown, the hometown founded by his father, that provided the setting for his Leatherstocking Tales.

In the context of reading so much about a place in America believed to have hallowed ground, inconveniently, my parents had little interest in sports, instead focusing on art, architecture, and antique furniture as their hobbies. Thus, asking Mom and Dad to take a few days off and drive to the National Baseball Hall of Fame in Cooperstown, New York, for the purpose of examining baseball artifacts had the same odds of getting a "Yes" as asking them to take me to Antarctica for the purpose of studying penguins.

Recognizing my dismal prospects for getting to Cooperstown in those years when vacation choices depended entirely on my parents' financial support, one Sunday afternoon in April 1972 during my senior year of high school, at a time when our family lived in Westport, Connecticut,[1] an idea popped into my mind that seemed to guarantee the opportunity for me to see the Baseball Hall of Fame one day. Possibly inspired by James Fenimore Cooper's description of the area as

---

1 From 1953 until January 1970, our family lived in Texas. Then, during my sophomore year of high school, my dad's company transferred him, and we moved to Connecticut.

Cooperstown—described by James Fenimore Cooper as "a place of solemn solitude and sweet repose with a placid view of heaven" on the banks of Lake Otsego, which Cooper called "Glimmerglass."

"a place of solemn solitude and sweet repose ... with a placid view of heaven," my brainstorm just had to be shared with someone, and my father happened to be nearby. "Dad, when I get married, whenever that is, sometime after college, no matter who the girl is, I'm going to take her to Cooperstown, New York, on our honeymoon. That way I know I'll get to the Hall of Fame."

My father looked at me with an expression of total incredulity, wondering how any child of his could have thought of something so inane, and to his everlasting credit calmly replied, "Talmage, I have no idea whom you'll one day marry. But whoever it is, I will not allow you to do that to a young woman on that special occasion. Let's pick a weekend next month and go to Cooperstown, so you can get this ridiculous thought out of your mind."

My dad kept his word. A few weeks after that fateful conversation, Memorial Day weekend 1972, we traveled to Cooperstown. Being thrifty children of the Depression, my parents never considered the possibility of staying at the Otesaga, the grand (and expensive) hotel in Cooperstown located between Main Street and Lake Otsego. No, for less than half the Otesaga's price, we stayed at a clean but aging motel on the lakeshore, right next to the dock where the big boat departs for tourist rides. Shortly after we arrived in the village, an incident occurred that earned a permanent place in our family's lore of outrageous stories, and primarily involved my dad, a man who regards baseball with the same level of affection he has for junk mail.

Every year, when spring arrives and pollen fills the air, my father's sinuses explode. Tears pour out of his eyes and his cannonball blast sneeze starts going off, causing him to become quite a spectacle for those in his immediate vicinity. As soon as we got to Cooperstown, Dad suffered a particularly raging case of hay fever, necessitating his seeking refuge in the first available air-conditioned place, but in a village that has few uncomfortably hot days each year, finding such a place wasn't easy. Like most of the inexpensive inns in the town, our lakeside motel offered no refrigerated air (as it was then called), so the nearest place where my father could remove himself from the pollen was the newly air-conditioned Baseball Hall of Fame. There, as soon as he bought his admission ticket and got through the front door, he immediately sat himself down and attempted to gain control of his sinuses in the first available chair, which happened to be right next to

Honus Wagner's locker.

On that holiday weekend, the Baseball Hall of Fame naturally had a steady stream of visitors, most of whom (like me) had come to examine treasures associated with their favorite baseball-playing icons. As scores of visitors moved through the room where Wagner's locker stood, they became distracted by the sight of a grown man sitting nearby, handkerchief in hand, tears streaming down his cheeks, who appeared to be wallowing in the deepest kind of grief. One compassionate gentleman stopped and tried to comfort my father (a man as allergic to baseball as he was to pollen), "Hang in there, fellow. I loved Ol' Honus, too."

Sitting in a chair beside Honus Wagner's locker at the Baseball Hall of Fame, my baseball-averse father appeared to be grieving for the old shortstop as tears of hay fever allergy poured from his eyes.

The museum in 1972 was nice but unspectacular, and still paid substantial homage to Abner Doubleday with both his portrait and the alleged "Doubleday Ball" displayed in the main lobby, while glossing over Abner's not having been the man who invented the game. In those days, unimaginative displays filled the rooms and no theater existed for showing films. The only presentation that made a lasting impression on me was a wall of framed photos featuring fuzzy cheeked boys in their days as Little Leaguers, who had grown up and gone on to play in the major leagues. One picture was of my favorite player, Carl Yastrzemski, who seventeen years later would become the first man to have played Little League Baseball and then be inducted into the Hall of Fame (in 1989). Another was of a young Rollie Fingers who would go on to grow out some of his whiskers and adorn his face with a "Snidely Whiplash" handlebar mustache, and who at that time had just started moving down a performance road that ultimately led to his receiving a plaque at the Hall exactly twenty years later.

After leaving the Hall of Fame, we walked down Main Street to the other important baseball edifice in town—Doubleday Field, and a sign there mentioned that the ballpark had been built on the site of Elihu Phinney's cowpasture, where "it was believed" former Cooperstown resident Abner Doubleday had taught local boys how to play his new game back in 1839. As I would learn two decades later in doing research for my first book, putting young Doubleday on Phinney's cowpasture was an idea that sprang from the text of the decisive letter to the Mills Commission (the entity charged with determining exactly how, when, where and by whom the game was invented) written in 1907 by former Cooperstown resident Abner Graves, who soon thereafter would reside in an insane asylum. In the spring of 1972, however, the many facts regarding Graves' letter lacking credibility were not known to me. Just as a young child believes in Santa Claus, the inadequacy of my baseball history scholarship that day allowed me to believe in Abner, unaware of the historical facts downplayed in the museum, that (i) Abner Doubleday never played baseball in Cooperstown or anywhere else, and (ii) it was Alexander Cartwright in 1845 who had first come up with rules to the new "base ball" game he and his buddies played at a park named Elysian Fields in Hoboken, New Jersey.

In that blissfully ignorant mode, gazing out at the radiant green grass of Doubleday Field, with the words "Elihu Phinney's cowpasture, Elihu Phinney's cow pasture ..." turning over in my mind, it took little imagination to reflect on this setting 133 years ago when Abner the teenager elevated the European game of rounders to something different and better.

In examining every aspect of the ballpark whose location now rested on Doubleday's chosen field, of particular note were the weathered bricks that extended beyond the exterior façade all the way into the dugouts, reminding me of the bricks around my grandparents' fireplace where our family gathered for Christmas every year. Making this mental brick connection shifted my imagination into high gear, six years before the Yale Alumni Magazine published Bart Giamatti's "The Green Fields of the Mind," and more than a decade before a Hollywood producer created a movie about a *Field of Dreams*. Looking at the baseball field framed by the bricks, and seeing the rooftops of homes just past the outfield fence, it wasn't hard to visualize a game being played here by ballplayers wearing thick flannel uniforms (like

In the spring of 1972, seeing Doubleday Field for the first time, my mind made a free association brick connection that soon led to an alignment in my mind between Abner Doubleday and Santa Claus.

those displayed down the street at the Hall of Fame) in this intimate ballpark, in this Norman Rockwell-esque town, under this gleaming sunshine. Surely playing a game under such ideal circumstances would lift every ballplayer's soul to the same mountaintop level of euphoria he had once had in childhood on cold December nights, sitting in front of a blazing brick hearth, wearing flannel pajamas, drinking hot chocolate, and knowing Saint Nick would later that night land on the rooftop and come down the chimney.

The green field in my mind raised two questions that afternoon: First, could life possibly get any better for an American male than playing a baseball game on the hallowed ground of Doubleday Field under the May sun? The second question flowed from the first—regardless of the actual circumstances surrounding baseball's origins, was there some sort of connection (mythical, mystical, or otherwise) between Abner Doubleday and Santa Claus as purveyors of wonder and joy? Christmas with the family might be as uplifting as playing baseball at this park, but nothing, not even Christmas, could be better than those ideas percolating in my head looking out at the freshly-mown baseball diamond made from Phinney's cow pasture in Cooperstown, New York, on that spring day in 1972.

Imagination, however, can take someone only so far. As we left the village after that Memorial Day weekend, despite a marvelous first encounter with baseball's bliss station in James Fenimore Cooper's Leatherstocking Country, alas, the ultimate Cooperstown experience had not yet been fulfilled. Our visit had not coincided with the annual real-life celebration, surely better than any imaginary dream, when the living Hall of Famers come to town and two major league teams actually play a ballgame on Doubleday Field—an event known in baseball circles as "Induction Weekend."[2]

Passing reference has already been made in this book (in Chapters 2 and 5) to my first Induction Weekend in July 1989, attended in the company of my wife, Claire, along with Peter and Liz Haveles, and the fact that it inspired me to become a baseball writer. Our making this rendezvous emanated from a decision made in 1974 while Peter (my former adversary on the high school debate circuit) had become my summer school dormitory roommate for six weeks in Austin. Sometime during those weeks, as passionate fans of the Boston Red Sox in general and Carl Yastrzemski in particular, Peter and I made a pact that we would go to Cooperstown for Captain Carl's induction into the Baseball Hall of Fame—whenever that was, presumably some time in the 1980's. When Yaz retired at the end of the 1983 season as the first American League player ever to amass more than 3,000 hits and 400 home runs in a career, we both marked our calendars for 1989, when our man would surely enter the Hall as soon as he became eligible.

It came to pass. Carl Yastrzemski got in on the first ballot, and the

---

2 In 2003, the Hall of Fame's leadership decided to split up Induction Weekend and the Hall of Fame Game, spacing them two months apart so as to have two huge tourist weekends each summer instead of just one. Before then, both happened on the same weekend.

Cheering for Carl Yastrzemski on his Induction Day turned me into a kid again, and my wife, Claire, went with the flow.

Bostons and the Haveleses made plans to be in Cooperstown for his induction into the Hall of Fame. And to add to the festivities for that long-awaited weekend, since Yaz would be getting his plaque alongside Johnny Bench, Major League Baseball arranged for the Boston Red Sox to play the Cincinnati Reds in the Hall of Fame Game on Doubleday Field, bringing back the ballclubs whose play in the seven-game 1975 World Series featuring Yastrzemski and Bench had dramatically revived national interest in the game. My friend Dr. Bobby Brown, President of the American League at the time, arranged to get us four tickets to the ballgame that had been an instant sellout.

Then we hit a bump in the road, adding another Cooperstown story to my permanent repertoire. Peter's sole responsibility in the planning of our odyssey had been to secure hotel rooms for the two couples. Months in advance of our departure, he confirmed with me that all was set, he had made reservations at a local bed-and-breakfast in the village and had sent in the deposit. However, a week before my wife and I were to leave Texas for New York, Peter phoned my office, and spoke in an uncharacteristically shaky voice: "Uh, Talmage, bad news. I just called the bed-and-breakfast where we were going to stay, and the owner said she never received my deposit, so we don't have rooms. And because all of New England's coming to honor Yaz, and all of Ohio's coming for Johnny Bench, there's not a room available within a hundred miles of Cooperstown. I'm not sure what to do."

Fortunately, my obsession for all things Cooperstown had stayed with me from that trip to the village in 1972 through the summer of 1989, meaning the Glimmerglass Opera (whose seasons are acclaimed each year by the *New York Times* and *Wall Street Journal*) had moved into my bailiwick. To appease our wives for having to absorb an overdose of baseball, we'd already purchased tickets to see *La Traviata* on our Saturday evening in Cooperstown.

Upon learning of not having a place to stay in Otsego County, I immediately called the opera's box office, explained our dire situation, and offered to make a contribution to the opera company if they could help us find lodging. The opera rep said she had good news and bad news. The good news was that the Glimmerglass Opera had reserved a block of rooms at a nearby motor inn for its patrons during the weekend; the bad news was that they had only one room left though it did have two double beds.

By 1989, Peter Haveles and I had been close friends for eighteen years, and had been in each other's weddings (mine in Dallas, Peter's in Boston) in the mid-eighties. All that was fine, but my wife, Claire, barely knew Peter, Liz Haveles barely knew me, and Claire and Liz barely knew each other. With no other sleeping accommodations available anywhere close to our intended destination, we accepted the notion of all staying in one room, thereby rapidly accelerating the growth of these new friendships involving two modest women and two snoring men in one small room with beds two feet apart, and sharing one small bathroom. Fortunately for Peter and me, our wives knew we had spent fifteen years waiting for this weekend, swallowed the bitter room accommodation pill like good soldiers, and went with the flow.

Saturday morning in Cooperstown, Peter and I headed off early into the village, allowing Claire and Liz to wake up at their own pace without any men in their presence. When we got into town, Peter demonstrated once and for all that he was the right guy to be with for my first Induction Weekend. We found a diner in town that made take-out egg-sausage-and-cheese sandwiches, and then Peter uttered an idea that was so good, all was forgiven for mishandling the hotel reservations. "Let's eat breakfast at Doubleday Field."

Sacks of hot food and cold milk in hand, we walked up to the site of Phinney's cowpasture, sat ourselves down in the grandstand behind first base, and immediately noticed television cameras all over the place and familiar faces walking around on the diamond. "Who's that short little preppy looking guy standing over by third base with a microphone in his hand? Looks like, yeah, that's Bob Costas." "And who's that guy in the half-frame glasses who keeps walking off the field and into the first base dugout checking out the equipment? Hey, that's Brent Musburger." Having seen Chris Berman the night before walking past the Hall of Fame, for Induction Weekend 1989, with first ballot superstars Yaz and Bench coming into the Hall, Commissioner Bart Giamatti here to emcee the ceremony while in the big middle of baseball's investigation into Pete Rose's gambling activities (in the midst of rumors that Rose might even come to town for the weekend just to tense things up a little), it became apparent that there were no rooms in the inns for the Bostons and Haveleses because the national media had joined the folks from New England and Ohio in taking over the town and filling up every available place for lodging.

The national television buzz, the taste of the hot breakfast sandwiches washed down with milk, the bricks and grass of Doubleday Field appearing exactly as remembered from seventeen years before, the sun shining, and the fellowship of being with a friend who had matched my life path from high school debate to college to law school to working in a big city law firm to marriage, all done while staying focused on Carl Yastrzemski, Fenway Park, and the Boston Red Sox— just as in 1972, the euphoria of Cooperstown was back, and maybe even stronger than before because this was real life, not imagined, though imagination had come in handy to connect all the dots in the picture that morning at Doubleday Field.

After finishing breakfast, full of ourselves as only ten-year lawyers can be, we left Doubleday and walked over to a batting cage on the lot outside the field, thinking that on this beautiful day in this magical place, we just had to take some swings and prove to the world that we still had the wherewithal to drive the ball. Everyone has strengths and weaknesses. That morning, we learned that our skill sets as attorneys and slow-pitch softball players bore no relationship to the talent needed to hit an 80-mile-an-hour fastball or a 70-mile-an-hour curveball coming out of a pitching machine. We grimaced at our ineptitude, pleased that our wives had not witnessed their cocky husbands fully equipping themselves in batting helmets and gloves, and then flailing away in futility at almost every pitch that came our way.

On Sunday morning, before the afternoon induction ceremony, Dr. Bobby Brown and his wife, Sara, took our Cooperstown experience up a notch by inviting us to meet them at the grand Otesaga Hotel, where we would pick up our tickets for the Red Sox-Reds Hall of Fame Game scheduled for Monday. Accepting the Browns' invitation put us into a new realm as baseball fans because during Induction Weekend, the only people allowed inside the gates of the Otesaga are Hall of Famers, baseball dignitaries, and their families and guests. The Browns' allowing us to come inside the gates and into the hotel meant we would enter Cooperstown's inner sanctum where the living baseball gods gather.

In this "as good as it gets" environment, being suave was not an option for someone of my Great Unwashed ilk. Since we'd be going straight from the Otesaga to the induction ceremony, I entered the front door of the grand hotel wearing my full Carl Yastrzemski appreciation uniform—a Boston Red Sox cap and uniform shirt with the number 8 on the back, which drew laughs from the Browns but also attracted some stares from nearby Hall of Famers who surely wondered, "Who let this guy in?"

We had a glass of iced tea with the Browns, looking out at shimmering Lake Otsego (named "Glimmerglass" by James Fenimore Cooper) on one side of us, while dozens of Hall of Famers socialized with each other on the other side. At that point, my mind's green fields moved into a harvest mode, feeling the same level of awe that had filled me twenty years before when Neil Armstrong walked on the moon. Peter and I had waited fifteen years for this weekend, but never had we imagined sitting on a patio in the immediate presence of our boyhood heroes.

After we finished the tea, and received the handoff of Hall of Fame Game tickets, it came time to leave the Otesaga and head toward Cooper Park where the induction ceremony was held in those days on the steps of the Hall's library.[3] As Sara Brown walked us out to the hotel gates, still carrying one white pearl of a baseball that was burning a hole in

3 In 1992, largely due to the overflow crowd for Carl Yastrzemski and Johnny Bench at the 1989 induction ceremony, the Hall of Fame's leadership moved the ceremony across town to the field beside the Clark Gymnasium.

The Otesaga Hotel, the second grand structure of Cooperstown, is where the baseball gods stay during Induction Weekend.

my pocket, summoning up all my courage, I asked the ever gracious Sara if she would mind getting Bart Giamatti to sign it. When she agreed, fireworks exploded in the sky above my mind's green field, knowing my most coveted autograph had now been secured.

There are few moments in life, less than five for most people, when circumstances come together in such perfect harmony that the act of walking lifts a mere mortal off the ground and up into the air of full-blown exhilaration. Movie stars talk about having the feeling of walking on air when they glide from their auditorium seats up onto the stage to accept the Academy Award. Golfers have it when moving down the fairway after making a hole-in-one. Parents experience it when they escort each other around the hospital's maternity ward carrying their first baby. Benjamin and Rosamund Zander describe it in their book, *The Art of Possibility* (Harvard Business School Press, 2000): "There are moments in everyone's life when an experience of integration with the world transcends the business of survival ... Some find admission to the realm of possibility at a religious gathering, some in meditation, some by listening to great music. Often people enter this state in the presence of natural beauty or the sight of something of infinite magnitude—an expanse of ocean or a towering sky. These are moments when we forget ourselves and seem to become part of all being."

The half-mile journey from the Otesaga Hotel to Cooper Park on July 23, 1989, was one of those moments. Aligned with my true blue baseball buddy and our marvelous understanding wives who loved us in spite of the pitiful room accommodations, we now found ourselves with great tickets, obtained for us by the President of the American League, to see the Red Sox play the Reds the next day at the Doubleday Field of Dreams Ballpark; we had just rubbed shoulders with dozens of Hall of Famers and baseball dignitaries at the tight-security Otesaga Hotel; we were walking past one perfectly restored two-story house after another on narrow streets shaded by massive trees, as if on the movie set of *It's a Wonderful Life*, on another dazzling sunny day in Cooperstown; and we were about to see our all-time favorite player, Carl Yastrzemski, be inducted into the Hall of Fame in a program emceed by my all-time favorite baseball philosopher, Commissioner Bart Giamatti, whose autograph I would soon have.

With all those facts synchronizing, my feet never touched the sidewalk on that slow-motion walk to the induction ceremony,. To use the Zanders' words, this was "an experience of integration with the world" that transcended "the business of survival," when I forgot myself (for a few moments) and seemed "to become part of all being." There may not be a Santa Claus, and Abner Doubleday may not have invented baseball on Elihu Phinney's cowpasture, but by golly, on that walk I knew one thing for sure—no Christmas had ever taken me to the point of walking on air, yet the events of July 23, 1989, had combined to produce that very result.

By the time the Hall of Fame Game ended on Monday, and it was time to go back home to Texas, baseball had gone from being an enjoyable hobby to something growing inside my soul.[4] The flight home allowed me to compose a long and winding thank-you letter to

---

4 Another bump in the road came the next day. The Cincinnati Reds' plane got grounded in Montreal, and instead of a Red Sox-Reds game, we saw an intrasquad game played between two teams of Bosox—though seeing nothing but our cherished Red Sox play baseball on Doubleday Field was not such a bad thing.

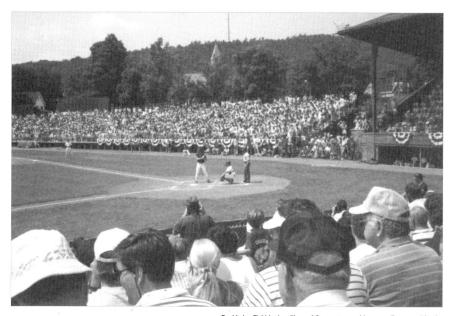

Doubleday Field in the village of Cooperstown with an overflow crowd for the 1989 Hall of Fame Game—as red, white, and blue a scene as America has to offer.

Dr. Bobby Brown for getting us tickets to the ballgame and for inviting us to the Otesaga, writing in riffs about what baseball in general and the Induction Weekend in particular meant to me. My pen took off onto page after page as my stream of consciousness transformed itself into a roaring river. In the midst of this metamorphosis, the sudden desire to keep writing about baseball, not just in letters but for publication, found its way onto my immediate to-do list. After all, wasn't writing for publication how Bart Giamatti got his start in baseball's arena?

First shot out of the pen upon our return to Texas was my effort to turn the guts of my letter to Dr. Bobby Brown into something prosaic. Though never published before, my essay entitled "Images From The Glimmerglass" expresses the particulars on the 1989 Induction Weekend's lasting impact.

We could forgive the heat, the crowd, and that you could not see the stage. We came to Cooperstown, New York, on July 23, 1989, to hear, glimpse, and remember Carl Yastrzemski, Johnny Bench, Red Schoendienst, and umpire Al Barlick. Their induction into Baseball's Hall of Fame made official what fans had determined years before—that these men are legends in the American mythology of baseball.

While waiting for the ceremonies to begin, we listened. Sons corrected fathers, but fathers insisted, with the leverage of experience. Wives questioned husbands, who answered with a sublime arrogance. All focused on their common passion—the Players of the Game. No one talked of income tax, visitation, SAT, work, or school, because the occasion compelled a disconnect from all forms of gritty reality.

Why more than 30,000 in this village of 2,400? Why 400 sportswriters? Why Tip O'Neill? Why the extended lines at the post office to get the Gehrig stamp, at the Hall to see the new wing, and at the stores to get an autographed ball or a commemorative bat? Why not spend this time studying computers, learning a foreign language, or helping the needy?

We gave our undivided attention to these activities because we live in America and, for these select men, induction into the Hall of Fame consummated their American Dream. That makes a happy story for them and for us. Their speeches made it clear that each did it through the support of families, teammates and coaches, faith, hard work, and a persevering attitude that collectively allowed them to excel at the game known as our National Pastime.

Baseball sent Yaz from a Long Island potato farm to Triple Crown Impossible Dream glory, took Johnny from an Oklahoma dust bowl town of six hundred to lead the Big Red Machine, and allowed Red to escape from an Illinois coal mine to play, coach and manage in seven World Series. These American Pygmalions emerged from the pack in playing this game where the best hitter gets one hit every three at-bats for only a couple of years, the best starting pitcher wins only six out of every ten decisions over his career, and a single-booted ground ball extinguishes fifteen years of stardom. (Sorry, Bill Buckner, but a Red Sox fan never forgets.)

Luck plays no part in Cooperstown's selection, and neither does a hot streak, a dramatic home run, a no-hitter, a great year, or a great three years. The men who make the Hall put it together for at least a decade, and usually closer to a score. Bobby Thomson hit the most famous home run in baseball history, and he is not in the Hall of Fame. Don Larsen pitched the only perfect game in the World Series, and he is not here either, nor is Denny McLain, the only man in the last fifty years to win thirty games in a season. Finally, and most incredibly, Roger Maris and his Babe Ruth-defying sixty-one home runs in 1961 are not here. A moment in the sun can become a flash in the pan. Selection to the Hall of Fame comes only through maintaining a career marked by sustained excellence of performance, and that is the lesson of this Induction Day.

For those whose fastball refuses to go ninety, whose bat fails to connect consistently, and whose throws from the hole never beat the runner, the niche for us mortals must be elsewhere. Ultimate success for us (like these Hall of Famers) will come only from sustained excellence of performance in the particular niche suited to our particular talents. A Hall of Fame career in any number of vocations can come through the support of family, mentors, faith, and personal dedication.

Baseball at Cooperstown—the American Dream lives for all of us in the reflection coming off the Glimmerglass.

After finishing that essay, my baseball musings made it into print two months later when the *Dallas Times Herald* ran my Giamatti tribute shortly after his death (which appears in Chapter 5). Then a wonderful guy named Steve Lehman gave me opportunities to write essays and book reviews for his baseball creative writing periodical, *Elysian Fields Quarterly*. Next, a talented writer in Fort Worth named Jeff Guinn guided me into the challenge of pursuing the writing of a baseball history book. And then, once my idea for a book about baseball's pivotal year of 1939 had clarified itself to the point of my knowing it would definitely work, I traveled back to Cooperstown to do the necessary research at the National Baseball Library in early February 1993.

Because the Otesaga is closed in the winter, I followed the Cooperstown Chamber of Commerce's recommendation and stayed downtown at the west end of Main Street at the Cooper Inn, owned by the Clark family, who for over a century and a half have had title to much of the town, including the Baseball Hall of Fame and the Otesaga Hotel.

On Sunday evening, January 31, 1993, in the dead of winter, I arrived at the Cooper Inn in time to walk down snow-covered Main Street, and get dinner at the Tunnicliff Inn, a local tavern with a good television, allowing locals and the town's one visitor to gather and watch Super Bowl XXVII matching the Dallas Cowboys against the Buffalo Bills. The game's first half was close, and as the only Cowboy fan in the place, I absorbed the other patrons' glares, as they (like the Hall of Famers at the Otesaga in July 1989) wondered, "Who let this guy in?" Believing in discretion as the better part of valor, I left the establishment at halftime, went back to my room at the inn, and whooped and hollered to my heart's content as the Cowboys obliterated the Bills in the second half.

The Cooper Inn gave the appearance of having its own rich history, and an information card in the foyer recited that it had been built and inhabited in the early 1800's by the youngest son of none other than (drum-roll) Elihu Phinney! A book on Cooperstown's history there in the breakfast room for guests' perusal provided more information on dear departed Elihu. It turned out that the man whose cowpasture became the site of Doubleday Field also owned and operated the first newspaper in town. Beyond that, in a remarkable display of

NEW YORK STATE HISTORICAL ASSOCIATION, COOPERSTOWN, NEW YORK, RESEARCH LIBRARY, SPECIAL COLLECTIONS, GIFT OF ALEXANDER S. PHINNEY

Elihu Phinney—entrepreneur, gentleman farmer, and Renaissance Man of Cooperstown—on whose cowpasture Doubleday Field was built.

Yankee ingenuity, Phinney decided to grow his revenues by finding ways to use his printing presses full time, expanding his repertoire of publications to include Bibles, textbooks, and almanacs. Elihu Phinney had undoubtedly been the area's Renaissance Man, maintaining livestock in his pasture while manufacturing books and newspapers on his business premises. Learning of his life, entrepreneurship, and contributions to expanding local consciousness made the Cooper Inn's grounds seem every bit as hallowed as the land for the diamond at Doubleday Field.

In early February 1993, the National Baseball Library resided in temporary quarters at an old theater on Main Street located conveniently (for my purposes) across the street from the Cooper Inn, where it would stay until construction of a larger facility, which opened in 1994. Entering the library on Monday morning in the midst of sub-zero temperatures that kept most of the town's residents off the streets, it became apparent that these five days of research would be the quietest week of my life.

In those days before Al Gore invented the Internet, coming to Cooperstown and keeping butt in chair at the National Baseball Library was essentially the only way to pursue meaningful research concerning baseball history. Not even in law school had I ever read nonstop from a Monday morning until a Friday afternoon with such complete, constant concentration, poring over the library's thick files dedicated to the baseball heroes and events of 1939—Lou Gehrig, Joe DiMaggio, Ted Williams, Bob Feller, Red Barber, Leo Durocher, Bill McKechnie, Satchel Paige, Bill Klem, Al Schacht, the formation of Little League Baseball by Carl Stotz, and, of course, Abner Doubleday and the entire crew associated with baseball's centennial year when the Hall of Fame opened its doors.

The library's temporary venue at the theater had a grand total of four small work tables, meaning the few who entered that tiny space during my week in the village would necessarily get well acquainted. As in my prior visits to Cooperstown, I again found myself in the right place at the right time. During my research time at the National Baseball Library, I shared table space and had meals with the likes of John Thorn (lead historical consultant for Ken Burns in his nine-part documentary, *Baseball*, which debuted on PBS a year and a half later in September 1994); Bill James (already recognized then as the leading baseball statistical analyst ever, whose perspective on the game would ultimately shape the talent evaluations of every general manager in baseball— most notably Oakland's Billy Beane and Boston's Theo Epstein); and last but not least, Rob Neyer, a pleasant young man doing work there as a freelance researcher for Bill James. A few years later, in his own right, Rob emerged as one of the game's top analysts, the author of bestselling books, and the lead baseball columnist for ESPN.com.

John Thorn gave me a verbal preview of Ken Burns' massive history/ film project, and correctly predicted that the documentary would turn Negro League legend Buck O'Neil into a television superstar. Bill James was working on forming a final opinion on the 1989 confrontation between Pete Rose and Bart Giamatti as part of his book that came out a year later, *The Politics of Glory: How Baseball's Hall of Fame Really Works* (Macmillan, 1994), and even asked for my assessment (as a litigator) about certain aspects of their trial proceedings. Most important to me and my book, Rob Neyer agreed to do freelance work for me (at the very reasonable rate of $7 an hour), as I could already see that there would be research rabbit trails ahead that would have to be run (which I, as a full-time practicing lawyer, didn't have time to run) in connection with some of my chapters to make sure the history in my book was accurate.

During that week, my friend Paul Rogers, then the Dean of the SMU Law School in Dallas, arranged his schedule to come to Cooperstown for a day, needing to be in the area anyway for a conference in Syracuse. During his twenty-four hours in town, Paul also felt the pull of the village. A few months later, he embarked on writing his own first baseball history book, teaming up with his childhood hero Robin Roberts on *The Whiz Kids and the 1950 Pennant* (Temple University Press, 1996).[5]

At this otherwise bleak time of year, Paul Rogers encountered during his one day in Cooperstown what struck me during my one week there, i.e., at this time, when the village had no other tourists milling around and not many resident pedestrians, for all intents and purposes, we had the National Baseball Hall of Fame and the town of Cooperstown all to ourselves. With no distractions, we soaked up the local scene gliding through town and the Hall of Fame museum at our own deliberate pace as if in slow motion, like the professional athlete who finally hits his stride, expressing our doubts that there could ever again be a time spent visiting baseball's home plate when we could spend as much time as we wanted doing exactly what we wanted. The Zanders' "art of possibility" had become a ball in play and the snow in the air and on the ground made that surreal time even more serene.

5 Paul and Robin Roberts then collaborated on Robin's memoirs for their second book, *My Life In Baseball* (Triumph Books, 2003).

Three trips to Cooperstown, all made under different circumstances, in the presence of different people, all led to the same result. This was a place that glistened for the visitor—on the green grass of Doubleday Field in May, on the waters of Lake Otsego beside the Otesaga Hotel in July, and on the snow-covered sidewalks and rooftops in February. Beyond the physical setting, what added to the area's sparkle throughout the year was its serving as a gathering place for bringing disparate folks together to form special bonds and memories, be it an antique furniture-loving father and his adolescent baseballphiliac son at Honus Wagner's locker in the spring of 1972; two couples in the same cramped motel room rising above their dismal accommodations to mingle at the grand Otesaga Hotel with the President of the American League and the baseball gods in the summer of 1989; or two Dallas lawyer/historian wannabes connecting with leading scholars and analysts while the town was otherwise deserted, in the winter of 1993. Centuries before, the Iroquois tribe who had inhabited the area got it right when they named this place "Otsego," a word that in their language meant "place of the meeting."

I have had other trips to Cooperstown since February 1993. In 1997,

Main Street in Cooperstown in wintertime, a glistening place of snow-covered sidewalks and rooftops— it's the same today as it was in 1930 when this photo was taken.

The connection between boyhood Cooperstown resident Abner Doubleday and baseball forever confirms the power of myth.

Bobby Bragan allowed me to accompany him when Bobby's lifelong friend Tommy Lasorda received his plaque, and that visit is detailed in the final section of Chapter 8, devoted to my friendship with Bobby. In 1999, I organized a group of family and friends to go up for Nolan Ryan's induction, and that experience is described at the end of Chapter 4. Thanks to Hall of Fame President Dale Petroskey, I even got to speak at the Hall's Bullpen Theater in May 2005 after my book *1939: Baseball's Tipping Point*[6] was published, and returned again in the summer of 2007 for the induction of Cal Ripken and Tony Gwynn.

Each of these later trips compared favorably with the 1972, 1989, and 1993 visits to the village, in that (as described in Chapters 4 and 8) each produced its own separate "walking on air in slow motion" moments, and in the Zanders' words, created a time when "integration with the world" transcended "the business of survival." Thus, thirty-seven years of going to Cooperstown, New York, has confirmed my 1972 suspicion that somewhere out there in the vast mythological universe, Santa Claus and Abner Doubleday walk side by side.

---

6 My book first came on in 1994, and was entitled *1939: Baseball's Pivotal Year* (Summit Group, 1994). Then when Summit went out of business, the book went out of print until Rue Judd of Bright Sky Press gave it new life with a new title, and *1939: Baseball's Tipping Point* (Bright Sky Press, 2005) came out in March 2005.

Roger Maris hit his this 61st home run on October 1, 1961, demonstrating in this historic photograph his picture-perfect, left-handed baseball swing.

CHAPTER SEVEN

ROGER MARIS
The Man, his Record, and the Steroids Controversy

My first baseball season, remembered from beginning to end, was 1961, which arguably produced more drama on the diamond than any other year in history. In the big middle of the action were New York Yankee teammates Roger Maris and Mickey Mantle who battled all summer long to break Babe Ruth's single-season home run record. In America, like everywhere else, we like our heroes to be of the tragic variety. Chapter One in this book tells how Mickey Mantle filled that bill. This chapter proves that Roger Maris did the same.

One of the greatest baseball photographs ever taken is of Roger Maris, arms fully extended, driving the bat through his level swing at the climax of his 61st home run on Sunday, October 1, 1961—my 8th birthday. With that blast on the last day of the '61 season, Maris broke Babe Ruth's record for homers that had been in place 34 years.[1] Home run number 61 also ended the summer-long competition between Roger Maris and teammate Mickey Mantle (dubbed "the M&M boys" by the press) whose late season illness/infection caused him to stop short of challenging the Bambino after hitting his 54th homer.

The wirephoto of Maris' record-breaking homer locked into the mind of Baby Boomers across the country and still remains there for many of us,[2] embedded in the permanent memory bank. Just like Babe Ruth, no batting gloves, elbow pads, or helmet flaps covered Maris'

---

1 Ford Frick, Commissioner of Baseball in 1961 and an old crony of Ruth's, determined that Maris should have an asterisk beside his name in the record book because he set the record in a 162-game season. Ruth had hit his 60 home runs in 1927 when seasons lasted 154 games, and Maris only had 59 homers at the end of the 154th game in 1961. Although Frick never got around to actually putting an asterisk in the record book, in 1991, six years after Roger Maris' untimely death, Commissioner Fay Vincent overruled Frick's decision and announced that from that day forward until someone broke it, only Maris would hold the single-season home run record.

2 A framed version of it hangs on this writer's bedroom wall.

In April 1961, American League President Joe Cronin presents Roger Maris with the award for being named the league's Most Valuable Player in 1960.

body parts. No. All that appeared in the picture was a leanly muscled young man in a billowing short-sleeved, pin-striped uniform, socks and pants connecting at mid-calf, swinging a long thin bat with his bare hands, using every ounce of power his fully balanced body could generate. If Michelangelo had ever conceived of sculpting a block of marble into the perfect left-handed baseball swing, he surely would have used Maris' 61st home run photo as his model.

Roger Maris never had another spectacular season after 1961, which, to the surprise of many, actually pleased him, as he abhorred the celebrity status that accompanied his breaking Ruth's record. In '63, a back injury and severe muscle pulls in his legs cut short his season, allowing him to play in only 90 games. A broken bone in his right wrist with collateral nerve damage caused by a hard slide ruined his '65 season, permanently robbing him of his power stroke. His injury proneness and power outage led to the Yankees trading him to St. Louis for a journeyman in December 1966, where he ended his career after the '68 season.

To the surprise of many Baby Boomers who regard Roger Maris as the best baseball player of their childhood (because, in fact, he was exactly that for the three summers from 1960 to 1962[3]), the home run king never got inducted into the National Baseball Hall of Fame despite winning two American League Most Valuable Player Awards (1960 and 1961), playing a key role on 7 pennant-winning teams (the Yankees of 1960-1964 and the Cardinals of '67-'68) during a span of 9 years, and being recognized as one of his era's best defensive outfielders and base runners. Regardless of all these accomplishments, his .260 lifetime batting average and 275 career home runs simply don't measure up to the Hall's unstated statistical benchmarks for power hitter inductees.

After leaving the game following the 1968 World Series, Maris maintained a low profile, owned and operated an Anheiser-Busch beer distributorship in Florida with his older brother, Rudy (whom Roger called "Bud"), successfully raised a family of six children with his wife (and high school sweetheart), Pat, and died of lymphoma cancer at the age of 51 in December 1985.

---

3 In 1960, he had 39 homers (second only to Mantle's 40) and a league-leading 112 RBI's, and finished second in total bases with 290. In 1961, he led the league in homers, RBI's and total bases, with 61-142-366. In 1962, he had 33 homers and 100 RBI's, with a career high 34 doubles and 287 total bases, such that he had more extra base hits that year than when he won the MVP in 1960.

So who was this Roger Maris, this fellow who wore uniform number 9 for the Yankees and then the Cardinals, who broke Babe Ruth's single-season home run record and completely captured the nation's attention in the early 1960's, and then suddenly disappeared from our lives like a phantom?

Those who knew Maris well, from childhood all the way through his professional baseball and business careers, have provided biographers with a clear account of him. The essentials of his character are consistently chronicled in the four leading books that focused on Roger Maris: teammate Tony Kubek's *Sixty-One: The Team, The Record, The Man* (Macmillan, 1987); longtime New York sportswriter (who covered Maris' Yankee teams) Maury Allen's *Roger Maris: A Man For All Seasons* (Donald I. Fine, 1986); Pulitzer Prize winning historian David Halberstam's *October 1964* (Villard Books, 1994); and *The Sporting News'* Ron Smith's *61*: The Story of Roger Maris, Mickey Mantle and One Magical Summer* (McGraw Hill, 2001).

In no particular order, the seven most essential elements in the phenomenon of Roger Maris, as determined by those who studied his life the most and those who knew him the best, were the following:

- Baseball's single-season home run king was a superior all-around athlete with a sprinter's speed, a fearlessness of physical contact, and astonishing hand-eye coordination. As a two-time, all-state high school football half-back, he ran four kickoffs back for touchdowns in one game (still a national record), and was good enough to attract a scholarship offer from Bud Wilkinson in his heyday at the University of Oklahoma. As for the hand-eye, while with the Yankees, in addition to his hitting prowess, in order to "relax" in the clubhouse before games, Maris often played a labyrinth game that involved moving a metal ball past sixty holes on a winding track by means of shifting the game board up and down and side to side, and outplayed all his teammates by achieving his objective fifty consecutive times without a ball ever falling through a hole.

- Roger Maris spoke his mind to the press and anyone else, letting the chips fall wherever they fell. Halberstam's book mentions that during the '61 season, when asked by a reporter one too many times whether he believed he could break Babe Ruth's record,

"Roger Maris was the best all-around player I ever saw."—Mickey Mantle.

Maris replied, "How the f—- should I know?" Like Joe DiMaggio, he regarded himself first and foremost as a ballplayer whose main objective was to help his team win games, and beyond that, he felt no desire and believed he had no obligation to entertain the media with witticisms or newsworthy sound bites. His often brutal directness produced severe and frequent criticism from those with the job of writing about baseball, admitting, "I was born surly and I intend to go on being that way."

- Maris was the consummate team player, executing better than any of his compadres those skills not recorded in box scores—breaking up double plays with hard take-out slides; hitting the cut-off man with his throws every single time; advancing two bases on a single; and getting runners home from third base with fewer than two outs by either dribbling slow grounders to the right side of the infield or laying down bunts.

- When his body was healthy, Roger Maris played harder than anyone—a ballplayer whose games were remembered for his ferocious slides into infielders and catchers; all-out diving catches; and maximum-effort, cut-it-loose throws. In the Yankee tradition of Joe DiMaggio, he also played smart—with total aggression but without mental mistakes. These characteristics on the field endeared him to his teammates, as did his personality off the field, totally devoid of arrogance or insincerity.

- Maris was sensitive to criticism, never forgiving teammate Jim Bouton for accusing him of dogging it when he jogged (because of having to play with a pulled leg muscle) down to first base after hitting an infield grounder; a writer who blasted him in the newspaper for failing to appear for an interview because of his fulfilling a higher priority commitment to see a dying child in the hospital on the condition that the visit receive no publicity; or the Yankee Stadium fans who booed him because he wasn't Mickey Mantle and from 1962 to 1966 because he failed to duplicate his 1961 season.

- From a big picture perspective, Roger Maris made good decisions: being a faithful husband and devoted father in his family life; never letting his success on the field go to his head; negotiating a deal with Cardinals owner Augie Busch to play a final season in St. Louis in consideration for being awarded one of Busch's prized beer distributorships in the college town of Gainesville, Florida; receiving experimental cancer treatment by receiving injections of fluids from mice in his final days, knowing death was imminent but hoping the knowledge gained from his tests and treatments might save the life of a subsequent lymphoma patient.

- Finally, at his core, as the son of a railroad worker renowned for pounding railroad ties in forty-below-zero weather, Maris was a quintessential blue collar guy. He had no interest in being fashionable or quotable. He never aspired to be rich or famous, but sought only to provide financial security for his large family and enjoy a comfortable life with them and his many close friends, removed from the media that dogged his every step throughout his baseball career. He smoked unfiltered Camels; drank black coffee in the morning and Budweiser in the evening; ate mass quantities of food in general and hard shell crabs in particular (an irony since many in the sports media regarded him as a hard shell crab of a person); worked hard when he had to, but relaxed when he could; and made up his mind quickly when it came to making decisions. In short, Roger Maris was a simple, hard man, who saw the world in terms of right or wrong, black or white, good guy or bad guy, and nothing and no one ever fell in between.

Some excerpts from the books on Maris serve as proof for his having these seven essential components:

Historian David Halberstam: "He was pursued by a press corps he did not want to talk to, adoring fans whose adoration he did not seek. He responded by retreating deep into his shell, increasingly unhappy with how he was perceived by the fans, the writers, and even his employers … He was a player who never heard the cheers but always remembered the boos … He was a physical man, not a verbal one: he was skilled in the use of his body, not in the use of words … Maris lacked the skill and the desire to win fans over. He not only was boring, he liked being boring. He was a man absolutely without pretense, and he wore no face save his own. He was not graceful or subtle. He was almost always blunt, sometimes unspeakably so."

Sportswriter Maury Allen: "There were times when he was short-tempered, sometimes gruff, often curt. It was part of his stoic, private, shy personality. Most of his anger, especially on the field, was directed at himself. He was, as the ballplayers say, a red ass, an angry young man under certain circumstances … The man had a hard shell but he also had a certain trait, uncommon in sports, uncommon in life: a devotion to honesty—brutal, unfeeling at times, but always necessary. In personality, he was colorless. In performance, he was thrilling. He could be passionate about the art of hitting a baseball and cantankerous about discussing it. He seemed closest, most comfortable, warmest, even funniest with his trusted friends and tested teammates. Roger Maris never pretended to be anything other than what he was—a man who wanted nothing more than to excel at his chosen profession, and asked to be appreciated for his efforts."

Seven-year Yankee teammate Mickey Mantle (in Kubek's book): "I was asked the other day who was the best all-around player I'd seen, and I said Roger. I really believe that the sixty-one homers is the greatest feat in baseball history." (In Allen's book): "He was a hell of a player, a Hall of Famer for sure in my book. He was a terrific outfielder, a great base runner, a marvelous slider. He studied the game. He always concentrated…. I can still see that 61st home run of his go into the seats and I still get chills thinking about it. Even now, even this very minute."

One-and-a-half-year Indian teammate,[4] and eight-and-a-half-year American League opponent Rocky Colavito (in Allen's book): "Roger was a tough player, very determined to excel, and very strong-minded. If he made up his mind to do something his way, that was it. He was not a wishy-washy guy, which was one of the things I liked about him. He gave loyalty as a friend and expected loyalty in return. I think some of the things he said in New York put him in hot water with a lot of people, but Roger just couldn't be a politician. He couldn't say one thing to one guy and another thing to another guy. Roger Maris was as honest

4 Maris played with the Indians from 1957 to midseason '58; then with the Kansas City A's from midseason '58 to '59; then with the Yankees from 1960 to 1966; and finally with the Cardinals from 1967 to 1968.

and stand-up a person as I have ever known. As for his baseball ability, he belongs in the Hall of Fame. He was the most underrated ballplayer of my time."

Five-year Yankee teammate Ralph Terry (in Allen's book): "The only difference between us was that I laughed everything off. Roger didn't. If he trusted you and you crossed him, you didn't get a second chance. He could be real cold and cut you up if you did something he thought betrayed his trust. I'd laugh about it, kid a guy out of it and forget it. Roger wasn't that way. He was a very serious man."

Six-year Yankee teammate Tony Kubek (in Allen's book): "We were playing this game against the White Sox and struggling a little. If they won, we would be two or three games back and it might have been tough to catch up again. Whitey was on the mound in a 2-2 game about the seventh or eighth inning. The White Sox had the bases loaded, and Gene Freese hit a line drive into right center field. I figured it was easily a double, maybe a triple for three runs, and we were out of the game. I ran out to take the throw and I watched Roger chase after the ball. He could really run. He simply overtook that ball, jumped in the air and backhanded it before it hit the wall to end the inning, a tremendous catch. After the game, which we finally won 7-2, Whitey came over to me and said, 'If Roger didn't catch that, I was finished.' There was a lot of feeling in the clubhouse that Roger's catch had not only turned the game around for us but turned the season. He was as good a right fielder as I ever saw."

Seven-year Yankee teammate Clete Boyer (in Allen's book): "Roger was a tremendous baseball player. There were a lot of things he did people didn't know about. He was the best guy I ever saw in going from first to third, the best on breaking up a double play, the best in getting a run in from third with less than two out. I saw Roger many times, with a guy on third, hit the weakest grounder in the world to the right side, I mean weak, but the guy from third can score. That's a lot better than hitting a bullet that the first baseman catches."

St. Louis Cardinals manager Red Schoendienst (in Allen's book): "He was a very solid player for us, not flashy, just a guy who did his job, played hard, always made the right play and fit in with the guys. I tried not to play him too much, never played him in a day game after a night game, and really got out of him as much as we could. We won two pennants in those two years he was with us. I'd have to say Roger was the difference in our winning in those two seasons. Roger knew how to win."

Those heavily researched accounts by esteemed writers and first-person statements from his baseball associates combine to portray the man Frank Sinatra described every time he sang his theme song, "My Way." With clarity as to these essential components that made up the unusual and talented man who set baseball's single-season home run record, it is now time to relive the drama of Roger Maris' 1961 season, which comedian, movie director, and fellow Baby Boomer Billy Crystal called "the greatest season of my life."[5]

———————

The '61 season started slowly for the 1960 American League Most Valuable Player. In the first four games, he had a grand total of one hit—a single. After 10 games, the guy who had hit 39 home runs the year before still had not yet hit his first homer, and after 27 games, he only had 3. In his memoirs of the 1961 season co-authored with New Jersey sportswriter Jim Ogle, *Roger Maris At Bat* (Duell, Sloan and Pearce, 1962), Maris attributed his production delay coming out of the blocks to being preoccupied about his wife's health when her two-month pregnancy with their fourth child became jeopardized. By mid-May, the health of Pat Maris and the baby had stabilized for the good, and Roger could at last focus on his hitting.

His high-strung spirits were also calmed on the morning of May 22 when Yankee owner Dan Topping and the team's new general manager, Roy Hamey, took their reigning MVP to lunch, and told him to calm down, feel secure about his position in the starting lineup, forget about his batting average, and focus entirely on hitting home runs. If Maris would do that, they explained, everything would work out for the good. One other thing—just to be sure nothing was amiss with their right fielder, they arranged for Maris that afternoon to have his eyes tested, and, in fact, they were fine.

Beyond clearing his head over family health issues and job security,

---

5 In 2001, Billy Crystal directed the film 61* for HBO about the 1961 season. When he first saw actor Barry Pepper as a soldier in the movie *Saving Private Ryan*, Crystal exclaimed, "That's Roger Maris!" and proceeded to cast him for the role of Maris in his movie.

another important factor powered Roger Maris' home run explosion in 1961 that lasted from mid-May until early October—a lineup decision made by the Yankees' new manager, Ralph Houk. In 1960, then skipper Casey Stengel batted Mantle third and Maris fourth in the lineup, and the team was great, finishing in first place 8 games ahead of Baltimore, but then losing the World Series in 7 games to Pittsburgh. After the Series ended, the Yankee brain trust fired Stengel and replaced him with Houk, who had been one of Casey's coaches. Houk had seen American League pitchers pitch a little too carefully to Mantle, walking him 111 times in 1960, and even intentionally walking him 6 times to face Maris.

Houk decided that by moving Roger to third and Mickey to clean-up in the batting order, pitchers would throw more fastballs to Maris to minimize the risk of walking him and, thereby, having to face Mantle, the most feared hitter in the circuit, with a runner on base. This clearly worked to Maris' benefit, as he, like all great major league power hitters, greatly preferred fastballs over any other pitch.

With each week, more national sportswriters and photographers were assigned to cover the game's most dazzling single-season home run competition, which received even greater media coverage because they played side by side in both the same batting order and the Yankee Stadium outfield (Mickey in center, Roger in right), had alliterative last names, and even shared an apartment together with teammate Bob Cerv. Though Mantle had started the season quicker, hitting 7 homers in the team's first 8 games, Maris exploded past him in June, hitting 23 home runs in a span of 36 games.

In his book, Maris described how the competition with his outfield colleague helped both of them: "It was becoming obvious that Mickey and I were helping each other hit home runs. We were not only challenging each other, but also pacing each other. It is hard to say just how much we helped each other, but definitely the way we were going after home runs made each of us try that much harder."

By mid-July 1961, Maris and Mantle were clobbering the ball over the fence at an alarming rate, ahead of Babe Ruth's pace in his record-breaking year of 1927, and Commissioner of Baseball Ford Frick simply couldn't stand the idea of the Bambino, his old friend, losing his record. On July 17, Frick announced at a press conference that because Ruth had set his mark when seasons lasted 154 games, regardless of the fact that the League's expansion from 8 to 10 teams in 1961 had caused the season to be extended to 162 games, no one could knock the Babe out of the record book unless he passed Ruth's total within the season's first 154 games. If someone broke the record in Games 155-162, then he would be named in the record book with a "distinctive mark" beside his name alongside Ruth's name. *New York Daily News* sportswriter Dick Young suggested to the Frick that the "distinctive mark" should be an asterisk, because "everybody does that when there's a difference

of opinion." The Commissioner's decision most definitely heightened the season's drama. Ironically, on the day of Frick's announcement, in the second game of a double-header against Baltimore, Maris and Mantle both hit home runs in a game that ended because of a fifth-inning rainstorm that caused the homers to be forfeited because the game was called before five complete innings had been finished.

In a July 25 doubleheader against the White Sox at Yankee Stadium, Maris hit 4 home runs, with the last being his fortieth, exceeding his career high 39 from his 1960 MVP season. With over

A close friend of Babe Ruth, Commissioner of Baseball Ford Frick announced in mid-July 1961 that no one could "break" Ruth's record unless he did so in 154 games.

two months left in the schedule, the idea of breaking Babe Ruth's record all of a sudden seemed very achievable.

By early August, most Yankee fans decided they had to cheer for their desired winner and boo for the desired loser in the home run race, with the substantial majority backing Mantle as the preferred choice to break Ruth's record. In the book published by *The Sporting News* in conjunction with his HBO film, 61*, Billy Crystal explained why the fans preferred Mantle: "If anyone should break Ruth's record, it should be Mickey. He was supposed to be the one. It was his time, his ballpark. Who was this guy Maris with the bad haircut, this flash in the pan? He shouldn't be the one. Not him. We wanted the handsome, fun-loving Elvis in centerfield. He's the real Yankee."

In the early 1960's, the M&M boys served as baseball's most productive and most photographed dynamic duo.

Maris described the grandstand appreciation shift in his book—"The fans had been good to me ever since I came to New York, and I usually got a good hand. Now, it began to swing. The fans began to get behind Mickey. Now he would be cheered all the time, while the fans began to get on me. It wasn't vicious, but they got off Mickey and on me. I guess they figured I was only a 'rookie' with the Yankees and didn't rate ahead of Mick. Mantle began to notice it, too, and often kidded me about it. 'Hey, Rogge,' Mickey would yell, 'It's nice to have you around taking over the boo-birds. Nice to see them on somebody else for a change.'"

By August 13, both the M&M boys had hit 45 homers and were 16 games ahead of Ruth's pace. They knew they would have to be well ahead of it going into September since the Babe had ripped 17 homers during the final month of the '27 season. The M&M boys had become such national celebrities that they appeared together on the cover of *Life* magazine's August 18, 1961, issue, smiling in the front of a shadowy black-and-white photo of Babe Ruth. On August 22, Maris became the first major league hitter in history to have 50 homers before the end of August, and only the ninth player in history to ever hit that many in a single season.

By the end of that month, the Yankees traveled to Kansas City for a series with the A's, allowing Roger Maris to be home with his wife and four children, including newborn son Randy who arrived home from the hospital with his mom, Pat, during his father's four-day visit.[6] Amazingly, shortly before the series opened, a knucklehead writer for the Kansas City newspaper published the home address of baseball's biggest superstar, meaning that for the four days Maris rejoined his family, hundreds of unwanted visitors hung outside their home and knocked on the door seeking autographs. In his book, Roger said, "I don't think I've ever been more angry in my life. This was an unthinking, uncalled-for invasion of my privacy ... Before I left town, I made sure I let a few people involved with the paper know exactly what I thought about their printing my address."

On September 3, Mantle hit his 50th home run and for the first time in baseball history, one team had 2 players who had each hit 50 homers. As the summer wore on, some sportswriters decided to create

---

6 The Athletics moved to Oakland following the '67 season and have been there ever since.

Roger and Pat Maris with their four children at their Kansas City home late in the '61 season.

a human interest story, claiming that the home run competition between the M&M boys had started to sour their friendship and a feud between them had begun. As close friends and apartment roommates, the two slugging outfielders read and laughed at the fabricated stories.

Everywhere Mantle and Maris went during the month of September 1961, they were mobbed for autographs and attacked for stories and photos by the paparazzi. In those days, reporters had essentially unlimited access to the Yankees' locker room, and Maris found that the best way to avoid them was to stay in the trainer's room, the only off-limits venue in the clubhouse. To avoid the constant frenzy when not at the ballpark, Maris spent most of the time on the road secluded in his hotel room, and said the only time he ever felt any peace at all was on the field during ballgames.

As evidence of Roger Maris' peace of mind on the diamond, on the first page of his book, *Sixty-One*, Tony Kubek tells a story of Maris' calm in the heat of battle in a game at Yankee Stadium on September 17 against the Tigers. As Kubek stood at second base with Maris at the plate getting ready to hit, he stepped out of the batter's box and paused to watch a flock of Canadian geese fly across the sky. "The game just stopped because Roger Maris wanted to watch some geese." Finally, he

As Maris pressed on through September in pursuit of
Babe Ruth's record, the stress became evident.

stepped to the plate and proceeded to crush the first pitch for a 400 foot home run, his 58th of the season. After the game, Maris mentioned to Kubek, "I can still see those geese. Watching them was so peaceful."

By mid-September, on the verge of clinching the American League pennant over the pesky second-place Tigers, Maris admitted in his book that he "suddenly developed a burning desire to break the record. What really drove me toward the record and kept me battling when the whole thing got out of hand was all the people who had been knocking me. I was tired of hearing and reading that I was a lousy hitter and wasn't in Ruth's class. I became so irked with the whole situation that I felt I'd like to break the record just to hear them squeal louder."

Maris started the 154th game on September 20 against Baltimore with 58 homers, knowing that Commissioner Frick would not fully recognize him as the record breaker unless he hit 3 home runs that night. America believed he might just do it, and CBS televised the game nationally just in case, with the two most interested viewers being Pat Maris in Kansas City and Babe Ruth's widow, Claire, in New York City. Maury Allen in his biography of Maris said, "In more than twenty-five years as a sportswriter, it was the most dramatic, exciting, tension-filled game I have ever witnessed, even more than the Yankee pennant playoff in Boston in 1978 (won by Bucky Dent's eighth-inning home run), more than any championship series game, and more than any World Series game. It was one man against history."

In the first inning, Maris hit a rocket right into the glove of Baltimore outfielder Whitey Herzog, Maris' close friend and former teammate on the Kansas City A's. In the third inning, he made solid contact again, this time achieving the desired loft, blasting Milt Pappas' fastball over the right field wall for home run number 59. In the fourth, with sinkerballer Dick Hall pitching in relief of Pappas, Maris knocked the ball down the right field line, and it sailed over the fence, but was slightly foul. One pitch later, he struck out. In the seventh inning, in the face of a strong wind blowing in, he hit another long foul ball over the fence before skying a ball to deep right caught on the warning track again by Herzog. Finally, in his last at-bat, with 2 out in the ninth inning, and the Yankees safely ahead by a score of 4-0, the Orioles' final reliever, Hoyt Wilhelm, threw Maris three straight knuckleballs for strikes, the last one glancing off his bat handle back toward the mound and Wilhelm tagged Maris out, as Claire Ruth and Ford Frick both breathed a huge sigh of relief.

Regardless of Frick and his pronouncement on the need to break the record by the end of the 154th game, in the season's final week, Roger Maris still pursued the home run record. Unfortunately, he had to do it alone because Mickey Mantle left the Yankees' lineup in late September with a severe case of bronchitis, and his condition then worsened after receiving an injection of experimental medicine from a quack doctor recommended by broadcaster Mel Allen, which caused a massive infection in his right thigh, necessitating surgery to remove the skin around the infected area.

Roger Maris tied Ruth's single-season record on September 26, hitting home run number 60 against the Orioles' Jack Fisher, whose other claim to fame during his otherwise unspectacular 11-year career came when he served up the gopher ball to Ted Williams on September 28, 1960, almost exactly one year before Maris' 60th home run, in the final at-bat of Williams' career.

Roger Maris' quest for the record all came down to the final game of the season on Sunday afternoon, October 1. Amazingly, Yankee Stadium was only half full that day with 23,154 fans in attendance. Red Sox manager Pinky Higgins gave the ball to starting pitcher Tracy Stallard who, to his credit, threw pitches in the strike zone, refusing to pitch around Maris. In the first inning, Stallard got Maris to go after an outside fastball, causing him to fly out to the Red Sox rookie left fielder Carl Yastrzemski.

Then came the fateful fourth inning, with the game tied 0-0. Stallard's first 2 pitches were balls, and the crowd booed the Boston right-hander who decided the time was right to fire his best fastball. Instead of going low and outside where Bosox catcher Russ Nixon wanted it, the pitch flew into Maris' wheelhouse, belt-high over the middle of the plate, and he smashed it 365 feet, ten rows deep into the right field stands, driving the crowd wild.

After floating around the bases in a fog, the new home run record holder tried to enter the Yankee dugout, but his teammates blocked his path on the top step, and required him to stand and wave to the crowd. The historic homer allowed the Yankees to win the final game of the season by a score of 1-0, and also gave Maris his second consecutive American League RBI crown with 142 ribeyes, 1 ahead of Baltimore first baseman Jim Gentile. After finishing his extensive post-game interviews, and enjoying dinner with his wife and a few friends, Roger Maris had one last thing to do before the day ended. He asked his buddy, Big Julie Isaacson, to drive him over to Lennox Hill Hospital so he could visit Mickey Mantle, still there recovering from his surgery.

Maury Allen described what happened at the hospital that night. "Roger left Big Julie and took the elevator to Mickey's fourth-floor room. When he opened the door, there was Mantle watching television. Mick looked up, surprised grin on his face, and said to his teammate, 'I hate your guts.' The M&M Boys, Roger Maris and Mickey Mantle, who had combined to make 1961 the most electrifying year in baseball history, laughed together uproariously."

With the regular season over, not only had Roger Maris set a new home run record, but his New York Yankee team had done the same, compiling a record 240 homers (long before the designated hitter rule came into effect in 1973) that still stands today, with Elston Howard, Yogi Berra, Bill Skowron, and John Blanchard each getting at least 20 homers to supplement the production of the M&M boys.

In the World Series, the Yankees annihilated the Reds in 5 games, as AL Cy Young Award winner Whitey Ford (coming off his own greatest season ever with a 25-4 record) broke another record held by Babe Ruth by throwing 32 consecutive scoreless innings in Fall Classic play.

In Game Three, with the Series tied 1-1, Maris hit a home run in the ninth inning, allowing the Yanks to win 3-2. The homer broke Cincinnati's spirit, and the Yankees won the next two games handily 7-0 and 13-5, overpowering the demoralized Reds. Though Maris went only 2 for 19 during the Series, his home run to win the third game proved to be the most critical hit in that year's Fall Classic. Cincy manager Fred Hutchinson confirmed the impact of the homer. "It was the most damaging blow of the Series. It ruined a fine pitching performance by

Bob Purkey and, after the loss, we just couldn't seem to bounce back."

And that was that for the 1961 season. Maris endured a tough round of negotiations with the Yankees management the following spring before finally getting a raise from $37,500 in '61 to $72,500 in '62. He had a solid year in 1962 (33 home runs, 100 RBI's) over-shadowed, however, by Mantle's final American League MVP season, as together they again led the Yankees to the pennant, and then triumphed in another World Series championship over another set of M&M boys, Mays and McCovey, beating the San Francisco Giants in a tense 7-game match-up. The Bronx Bombers would not win another world championship after that for fifteen years until Reggie Jackson became "Mr. October" in 1977.

From 1962 until his career ended after the '68 World Series, Roger Maris suffered by having to play in the shadow of his once-in-a-lifetime season in 1961. With each passing year while in New York, even in 1964 when by all accounts he essentially carried the team on his shoulders during the season's second half and led them into that World Series immortalized by David Halberstam in his book, *October 1964*, he became increasingly estranged from the fans, the media, and the Yankee front office.

He finished his career in happily-ever-after fashion, however, away from the Big Apple's red glare, after getting traded to the St. Louis Cardinals. Following the '66 season, the Redbirds were the proverbial "one man away" from being a championship team, and in his two seasons with the ballclub, Roger Maris proved to be that "one man."

After retiring from baseball and becoming successful in the beer distributorship business in Gainesville, Florida, the call from the Baseball Hall of Fame never came to Roger Maris, to the surprise of his teammates and opposing players who witnessed the man in his prime. For years, he refused to return to Yankee Stadium for the annual Oldtimers Game or any other occasion, claiming to fear the prospect of being booed again by the fans.

George Steinbrenner finally persuaded Maris to return to New York in 1978, and the home run record holder appeared on the field at Yankee Stadium on a chilly April afternoon in front of almost 45,000 fans who stood and cheered themselves hoarse. Maury Allen described the scene: "Some seventeen years after that summer of '61, the slate seemed wiped clean. The fans—even if they were not the same ones as

NATIONAL BASEBALL HALL OF FAME LIBRARY, COOPERSTOWN, NEW YORK

Maris spent his last two seasons with the Cardinals, and was a vital cog on two pennant-winning teams.

in 1961—had forgiven Maris for not being Mantle, for driving Ruth from his lofty heights, for not showing more public joy, for surliness under stress, for an obscene finger (shot toward an insulting spectator above the Yankee dugout during the '62 season), for fighting back when he felt he had been abused. On this day, as it should have been in 1962, they cared only that this man had once electrified baseball, performed a heroic feat, slugged more homers in one season than any man who ever lived, and did it with determination, grace, and pride."

In the fall of 1983, Roger Maris developed cancer symptoms, and was soon diagnosed with lymphoma and treated with chemotherapy.

By the summer of '84, having already lost Elston Howard to an early death in 1980, George Steinbrenner decided he wanted to move quickly to give Maris the ultimate honor for a Yankee player. Eerily reminiscent of Lou Gehrig Appreciation Day on July 4, 1939 (when the Iron Horse in terminal decline with amyotrophic lateral sclerosis gave his "luckiest man on the face of the earth" speech), on July 21, 1984, surrounded on the field by many of his Yankee teammates and Elston Howard's widow, Maris appeared at the ceremony where his former team retired his uniform number 9 and also dedicated a plaque in his honor at Yankee Stadium's Monument Park beyond the center field fence that bore the following inscription:

> ROGER EUGENE MARIS—AGAINST ALL ODDS IN 1961, HE BECAME THE ONLY PLAYER TO HIT MORE THAN 60 HOME RUNS IN A SINGLE SEASON. IN BELATED RECOGNITION OF ONE OF BASEBALL'S GREATEST ACHIEVEMENTS EVER, HIS 61 IN '61, THE YANKEES SALUTE HIM AS A GREAT PLAYER AND AUTHOR OF ONE OF THE MOST REMARK-ABLE CHAPTERS IN THE HISTORY OF MAJOR LEAGUE BASEBALL. ERECTED BY NEW YORK YANKEES JULY 21, 1984.

The uniform number retirement and monument dedication ceremony would mark Roger Maris' final appearance at Yankee Stadium. His lymphoma worsened after that, and he died in Houston at M.D. Anderson Cancer Hospital and Tumor Institute on Saturday, December 14, 1985.

———

Regardless of the Hall of Fame's rejection, his disappearance from the public arena after his retirement from baseball after the 1968 World Series, and his tragic death at a young age, the memory of Roger Maris and his record-breaking swing stayed with Boomers for almost four decades. And it had started to fade when suddenly, in 1998, it came back to life in a vivid, bittersweet way. Bulked up like Mr.

Universe, Mark McGwire blew past Maris in early September 1998 and obliterated his home run record, blasting 70 homers that season. An equally massively-muscled Sammy Sosa competed with McGwire for the record throughout that summer and also bested Maris by hitting 66 home runs.

In August of 1998, when it became clear Roger Maris' record was going to be broken, and unaware (at the time) that McGwire's power blasts were artificially enhanced by drugs (and Sosa's likely were as well, given his enlarged physique, refusal to speak English to the Congressional investigation into steroids in baseball in 2005, and willful failure to respond to George Mitchell's drug use questionnaire during the investigation of 2006- 2007), I wrote a column for the *Dallas Morning News* addressing the subject of how having a new single-season home run king would impact baseball fans of the Baby Boomer generation.

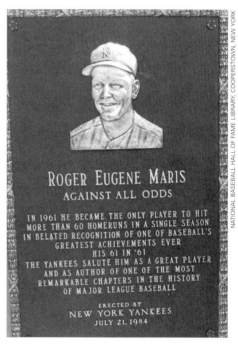

Maris' plaque at Yankee Stadium's Monument Park

For those of us who wax nostalgic, it is time to face the music. Records are made to be broken. In sports, sad but true, when a standard for unique achievement gets exceeded, the former record holder immediately loses his historical significance and descends into oblivion.

When we think of a consecutive game iron man in baseball, the sharp image appearing now is Cal Ripken as our memory of Lou Gehrig fades. Stolen bases? Today, it's Rickey Henderson who floats to the top in our sea of recall, while Lou Brock sinks below the surface.

As Mark McGwire and Sammy Sosa now hammer their way towards

home run history, the days of Roger Maris become numbered. Before the left-handed slugger loses his place in the record book, let's turn back the clock thirty-seven years, to the first real memory of sports for many of us now graying Baby Boomers, a time of black and white television, Doris Day, the Twist, the Mercury 7 astronauts, and John F. Kennedy.

In the summer of 1961, for the first time in decades, Babe Ruth's single-season home run record (60 in 1927) suddenly seemed vulnerable to two Hollywood-handsome New York Yankee outfielders. The challenger who burst out of the chute quicker, Mickey Mantle, was the most beloved player of his era. A pin-striped torch had passed from Ruth to Gehrig to DiMaggio to Mantle, and the switch-hitting Mick had already proved his mettle by leading the Bronx Bombers to eight American League pennants in his first ten seasons and winning the Triple Crown in 1956.

The other guy taking aim at the record was a new star. Roger Maris had joined the Yankees only the year before and promptly won the 1960 American League's Most Valuable Player Award, hitting 39 homers and driving in 112 runs. The quiet twenty-six-year-old North Dakotan preferred privacy to bright lights, but his left-handed, dead-pull hitter swing proved tailor-made for Yankee Stadium's close right field fence.

Three separate contingents of fans emerged as that summer's drama unfolded. Senior citizens, including then Commissioner of Baseball Ford Frick, still fawned over the Babe (who had passed away only thirteen years before in 1948) and wanted his record to stand forever. Those born shortly before and during World War II largely backed Mantle, who had already won over the Big Apple's huge core in his first decade as a Yankee in the 1950's.

Unlike his competitors for the home run record, Roger Maris had no fan base outside North Dakota, so he just went out and played hard. That approach to the game worked just fine for the kids of the Boomer generation, who wanted a new baseball hero we could call our own and applauded the efforts of the new kid on the block. In those days before batting accessories covered up the everyman look of baseball players, the sleek hitting Maris became the summer's poetry in motion. His sinewy arms rippled out from the short-sleeved uniform, turning on inside and even outside pitches with only his bare hands gripping the bat, and pulling them into the right field stands.

NATIONAL BASEBALL HALL OF FAME LIBRARY, COOPERSTOWN, NEW YORK

Mark McGwire, the man who broke Roger Maris' single-season home run record, and his two bodies.

In late September, Mantle went down with bronchitis and a serious infection in his leg that required surgery, leaving only Maris to face the press' constant frenzied demands in the first great sports media event of the television age. Reporters dogged the shy outfielder's every step, driving him into frequent irritability and such severe anxiety that a red rash started appearing on his face and clumps of hair started falling out of his blonde crewcut.

In the season's final game, on October 1, 1961, still needing one homer to top the Babe, and having heard more than an earful all summer long about the greatness of the Bambino, Maris shot at the press with his customary Midwestern directness: "Maybe I'm not a great man, but I damn well want to break the record. A season is a season." Maris ripped Number 61 off Boston right-hander Tracy Stallard in the fourth inning of the finale, and has now held the single-season record longer than Babe Ruth.

Sadly, the 1961 season essentially wore out Roger Maris, causing his power stroke to deteriorate rapidly after that year. From 1962 to 1964, he averaged only 27 homers per season, and then a serious wrist injury arising from a hard slide into home in June 1965 required post-season surgery that caused permanent dissipation of his strength, allowing him to hit only a total of 21 home runs in 1965-1966. The Yankees decided his days of being a productive player were over, and traded Maris to St. Louis in December 1966, and in his final two big league seasons there, he hit only 14 homers.

Roger Maris died in 1985 at the age of 51. Like many others (Jackie Robinson comes to mind most immediately) in the sports arena's limelight, the Yankee slugger's brief over-exposure to the paparazzi's infra-red glare burned out his life prematurely. Shortly before his death, Maris remarked to a friend, "It would have been a helluva lot more fun if I hadn't hit those 61 home runs. All it brought me was headaches."

Rest in peace, Roger Maris. For at least some of us forty-something-year-old fans, even if you lose your record this summer, your place in our memory is secure. The 1961 season baptized us into the pure springwater pleasure of our National Pastime, and your perfect home run swing rests in that special place Bart Giamatti called "The Green Fields of the Mind."

Roger Maris? Ah, yes. I remember him well.

Though Mark McGwire shattered Maris' record by hitting 70 home runs in 1998, he held the single-season record a grand total of 3 years before an equally artificially massive baseball specimen named Barry Bonds broke the record again during the 2001 season, hitting 73 homers. Yes, McGwire, Sosa, and Bonds all succeeded in hitting more than 61 home runs in a single season, but the cloud of steroids and Human Growth Hormone usage has hung over them ever since McGwire's and Sosa's flagrantly evasive testimony during the March 2005 Congressional hearings aimed at investigating the misuse of performance-enhancing drugs in baseball.

Though not appearing before Congress, prior to those hearings, Bonds' testimony to a San Francisco grand jury published in December 2004 reflected that he had used "the cream" and "the clear" during his record shattering seasons, but attempted to minimize his misconduct by claiming to be unaware that such drugs were steroidal, in spite of their substantially enlarging every part of his body, from the size of his feet all the way up to the circumference of his head. His incredible assertion that he didn't know what drugs he was using prompted my column aimed at generating hope in Mudville that with Major League Baseball's recognition of its runaway drug problem, maybe when the dust cleared, Commissioner Bud Selig might see fit to allow Roger Maris to regain the single-season home run record. Why? Because the record should belong to someone who hit his homers by driving the baseball over the fence using only his natural body and its natural power, unaided by transformational, enhancing drugs. I called the essay "The Empty Head Defense."

At the University of Texas Law School in the mid 1970's, our professors described hypothetical fact situations involving outrageous criminal or tortious conduct, and how perpetrators would attempt to defend their wrongful actions by saying, "Gosh, I didn't know the gun was loaded," or "Gee, I never thought using cheap materials might create a dangerous product." Teachers called it the "empty head" defense, and it never worked as a basis for excusing culpability because, in the words of my evidence prof, it had "sincerity problems."

Occasionally, the empty head defense works in real life. My (then) four-year-old cousin Jackie (name changed to protect the guilty) once threw ketchup on my grandmother's face. As Uncle George raised his hand to deliver an imminent spanking, Aunt Amy stopped the action with, "Now, George. Let's calm down. I don't know that we ever told little Jackie he couldn't throw ketchup."

The defense now enters the national sports scene in the context of baseball superstar Barry Bonds' admission to a San Francisco grand jury, published for the first time last week, that yes, he used "the cream" and injected "the clear" into himself, which turned out to be steroids. And in defense of his actions, the Giants' superstar outfielder said with a straight face, "I didn't know they were steroids." When his trainer applied the illegal stuff on and into his body, Bonds' justification for his actions now essentially goes like this: "I never asked what they were. I just said, 'Whatever.'"

At law school, whenever the empty head excuse was invoked, we laughed. And the ketchup story has been told in my family for over forty years and still makes us smile. Yet in this "death of outrage" era, not enough people are laughing at Barry Bonds' use of this legally ridiculous defense.

Speaking of "athletes" and "ridiculous," over the last few decades, many professional stars have developed the habit of referring to themselves in the third person. Presumably, these jocks are so internally disconnected they have lost track of who they are. Or have they?

In his first ten big league seasons, when most players are in their physical prime, a lithe Barry Bonds averaged 29 homers a year. But in the last nine years, this muscled up Schwarzenegger wannabe has had annual power production of almost 46 home runs. He looks in the mirror and sees that every part of his body has gotten pumped up as if inflated by an air hose at a gas station. He knows his jazzed up body puts extra velocity into his bat speed, causing the ball-on-bat connections at the plate that used to become warning track fly-outs to now sail over the fence, out of the ballpark, and into San Francisco Bay. These days, Barry Bonds can honestly speak of himself in the third person because, in fact, he knows he has been two different people.

Did Bonds eat more nutritious food, lift more weights, and train more during the off-season than the great power hitters who preceded him? Yes. Does that explain the vast statistical difference between the first and the second half of his career? For those who think so, George Strait hereby dedicates his song "I've Got Some Oceanfront Property in Arizona" to your gullibility.

Baseball Commissioner Bud Selig should now do to Barry Bonds what then Commissioner Bart Giamatti did to Pete Rose in 1989 for tarnishing the National Pastime—banish him from the game and thereby make him ineligible for Hall of Fame consideration. The "empty head" defense shouldn't work anywhere for a forty-year-old man—and it darn sure shouldn't work in Cooperstown.

———————————

What to do about the steroidal problem and how it should be addressed in the record book became clearer with the release of the Mitchell Report on December 13, 2007, a month after Barry Bonds was indicted for perjury in connection with his testimony to a San Francisco grand jury about his use of illegal drugs.

When Bonds, Sammy Sosa, Mark McGwire, Roger Clemens, and everyone else George Mitchell and his investigative team sought to question, chose to respond to the former Senator's invitation by refusing to tell their stories, thereby inhibiting Major League Baseball from getting the pertinent details on its massive steroid and Human Growth Hormone problem, that non-disclosure cover-up response cleared my thinking then, now, and forever as to the appropriate penalty for such misconduct. My column of December 20, 2007, advocated my position, and if Commissioner Bud Selig ultimately decides to go with my recommendation, the single-season home run record would again be owned by Roger Maris. I called the essay "The Numbers Make the Case."

———————

In his last 4 seasons with the Boston Red Sox, Roger Clemens won a total of 40 games and lost 39. After that fourth season, Boston believed the Rocket Man was past his prime at age 34, and did not attempt to resign him for the '97 campaign.

Clemens then joined the Toronto Blue Jays, and before anyone could say "Cy Young," the pitcher regained his dominance, going 21-7. The following year he hooked up with the team's strength coach, Brian McNamee, who in recent months told George Mitchell's investigative team that in the summer of 1998, he started injecting steroids into Clemens' buttocks in his room at the Skydome, driving Clemens to another 20-win season and his second consecutive Cy Young Award.

From there, McNamee followed Clemens to the Yankees, and the trainer told Mitchell he kept the steroids and Human Growth Hormone flowing into his prized client in New York, allowing the hurler to maintain his age-defying, power-pitching career well into the first decade of the twenty-first century.

What steroids and HGH did for Clemens' pitching, they also did for Barry Bonds' power hitting. Bonds went into his body-enhancing mode after Mark McGwire's own steroid-fueled power surge led to his gaining the national spotlight (and also enabled him to pocket tens of millions of dollars) in 1998 by shattering Roger Maris' single-season home run

Barry Bonds—before and after.

record. Till then, Bonds had had good, but not spectacular, power, hitting 40 or more homers in only 3 of his 13 seasons, and never more than 46.

Aided by drugs supplied by personal trainer Greg Anderson, all of a sudden balls hit by the Giants outfielder started flying out of the park, as Bonds knocked McGwire out of the books by hitting 73 home runs in 2001. Along with his power numbers, the formerly lithe ballplayer's body also expanded, his cap size growing a size, his feet growing 3 sizes, and his uniform shirt growing 10 sizes. By the summer of 2007, Bonds had blown past Hank Aaron's career home run record.

Charged by Commissioner of Baseball Bud Selig twenty months ago with the responsibility of investigating the steroid scandal, George Mitchell invited Clemens, Bonds, McGwire, and Sosa to be interviewed and/or at least fill out his questionnaires and give their side of the story, but they all refused. Since the Mitchell Report's release last Thursday, some of their lawyers have blasted the "hearsay" and "unsubstantiated" statements from the trainers/drug suppliers relied upon by the former Senate Majority Leader, while conveniently ignoring the facts that (i) Mitchell had no subpoena power in his investigation to compel Bonds,

Clemens, et al., to testify, and (ii) the star ballplayers absolutely ran away from the opportunity to make full disclosure of their past conduct.

The Mitchell Report, released on December 13, 2007, was led by a competent, high-integrity, experienced lawyer and legislator with a proven track record as a top-flight investigator. It not only tells the history of body-enhancing drug use over the past few decades by providing the names of users and suppliers, it also makes recommendations as to what Commissioner of Baseball Bud Selig should do about baseball's biggest problem on a going forward basis. Immediately following the report's issuance, Selig announced at a press conference that Mitchell's information provides him with "a call to action," and that he, in fact, "will act."

Here's one idea for Mr. Selig to "act" on. As for each of those players named in the Mitchell Report who refused to cooperate in the investigation, their records should immediately be extinguished, and their awards should be returned, just like what happens when Olympic athletes and Tour de France cyclists get caught competing while juiced. This "act" of record & award removal by Commissioner Selig should stay in place at least until those named players come forward, make full disclosure, and respond to a full interrogation regarding their activities.

Among other things, what this action by the game's top executive against Barry Bonds, Mark McGwire, and Sammy Sosa would accomplish is to restore Roger Maris and Hank Aaron back to their rightful place at the top of the page in baseball's home run record book. And stripping Clemens of his Cy Young Awards until he makes full sworn disclosure in the context of competent interrogation should remove the possibility of any knowledgeable baseball fan's daring to mention him in the same breath with the one and only Nolan Ryan, the guy who set his records the old fashioned way—by earning them—without having anything shot into his buttocks.

———————

In the twenty-first century, fans yearn for a superstar athlete with the characteristic Maury Allen described as being at the core of Roger Maris, "a certain trait, uncommon in sports, uncommon in life: a devotion to honesty—brutal, unfeeling at times, but always necessary."

David Halberstam evaluated the same subject with the same perspective, describing Roger Maris as "a man of old-fashioned values and loyalties, an honorable man who tried to live within his own code." Today, when we think of those who have hit more than 61 home runs in a season since the Yankees' Number 9, the image of them that comes to mind since 2004 when the steroid problem first made the sports section's front page is not that they have demonstrated "a devotion to honesty," or dedicated themselves to "old-fashioned values and loyalties, and been honorable, and dedicated themselves to living within their own code."

Roger Maris was part hardshell crab and part high-flying bird. In 1961, he lifted up the baseball world onto his strong but medium-sized shoulders and created an image, a legacy, and a non-steroidal record that stays with us to this day.

John Grisham and Lou Brock are as engaging in conversation as they are accomplished in their chosen fields of artistry. The two Bobbys of Fort Worth—Bragan and Brown—productive and generous in every step of their lives. I have dedicated this book to the two of them.

CHAPTER EIGHT

FRIENDS IN THE GAME
A Writer, a Minister, a Cardiologist, and a Goodwill Ambassador

Like many ventures in life, baseball creates opportunities for making friendships. Sometimes, the game even opens doors to connecting with celebrities. In my case, some of the celebrities I've met through baseball have become my friends. This chapter tells the story of four favorites.

F or a baseball fan, it doesn't get any better than my lunch on December 5, 2006. Sitting in the Fort Worth Club's friendly confines, at a table in the corner next to a Christmas tree, my baseball soul brother, John Ledbetter, and I sat, ate, and savored one big league tale after another from Hall of Famer Lou Brock; former New York Yankee third baseman and American League President Dr. Bobby Brown; and Texas' "Mr. Baseball" Bobby Bragan, a Brooklyn Dodger teammate of Jackie Robinson, who later managed the Pirates, Indians, and Braves, and then became President of the National Association of Professional Baseball Leagues, the umbrella organization for all minor leagues.

In the midst of this baseball banter barrage, as each story raised the bar for the next ("Yogi Berra did this...," "Branch Rickey chewed on his cigar and said that...," "Bob Gibson threw at so-and-so's head..."), my cell phone rang. Answering it quickly, I heard a familiar voice: "Talmage Boston, this is John Grisham. What are you doing?" After telling John who was at the lunch table and how fast the baseball stories were flying, he sighed and capped the moment, "Man, you do get around."

Yes, baseball has gotten me around some special people through the years, none more special than the quartet of Messrs. Grisham, Brock, Brown, and Bragan, who converged at a Fort Worth lunch table on that sunny December day. These four friends, whom I've been lucky enough to meet through baseball, have covered much of our National Pastime's canvas in their own unique style since 1946. In my opinion, and in this book, they make up the absolute best the game has to offer when baseball is embraced at its highest level.

My perspective on Lou Brock and Dr. Bobby Brown, two of the most accomplished and humble men on Planet Earth, is that up until now, the story of their lives has not been covered adequately either by autobiography or biography.[1] Thus, the part of this chapter devoted to them is largely my historical account of their baseball careers and exemplary lives.

On the other hand, John Grisham has been an international celebrity for more than twenty years, and Bobby Bragan (with the help of collaborator Jeff Guinn) wrote one of the best sports autobiographies of all time, *You Can't Hit the Ball With the Bat on Your Shoulder* (Summit Group, 1992, foreword by Howard Cosell). Their life stories are, therefore, well known or readily accessible, such that the part of this chapter devoted to them is essentially my account of our friendships.

JOHN GRISHAM–BASEBALL'S ULTIMATE FAN

John Grisham is not only the most commercially successful writer in America, he's also one of its most serious baseball fans. How serious?

- John says his wife accuses him of being a serial baseball field builder because he provided the land and funding to build the field along Highway 6 near his home in Oxford, Mississippi; then, after moving to Charlottesville, Virginia, expanded his vision by erecting the massive Little League Baseball complex near his home there; then donated the money for a new diamond at St. Anne's-Belfield School; and then did it again for the new ballpark at the University of Virginia;

- He's now been the Commissioner of Little League Baseball in Charlottesville for many years;

---

1 Brock wrote his memoirs with a collaborator in a book, *Stealing is My Game* (Prentice-Hall, 1976), that didn't receive much attention, in large part, because (surprisingly) the co-author, Frank Schulze, had Lou tell his life story in the third person.

- He's a passionate supporter of college baseball, making appearances at fundraisers for the baseball programs at the University of Memphis in 2007 and Delta State University in 2008, without charging a fee, because when it comes to college baseball players, it's all about respect—respect for coaches, respect for umpires, respect for fans, and respect for the game;

- He has an extensive baseball library in his home, and is an ardent supporter of the National Baseball Hall of Fame and Museum;

- He played baseball at every opportunity all the way through high school, but his career came to an end in college when legendary Delta State University coach Boo Ferriss cut him as a walk-on and famously encouraged his downcast departing player to "stick to the books," because (like so many of us mortals) he just couldn't get around on a 92-mph fastball or synchronize his psyche to a curveball, though Grisham still maintains, "I can hit a change-up when I know it's coming";

- He writes about baseball—weaving it into a novel (*A Painted House*); choosing it for the subject of his first non-fiction book (*The Innocent Man*); contributing an essay to the National Baseball Hall of Fame's *Baseball as America* coffee table book (National

John Grisham with legendary coach "Boo" Ferris at a Delta State University fundraiser. "Boo" cut John from the DSU baseball team in 1974, and told him to "stick to the books."

Geographic 2002); occasionally reviewing baseball books for the *New York Times*; and preparing forewords to baseball books written by others;

- On the dust jackets of his novels that came out before his son reached adolescence, the only information Grisham provided the reader about himself was (i) his place of residence and (ii) the fact that he coached boys baseball;

- When given the chance in 1993 to interview any celebrity in the world for NBC News, Grisham chose Nolan Ryan;

- A lifelong fan of the St. Louis Cardinals who grew up listening to Harry Caray and Jack Buck broadcast the Redbirds' games on the radio, today he counts Cards manager Tony LaRussa as one of his closest friends, and his boyhood hero, Stan Musial (thanks to arrangements made by Baseball Hall of Fame President Dale Petroskey), attended and played the harmonica at Grisham's 50th birthday party;

- He authored the screenplay, co-produced, and played the role of Little League Commissioner in *Mickey*, a semi-thriller movie about youth baseball, starring Harry Connick Jr., released in 2004; and

- In his bestselling legal thriller, *The Appeal* (Doubleday, 2008), he drew on his experience as a Little League coach and commissioner, and had his appellate judge character, Ron Fisk (whose pro-tort reform opinions were bought and paid for by companies on the wrong side of trial court judgments assessing punitive damages), have an epiphany that transformed his pre-existing attitude toward aggressively limiting tort liability, due to his twelve-year-old star pitcher son's getting smacked in the temple by a rocket off an outlawed aluminum bat too light for its length, which caused the boy to sustain brain damage and end his promising career.

These facts only begin to rough up the horsehide cover on John Grisham's passion for the game. Through reviewing his books for Dallas newspapers and finally meeting him at the USA Kids Film Festival premier of *Mickey* in Dallas, I became acquainted with the

Upon learning the tragic story of former minor league baseball player Ron Williamson, John Grisham accepted the challenge of writing his first non-fiction book, *The Innocent Man,* and speaking to large groups, such as the 2007 State Bar of Texas Annual Meeting, about The Innocence Project.

bestselling author to the extent that he asked me to help him publicize the film a few months later, in April 2004, when it was released at over a dozen local theaters. Here were some of my thoughts on the man after we spent an entire day together pitching his baseball film.

As a middle-of-the-pack law student at Ole Miss in the late 1970's, John Grisham didn't always know the answers. In fact, he remembers one final exam where he came to the last question, and having no idea where to begin, just started writing, hoping to connect with at least part of his teacher's desired response. When he got his test back after the semester ended, the professor, Robert C. Khayat, wrote in the margin next to the answer, "John, none of this is right, but have you ever thought about becoming a fiction writer?" Stories like this flow out of America's all-time bestselling author like songs stream out of Tony Bennett in concert—they're constant, delivered effortlessly, and unforgettable.

Through a fortunate set of circumstances, I spent a day with Grisham when he came to town recently as part of the promotional effort for his superb new movie, *Mickey*. In the course of twelve hours spent at a half dozen media interviews, an SMU Athletic Forum head table luncheon appearance with Hall of Famer Joe Morgan, and an onstage discussion and screening of the film at Highland Park Methodist Church, I learned some things along the day's ride.

John Grisham never wrote anything for publication until his first novel, *A Time to Kill*, such that his training as a writer came entirely from his lifetime, voracious reading habits. As a boy, he blew through the complete Hardy Boys and Chip Hilton series because his parents rarely allowed him to watch television.

As the Little League Baseball Commissioner of Charlottesville, Virginia, where he's lived the last decade, during the spring and early summer of every year, John Grisham doesn't write at all. He spends those months organizing teams and scheduling games involving over 500 boys, and occasionally even rides a tractor to mow the seven fields he purchased, equipped, and donated to the community. "Riding a big mower helps clear my head. When I'm up there chewing on a cigar, no one ever tries to talk to me."

Grisham knows how to connect with people. One of the interviews he had while in North Texas took place at Rangers Ballpark in Arlington where KRLD radio has its studio. The station planned to run the interview later that afternoon on its Rangers post-game show. After exploring the author's athletic interests, the talk show host concluded with a final question: "So, John, what's your favorite professional sports team?" Without hesitation and with a big grin on his face, Grisham proved "his momma didn't raise no fool." There in the midst of pitching his movie to a Metroplex listening audience, the author knocked the broadcaster's last question right out of the park. "Why, of course, it's the Texas Rangers!" Unlike his law school days, the man now knows all the answers.

A few months after our *Mickey* day together, in making a deal with my publisher on the release of my first book, *1939: Baseball's Tipping Point* (Bright Sky Press, 2005), I had the responsibility of finding a "big name" to write the foreword. To my surprise, Grisham said "yes," and proceeded to write a two-page mini-masterpiece that captures his deep grasp of our National Pastime.

> I'm writing this in December. It's cold, and Christmas, unlike baseball, is not far away. It will be months before things thaw and the pitchers and catchers report early. It'll take half a year before you can buy a ticket for the bleacher seats, buy a hot dog and something cold to drink, and on a hot, sticky night watch three hours of our country's greatest game.
>
> Because there are no daily box scores in December, no standings or stats or injury reports, fans are forced to fret over other things. Unfortunately, our game feeds us a steady diet of problems. Most teams are losing money and cannot be competitive. Armed robbers disguised as sports agents are shopping their clients around to the fattest owners. The team-hopping by our favorite players makes us dizzy. Baseball fans are fiercely loyal, but these days loyalty requires hard work. And each week, there are more depressing revelations about illegal steroid usage and questions about bogus stats and hollow records. In the gloom of winter, with our game eroding before our eyes, what's a fan to do?

Go read a book. Take a trip back to the golden days of the game. Visit 1939, one of the most remarkable years in baseball's celebrated history. Talmage Boston begins his book with a rich account of the heartbreaking and at first quite mysterious decline of Lou Gehrig, the most beloved hero of the era. Gehrig's "luckiest man" speech still evokes emotions from even the most ardent of Yankee-haters.

1939 was a year for kids, though very talented ones. Twenty-year-old Ted Williams blasted onto the scene and staked his claim as baseball's greatest hitter, while twenty-year-old Bob Feller dominated the All-Star Game and won twenty-four games. A young Joe DiMaggio had his greatest year and led perhaps the greatest Yankees team ever to another World Series title. And in Williamsport, Pennsylvania, a man named Carl Stotz organized some local boys into teams. After struggling with several ideas, he named his program "Little League."

1939 was full of memorable baseball events. It was a year of change, as the game silently said farewell to its golden era and stepped into the modern one. All sixteen teams broadcast their games on radio. Televised baseball made its debut. Baseball under the lights became popular. On June 12, 1939, the Hall of Fame opened in Cooperstown with a celebration of the game's first 100 years.

It was a year of great change, both in baseball and in the country. In so many areas of our national fabric—civil rights, the industrial age, the flood of immigrants, regional conflict, transportation, entertainment, depression, war, even greed and scandal—the history of baseball reflects the history of our country.

Talmage's book is a delightful chapter in this great history; perfect for frigid fans dreaming of spring or sweating ones waiting in line for tickets in the bleachers. It's also a gentle reminder that the game has always had its problems. It always will, and it will always survive because of its greatness.

In December 2004, as I spoke to Grisham on the phone about his foreword, he injected into the conversation the foremost subject on his mind that day, which ultimately resulted in the following essay that became part column, part book review for our community newspaper:

───────────

"Talmage, did you read the *New York Times* obituaries yesterday? Find it. Quick. Read the obit of a guy named Ron Williamson. It's the most dramatic life ever—small town baseball hero heading for professional glory blows out his arm, falls into manic depression and alcoholism, gets convicted of murder and sentenced to death. After spending years on Death Row, his conviction gets reversed because DNA testing proved him innocent. After his release, he finally gets to walk around Yankee Stadium and see what he missed. I think his story is going to be my first non-fiction book.'"

From that day on, for the next 18 months, John Grisham researched Williamson's life, interviewed those who had played roles in it, and wrote *The Innocent Man: Murder and Injustice in a Small Town* (Doubleday, 2006), which immediately shot to #1 on the *New York Times* non-fiction bestseller list. The author transformed a 661 word obituary into a 352-page book that may exceed his fiction as a story that holds the reader by the throat until the final chapter ends.

Suffice it to say, the policemen, lawyers, and judges of Ada, Oklahoma, portrayed by Grisham as bumbling, self-righteous buffoons, will not be giving copies of *The Innocent Man* to their friends as Christmas presents this year.[2] The book rakes them over the coals, pours gasoline on their remnants, and then lights up the sky with their debris.

How in the United States of America can such a travesty of justice occur as was perpetrated on Ron Williamson? Easy. Grisham's *The Innocent Man* demonstrates that American criminal justice systems are, and will always be, in the hands of fallible people who sometimes

2 In fact, in 2007, the Ada district attorney sued Grisham for libel.

believe that getting convictions is their most important responsibility—more important than adhering to the constitutional notion that even an indicted individual is supposed to be presumed innocent until proven guilty.

Though Ron Williamson was a sports hero as a teenager in Ada, when he returned home after his minor league career ended, he morphed into a jerk—a loud, lazy, hard-drinking, skirt-chasing, has-been jock—whom local residents grew to loathe. As his mood swings and depression spiraled into full blown mental illness, he changed from being somewhat unappealing to downright despised. When the murder of a 26-year-old woman went unsolved for 5 years, Ada's law enforcement and jurisprudential sectors decided, against all credible evidence, that Ron should be the person convicted of the crime, then imprisoned, and finally executed.

Some samples of Grisham's way with words in telling this stranger-than-fiction story—

> In rural Oklahoma, virtually all funerals take place with the casket open and positioned just below the pulpit ...The reasons for this are unclear and forgotten, but the effect is to add an extra layer of agony to the suffering.

> Like most crime labs, Oklahoma's was underfunded, understaffed, and under enormous pressure to solve crimes.

> Nothing makes a small town bar scatter more quickly than a capital murder case. The lawyers flee to their offices, lock their doors, and unplug the phones.

> When you're on trial for your life, hire either the best lawyer in town or the worst. Greg had unwittingly hired the worst, and now he had a new trial.

In 2005, Malcolm Gladwell had a bestseller entitled *Blink: The Power of Thinking Without Thinking* (Little Brown) that focused on the circumstances in which instantaneous decisions are made based on limited information. As one of the many examples, Gladwell reveals, "in

The night before his speech at the Texas 2007 State Bar Convention, John Grisham joined me and my wife, Claire, at Corpus Christi's Whataburger Field, where we were hosted by Nolan and Reese Ryan.

the military, brilliant generals are said to possess *coup d'oeil*—which translated from the French means 'power of the glance': the ability to see and make sense of the battlefield immediately."

In researching and writing *The Innocent Man*, John Grisham has proven he has *coup d'oeil*. Responding to a newspaper obituary absorbed in one glance, he has proceeded to create a book worthy of the Pulitzer Prize.

For our most recent baseball experience, in June 2007, at my invitation, John Grisham again came to Texas to serve as the keynote speaker for our Annual Meeting of the State Bar of Texas in San Antonio.[3]

True to his baseball passions, he flew in the night before his speech so we could attend a Corpus Christi Hooks (the Houston Astros' AA team that plays in the Texas League) ballgame against the San Antonio Missions (the San Diego Padres' AA team) at scenic Whataburger Field overlooking Corpus Christi Bay, and enjoy the privilege of Nolan Ryan's

3 In fact, he made his December 2006 phone call to me at the Fort Worth Club (described in this chapter's opening) for the purpose of accepting that speaking engagement.

company in his owner's suite. It was the first time they had been together since John's '93 interview of Nolan for NBC at Arlington Stadium during his (and that old ballpark's) final big league season.

When Nolan Ryan and John Grisham get together, baseball stories start to roll. John likes to spin tales about his special focal points—Mississippi State hardball heroes (ranging from Will Clark to Buck Showalter to Jonathan Papelbon), his close friend Tony LaRussa, and how he goes about sizing up Little League players' growth potential as their commissioner in Charlottesville, Virginia ("Knowing the size of the mother is the key!")—while Nolan (like most Hall of Famers I've met) remembers the details of his every encounter on the diamond.

Before the ballgame started, they matched up on a pitch-by-pitch basis, as to the particulars of the first time Nolan Ryan faced Will Clark, which at-bat resulted in a Clark home run. Nolan laughed as he remembered the situation: "I had a great plan for Will, but it fell apart on the execution side. I knew which pitches to throw, but they didn't quite hit the target."

Nolan had just finished reading John's book, *The Innocent Man*, and commented on how frequently professional ballplayers fall into a downward spiral once their playing days end. That observation shifted John into high gear about how coming out of high school his protagonist, Ron Williamson, was projected by the folks in his Oklahoma region to be "the next Mickey Mantle" until alcohol, drugs, a blown-out throwing arm, and his unmedicated bipolar depression all combined to make him the absolute scourge of his hometown neighbors, to the extent that they conspired to orchestrate the judicial lynching of an innocent over-the-hill, mentally-ill jock.

The subject of managers came up. Those wound extraordinarily tight[4] can sometimes motivate their teams to play for them (as LaRussa has throughout his successful career) over the course of a long season, and sometimes they can wear their players out with their hyper-intensity (as Showalter has now done with three different big league teams). After an extended pause, before answering my question as to his favorite manager during his pitching career, Nolan Ryan finally recalled Dave Garcia, his skipper with the Angels for parts of two

---

4 Grisham likes to say that if you go up to LaRussa before a ballgame and ask, "Tony, how are you doing?" He'll respond, "I'll tell you in 3 1/2 hours, after the game."

seasons, as a manager for whom he genuinely enjoyed playing. Former military veterans Gil Hodges and Bill Virdon, who had managed Ryan while he pitched for the Mets and Astros respectively, had both been largely uncommunicative due to their stoic and stern personalities, but the former pitcher recognized that it was those very characteristics that had made them good soldiers.

Of course in June 2007, as Barry Bonds headed toward breaking Hank Aaron's home run record, the subject of steroids came up. Nolan's last year to pitch in the big leagues had been in 1993, but even then he said he could recognize which players were using them, not only because of their expanding physiques, but also by their unpredictable mood swings. John and I shook our heads in amazement when Nolan told us that the final contract between the owners and players union in place in the early nineties, at the end of his career, contained absolutely no provision for drug testing.

As the conversation continued, once the Hooks-Missions game started, in the tradition of great baseball fans, John and Nolan stayed engaged with each other in their swapped stories and comments, but kept their eyes glued to the action. When a Hooks base runner failed to run home in the sixth inning on what was a clear scoring opportunity in the tight ballgame, both men sprang to their feet simultaneously, exclaiming in dismay over the runner's failure to achieve the desired result.

When it was time to go, our gracious host bid us adieu, exhorting John, "Next time you come to Texas, come see a ballgame with me at the Dell Diamond in Round Rock!" I suspect John Grisham will one day find a way to make that happen as that night in Corpus Christi he delighted in hearing Nolan's stories and baseball insight as much as he had once savored the Hall of Famer's dominant pitching performances.

The next morning, at the State Bar's Annual Meeting, in giving a press conference before his keynote speech, John started the session by telling the San Antonio media he was happy to travel from Virginia to Texas for the chance to speak to the state's lawyers and judges, but what made the trip truly special was having the opportunity to spend an evening at the ballpark with Nolan Ryan—a profound statement of priorities from the game's ultimate fan.

LOU BROCK—BASEBALL'S HORATIO ALGER

Lou Brock played offensive baseball for the St. Louis Cardinals like Jackie Robinson once did for the Brooklyn Dodgers—hitting line drives with some power, and driving pitchers, infielders, and catchers nuts by keeping his pedal to the metal while motoring around the base paths.

Ten years ago, a client of mine, who was then pursuing a business venture with Brock, arranged for me to have dinner with Lou and his gracious wife, Jackie, and since then, our paths have crossed several times. Shortly after that dinner, Scribner's offered me the opportunity to write the profile on Lou Brock for its *Encyclopedia of American Lives: Sports Figures*, and I have expanded that profile for purposes of this book to include the additional information gained from him during our visits at a half dozen fundraising events in 2006 and 2007, as well as at St. Louis Cardinals Legends Camp (see the end of Chapter 9). Every encounter I have had with Lou Brock enhances my appreciation of him as both a wonderful human being and an extraordinary ballplayer. The details of his life reflected in my profile below prove that in baseball and in life, nice guys can and do finish first.

The seventh of nine children born to a family of sharecroppers in El Dorado, Arkansas, Lou Brock's humble beginnings didn't suggest that he would have the calculating mind and intense concentration that carried him to baseball stardom. His father abandoned the family when Lou was two years old, prompting his mother, Paralee, to move her brood to the anticipated greener pastures of Collinston, Louisiana, population 300. For the first four years in the new venue, the family lived in a two-bedroom house with no running water or electricity.

By the time Lou was six years old, his mother remarried, and the expanded clan moved to a larger home in town, big enough to accommodate a Collinston schoolteacher as a boarder. The teacher saw some potential in Lou and inspired the introverted, but quick-thinking, boy to set his sights on taking his education beyond high school and aim for college as a means of attaining a better life. She also unintentionally opened Lou Brock's mind to the world of the National Pastime by having him read a baseball history book aloud to his third grade class as punishment for an act of misconduct involving the slinging of spitballs. From that reading exercise, Lou decided that if major league ballplayers in the early fifties were receiving $9 a day just in meal money, then pursuing a career in professional baseball might well be a possible future means of enhancing his standard of living.

Working in the cotton fields, when not with the teacher-boarder or in the classroom, Lou Brock never played on a baseball team until he started Union High School in nearby Mer Rouge, Louisiana. By his senior year, however, his skills had progressed to the point where he hit .540, along with being the team's star left-handed pitcher. The young athlete's performance as a student matched his accomplishments on the diamond, graduating third in his class of 105, and representing his school in statewide interscholastic science and math competitions.

After finishing high school, Lou Brock entered Southern University in Baton Rouge, majoring in mathematics on a work-study scholarship because his family had no money available for tuition, room, or board. At Southern, to keep the academic scholarship required maintaining a B average, which Brock narrowly missed in his first semester. In the spring, he attempted to stay connected to the college by shagging flies for the school's baseball team, pushing himself to the point of physical collapse in an effort to impress Southern's baseball coach, Emory Hines, enough to give him an athletic scholarship. After four weeks of high-intensity ball-shagging, when Hines finally gave Lou the chance to bat, he hit 3 out of the first 5 pitches over the right field fence, and received an athletic scholarship on the spot. His ballplaying days at Southern soon took off, as he hit over .500 his sophomore year, helping his school become the first historically black college to win the NAIA baseball championship.

These heroics merited Brock's being selected to play for the United States baseball team in the 1959 Pan American Games in Chicago. While there, he befriended a young boxer named Cassius Clay (who would later change his name to Muhammad Ali); college basketball stars Oscar Robertson and Jerry West; and most importantly, American sprinter Deacon Jones, who introduced the young outfielder to his friend, Jesse Owens, at the University of Chicago track, where the former Olympian champion proceeded to teach the young baseball speedster take-off and acceleration techniques that would serve him well for the remainder of his ballplaying career.

By his junior year at Southern, major league scouts had taken note of Brock's skills. In particular, Chicago Cubs scout Buck O'Neil could see the young ballplayer had a perfect baseball physique (big shoulders, a small waist, and essentially no body fat) and a hunger for excellence, which led Chicago to sign Brock in 1961 for a $30,000 bonus. Lou spent less than one season with the Cubs' Class C minor league team, where he led the league in every offensive category, before receiving the call-up to Chicago at the end of the 1961 season. The Cubs immediately entrusted their young phenom with the team's biggest star, Ernie Banks, pairing them as roommates on the road. Banks gave Brock advice that stayed with him the rest of his career: "Don't think about it being Sandy Koufax or Don Drysdale out on the mound. Think of only the white ball coming in that you have to hit. You've got to dehumanize the pitch, and disconnect the person who throws the ball from the ball itself. Take the reputations and personalities out of the context. It's just you and the ball."

Ernie Banks told Lou Brock during his rookie season, "You've got to dehumanize the pitch, and disconnect the person who throws the ball from the ball itself."

With the Cubs, the game that had come so easily to Lou Brock since high school suddenly became difficult. For almost 2½ seasons, he struggled to hit .260, fielded poorly in right field while facing Wrigley Field's blinding sun, and never received the green light to steal bases. It appeared his big league career would be short and undistinguished as his failures with the Cubs caused Brock to lose what author David Halberstam called "that most critical of athletic abilities: the capacity to relax and just play." Then in a game against Cincinnati in early June, Vada Pinson blasted a rocket to Wrigley's right field wall that Brock believed he had no chance to catch, but for which, despite the seeming impossibility of execution, he ran hard, jumped high and stuck his glove into the ivy. Not believing he had made the catch, he spent several seconds searching for the ball in the ivy, when a teammate suggested to Brock that he look in his glove. Lo and behold, the ball had stuck in the pocket, prompting Lou Brock to laugh out loud. That laughter following his catch of Pinson's blast allowed the young outfielder at last to turn loose of his tension. In that relaxed mode, in his final days as a Cub, Lou

Brock's hitting career took off.

Unaware of the emotional breakthrough that had occurred in Brock with the catch of Pinson's liner, the St. Louis Cardinals' brain trust, struggling in mid-June 1964 to find the missing piece for their under-achieving team, traded veteran pitcher Ernie Broglio to Chicago for Brock in what would become one of the most one-sided deals in baseball history.[5] Broglio won a total of 7 more games in his career after the trade, while Lou Brock ignited the Cards' offense for the next 16 seasons. Cub fans still regard the Broglio-for-Brock transaction as the worst trade in team history, though when the trade was announced, *The Sporting News* proclaimed that the Cubs had gotten the better end of the deal. To this day, Lou Brock insists that Ernie Broglio had a better curveball than Sandy Koufax, and Brock and Broglio have remained friends ever since their famous trade.

During 1964, Lou Brock managed to hit only .251 for the Cubs in the season's first 52 games, and then jacked up his average with the Cardinals by almost a hundred points to .348 after the Broglio trade. Besides acquiring a relaxed mindset in his final games with the Cubs after making the emotional watershed catch on Pinson, what else could have made such a difference in Brock's performance after he changed teams? He has a quick answer to that often-asked question: "With the Cardinals, I saw immediately that a player *had a right to fail.* Failure at one thing was permissible in the interest of letting you succeed at another." Losing the fear of failure as a member of the Cards inspired Brock's timeless observation that has universal application, "Show me a man who's afraid to look bad, and I'll show you a guy you can beat every time."

Despite having a sensational infield (Ken Boyer-3B, Dick Groat-SS, Julian Javier-2B, and Bill White-1B, who each started for the National League in the 1964 All-Star Game), a promising rookie catcher (Tim McCarver), a prize centerfielder (Curt Flood), and 3 starters (Bob Gibson, Ray Sadecki, and Curt Simmons) who were all good enough to win at least 18 games that year, it was the addition of Lou Brock that made the difference for the surging 1964 St. Louis Cardinals in blowing past the collapsing Phillies (who still had an 11-game lead as late as August 23) to win the first National League pennant for the Redbirds since 1946.[6]

5 Broglio had had an 18-8 win-loss record in 1963 with a 2.99 ERA.
6 As of July 24, 1964, St. Louis had a record of 47-48, but led in large part by their new left fielder, they went out and won 46 of their last 67 games.

"With the Cardinals, unlike with the Cubs, a player had a right to fail. Failure at one thing was permissible in the interest of letting you succeed at another. Show me a guy who's afraid to look bad and I'll show you a guy you can beat every time." — Lou Brock

In the Fall Classic, the upstart Cardinals proceeded to beat the Yankees, in Mickey Mantle's and Whitey Ford's last postseason hurrah, which was profiled by David Halberstam in his *New York Times* bestseller, *October 1964* (Villard Books, 1994), as a racial drama as much as a postseason baseball series (the predominantly non-Caucasian Cards besting the pre- dominantly Caucasian Yankees).[7] In that 7-game Series, Lou Brock hit an even .300 and knocked in 5 runs.

In 1965, Brock picked up where he left off from '64, and was hitting .370 until May 26, when he made the mistake of making Sandy Koufax mad—so mad that baseball's premier pitcher of the era deliberately hit him with a pitch and broke his shoulder blade after Lou succeeded too many times in getting on base with bunt singles.[8] In her bestselling book, *Sandy Koufax: A Lefty's Legacy* (Harper Collins, 2002), author Jane Leavy described the incident:

> On May 26, Koufax faced the Cardinals and his nemesis, Lou Brock, in Los Angeles. In the first inning, Brock led off with a bunt single, stole second, stole third, and scored on a sacrifice fly. In the dugout, Drysdale told rookie Jim Lefebvre, "Frenchie, I feel sorry for that man."
>
> When Brock came up again in the third, Koufax hit him hard and with intent. "So darned hard that the ball went in and spun around in the meat for a while and then dropped," catcher Jeff Torborg said.
>
> It was the first time, the only time, Koufax threw at a batter purposefully. He didn't brag about it. He didn't tell anyone he was going to do it. He didn't acknowledge it until long after his career had ended. "I don't regret it," he told fans more than a quarter century later. "I do regret that I allowed myself to get so mad."

7 Brock believes that Halberstam's historical assessment of the '64 Series as a racial breakthrough Fall Classic is flawed. He notes that the 1955 Brooklyn Dodger team that beat the Yankees was as completely integrated as the 1964 Cardinals, and the '55 Yankees had no African-American players at all, whereas the '64 Yanks had Elston Howard and Al Downing.

8 Even the greatest pitchers have at least one weakness and Koufax's lone negative in his prime was that he had trouble fielding bunts.

It took the remainder of the '65 season after the Koufax beaning for Brock to regain his hitting form and lose his fear of inside pitches as his shoulder slowly healed.

During the remainder of Brock's career as his era's premier speedster, three seasons stand out. In 1967, he became the first player in baseball history to hit at least 20 home runs and steal 50 bases in a single season, leading the league in stolen bases (52), runs scored (113), finishing second to Roberto Clemente in hits (with 206), second to Hank Aaron in total bases (with 325), hitting 21 homers, and driving in 76 runs while batting lead-off for the Cards, helping St. Louis blow past the second place Giants by 10 $\frac{1}{2}$ games. Then in the World Series, Brock hit .414, getting 12 hits, scoring 8 runs, and stealing 7 bases in leading the Cardinals' offense, while Bob Gibson took care of the pitching, driving the National League pennant winners past the "Impossible Dream" Boston Red Sox.[9] Throughout the '67 season, the American League had no player who was even remotely close to having Lou Brock's skill set, and they had no clue as to how to handle his offensive game. Brock told me, "They didn't know what to do with me." For these postseason heroics, he received the Babe Ruth Award, given annually by the New York Chapter of the Baseball Writers Association of America (from 1949 to 2002) to the player having the best performance in the World Series.

The running show demonstrated by Lou Brock against the Bosox in '67 had never been seen before in World Series competition. His chief base-stealing competitor in the sixties, the Dodgers' Maury Wills, managed to steal only a total of 6 bases while playing in the '59, '63, '65, and '66 Fall Classics, and neither Jackie Robinson nor Ty Cobb ever stole more than 2 bases in any World Series. The only postseason base-stealing performance even remotely close to Brock's was by Pepper Martin when he stole 5 bases in 7 games against Hall of Fame catcher Mickey Cochrane in leading the 1931 Cardinals past Connie Mack's Philadelphia A's.

Brock maintained his torrid offensive pace in 1968 (dubbed by sportswriters as "The Year of the Pitcher"), leading the National League

---

9 Ironically, Elston Howard was the starting catcher for the Yankees in the '64 Series and for the Bosox in '67. Whereas Lou Brock did not even attempt to steal a base in the '64 Fall Classic, he ran wild on the aging Howard three years later. In explaining the difference between his inclination to steal bases in those two series, Brock says that in the three years between '64 and '67 Howard became "a different player who lost his capacity to throw out the top baserunners."

in doubles (46), triples (14), and stolen bases (62), as the Cardinals again ran away from their competition, ending the season 9 games ahead of the runner-up Giants. In the Fall Classic against the Tigers, Brock amazingly found a way to elevate his game above the previous year's spectacular Series, hitting .464 with 13 hits and 7 stolen bases, moving legendary baseball scribe Leonard Koppett to remark, "Lou Brock is the most brilliant Cardinal of this (or any) Series." Unfortunately for St. Louis fans, despite Brock's heroics, Detroit came back from a 3-1 deficit behind the dominant pitching of Mickey Lolich and beat the Cardinals in 7 games.

Lou Brock's final great season came in 1974 when, at the age of 35, at the behest of National League President Chub Feeney who was looking for a way to keep the spotlight on his league after Hank Aaron broke Babe Ruth's record early in the '74 season, Brock shattered Maury Wills' 1962 single-season stolen base record (of 104) with 118 thefts.[10] Feeney instructed the national media to showcase Brock's ability, even at an advanced age for a speed merchant. In that spotlight, baseball fans could see Lou Brock's totally unique approach to stealing bases. How was it unique? First, he used a very short lead-off (which minimized the number of pick-off throws, thereby conserving his energy and also minimizing the number of hard slap-tags on the body administered by the likes of strongman Willie McCovey). Second, his capacity to read pitchers' moves was executed with the clarity gained from watching films of them made by Lou with his own camera, allowing him to start his dashes earlier than other players. Finally, Brock concluded his thefts with his patented pop-up slide which allowed him to avoid collisions with the knees of tough-guy middle infielders like Bill Mazeroski, and also put him in a position to advance to third base more easily when balls got past the infielders. The pop-up slide became for Lou Brock what the basket catch was for Willie Mays.

Ironically, Brock, the humblest of men off the field, has often spoken of the essential element that allowed him to become a successful base stealer: "It takes base running arrogance. You must believe and envision that you are a force, and then must communicate that attitude to the opposition. It requires complete and total confidence." For his record-setting performance in '74, *The Sporting News* named Brock

---

10 Brock's single-season stolen base record was broken in 1982 by Rickey Henderson, who had 130 thefts that season. Henderson also would later break Brock's career record with 1,406 thefts.

National League Player of the Year.

By breaking Wills' single-season record in '74 and Cobb's career stolen-base record in '77, Lou Brock at last started to receive the public recognition that had eluded him for much of his career, as reflected by his failing to become a starting National League All-Star outfielder for most of his great seasons with the Cards because of having to compete against icons Hank Aaron, Willie Mays, and Roberto Clemente. In his final seasons, baseball's three most prestigious awards, which recognize exemplary conduct on and off the field, all came Brock's way as he won the Clemente Award in 1975 (given by the Commissioner of Baseball to the player "who best combines good play on the field with strong work in his community"), the Lou Gehrig Award in 1977 (given to the player "who gives back to his community and strongly exemplifies the integrity, spirit, and giving nature that Gehrig possessed"), and the Fred Hutchinson Award in 1979 (given to the player "who has shown strong commitment to his family and community").

Most amazing, in 1978, while still the starting left fielder for the Cardinals, the National League created the "Lou Brock Award," given from that year forward to its single-season stolen base leader, the first and only time an award has been named in honor of an active big league player. Brock believes League President Chub Feeney may have decided to give him this honor as a way of saying thank you for Brock's keeping the spotlight on the league throughout 1974 in such a positive way by breaking Wills' record.

When Brock ended his career in 1979, he was the major leagues' career stolen-base leader, and had become only the fourteenth player in baseball history to obtain 3,000 career hits.[11] With these marks, and in light of his leading the league in stolen bases 8 times, making 6 All-Star teams, and compiling a .391 World Series batting average in 21 games (the highest lifetime Series average of all time for a player having at least 75 at-bats), Lou Brock became a Hall of Fame first ballot inductee in 1985.

Fellow Hall of Famer Bob Gibson summed up his teammate: "Lou Brock is the best damn money-player I ever saw on the Cardinals." First baseman Bill White quantified Brock's value with more concrete

11 Brock finished his career strong, hitting .304 (after falling to .221 in '78) for which he received *The Sporting News'* Comeback Player of the Year in 1979.

A major source of Lou Brock's success as a base stealer came from the take-off acceleration techniques he learned from Olympic gold medal sprinter Jesse Owens.

specificity: "Lou Brock is worth one run a game." Both observations, along with his statistical records, accurately reflect why in 1998 *The Sporting News* ranked Lou Brock 58th among the 100 greatest baseball players of all time.

After retiring from baseball as a player, Lou Brock and his wife, Jacqueline, became ordained ministers, serving the Abundant Life Fellowship Church in St. Louis, and supporting young people through the Lou Brock Foundation, which has provided over $300,000 in scholarships for students in both St. Louis and Northeast Louisiana (where Lou grew up).

By serving as a role model, educational spokesman, and minister, Brock (i) has received honorary doctorate degrees from Washington University (in St. Louis), Southern University (his alma mater), and Missouri Valley College; (ii) has been inducted into the sports hall of fame in Louisiana, Missouri, and Arkansas (where he was born); and (iii) was named a 2002 recipient of the Horatio Alger Award given by the Alger Association of Distinguished Americans to those whose "lives exemplify dedication, purpose, and perseverance, who have succeeded in spite of adversity, and share a message of hope with young people, encouraging them to pursue their dreams through higher education."

Most recently, Lou Brock has embarked on a mission of history,

NATIONAL BASEBALL HALL OF FAME LIBRARY, COOPERSTOWN, NEW YORK

At the request of National League President Chub Feeney, Lou Brock broke the single season stolen base record in 1974 at the age of 35.

pursuing the moment in history when the first pitch in a twentieth century major league baseball game was made to an African-American batter. In that historic encounter, on April 15, 1947, the Boston Braves' Johnny Sain (then one of the premier pitchers in the game, coming off a 20-14 record in '46) threw a curveball for a called strike against Jackie Robinson, and with it, the American Civil Rights movement got under way.

Since childhood, Brock had admired Robinson as a ballplayer and as a man, but recognized on reflection in recent years that the Great Jackie's place in history could have been denied if Sain had followed the advice of many bigots in the spring of '47 and aimed his first pitch at the black batter's head. So beginning in March of 2006, with the aid of his friend Joe Vonder Haar, and Joe's daughter, Melissa (an aspiring young writer, serving as Lou's collaborator), Lou Brock started traveling across the country obtaining the oral history of *The Pitch*, interviewing Sain at length (before the pitcher's death on November 7, 2006), as well as members of the '47 Braves, other friends of Sain's, and teammates and opponents of Jackie Robinson, in an effort to re-create the complete perspective on that historic moment.

I had the privilege of arranging and sitting in on Brock's interviews of Dr. Bobby Brown and Bobby Bragan during the course of this project and hearing their conversations about the men involved, the event in question, and what they thought it meant to American (not just baseball) history. As the son of sharecropper parents and the descendant of slaves, Lou expressed his visualization of the plight of blacks in America all the way from their African deportation through Jim Crow and the "separate but equal" malaise, with all that history running through his mind as if in a high-speed movie, and playing itself out in his imagination at the pace of Johnny Sain's smooth windup and first pitch to Robinson. For Lou Brock, Sain's treating Jackie Robinson like any other National League batter on that fateful day—just trying to get him out and not trying to hurt or kill him (batters in 1947 did not wear protective helmets)—that first pitch meant the playing field in America in all sorts of endeavors, not just baseball, had officially become level.

Lou Brock entered the Baseball Hall of Fame in 1985 as a first-ballot inductee.

Bobby Bragan embraced the idea but cautioned, "Now Lou, don't forget about Abraham Lincoln's role in all this. Johnny Sain may have thrown the first pitch, but it was Lincoln who started the Civil Rights movement with the Emancipation Proclamation. Abe's the guy who put the ball in Sain's hand." Every 5 minutes for the rest of their 90-minute conversation, Bobby kept interjecting, "Just don't forget about Abe Lincoln!"

The final published product of Brock and Vonder Haar's *The Pitch* should come off the presses in 2009. We can only hope the book will be as well received as Lou Brock has been received since he joined the St. Louis Cardinals in the middle of the 1964 season, relaxed into ballplaying excellence, lost his fear of failure, and shifted his Horatio Alger-like, rags-to-riches life into a higher gear.

DR. BOBBY BROWN—THE MAN WHO KEPT MOVING FORWARD

After I moved to Dallas, following law school graduation in the fall of 1978, my first girlfriend was Bobby Brown's older daughter. Our courtship ended after a year, but my friendship with Dr. Brown has now lasted almost three decades. To the disappointment of many, due to his steadfast humility, he has refused to write his memoirs, meaning many of the details of his life story (like Lou Brock's) are not well known, despite having an outstanding baseball career (both as a player and an executive) along with substantial connections to some of the game's most celebrated figures—Casey Stengel, Mickey Mantle, Joe DiMaggio, Yogi Berra, Whitey Ford, Jackie Robinson, and Bart Giamatti, to name a few. In 1996, I wrote an essay on the amazing life of Bobby Brown for *The Baseball Research Journal* published by SABR, which appears below in substantially expanded, updated form.

What has impressed me most over the years about Dr. Brown's eventful life is that he never allowed himself to rest on his considerable achievements, always keeping himself open to new challenges in new arenas, and elevating himself to a higher position at every key stage in his life, creating arguably the most successful multi-dimensional career of any American since 1946. His amazing life is full of rich details at each juncture, establishing why Tom Brokaw named the men and women of Bobby Brown's era "The Greatest Generation."

As a New York Yankee in the late DiMaggio-early Mantle era, i.e., 1947-1954, Bobby Brown possessed an offensive game devoted to spraying line drives, an appropriate style of hitting for a man whose life has proven to be a line drive of constant achievement in different directions. In a society needing role models for its youth, none has better lifetime credentials than the man who has been a World Series hero, esteemed cardiologist, and statesman-like American League President, thereby earning the distinction of being selected as the only American athlete enshrined in three college (Stanford, UCLA, and Tulane) halls of fame due to his athletic prowess and exemplary life.

Childhood and Amateur Career: 1924-1945—Baseball and the media like to promote the image of the game's impact on fathers and sons—playing catch and going to games together as the ball gets tossed and the bat gets handed from one generation to the next. Unlike in the

Mantle and Piersall families (see Chapter 1), the wholesome image actually fits the relationship between Bill Brown and his son, Bobby, an emotionally healthy baseball father-son combination if there ever was one.

Bill Brown played the game well enough as a young man to compete at the semipro level and think about pursuing a big league career. When he learned that the money paid ballplayers in the early twentieth century didn't compare with what a successful business executive could make, Bill reluctantly abandoned his dream of playing professional baseball, but never lost his love for the game.

Under his dad's watchful eye, Bobby started swinging a bat at age five. Grade school years opened up the world of ballgames, starting with softball games at recess, lunch, and after school. In a year or so, hardball entered the picture. By the time he was eleven, he performed so well at a baseball school for kids sponsored by the Seattle Indians (the city's team in the Pacific Coast League), that when the fielding, throwing, and hitting competition ended, Seattle's Broadway American Legion team coach invited Bobby to join his ballclub, putting the pre-teen phenom on a roster filled with high school players.

In 1937, the Brown family moved from Seattle to Maplewood, New Jersey, where Bobby immediately began making a name for himself in area baseball—starring not only for Maplewood's American Legion Team (for teenagers), but also for two adult teams. In the summer of 1938, Bobby Brown attended a tryout held by the New York Yankees' top farm team, the Newark Bears. Knowing the tryout was for boys eighteen or older, the spunky thirteen-year-old claimed to be eighteen when he filled out his application form, hit a slew of rockets, and Yankee scouts in attendance quickly picked up on Bobby's flawless left-handed swing.

When Bobby Brown turned fifteen, in the fall of 1939, his high school coach amazingly assigned Maplewood's top young baseball superstar (who had already stood out in area adult leagues) to the junior varsity. Father and son both took the news hard, and father Bill Brown did something about it. After speaking with the coach, and learning he had made his selections for varsity and JV without the benefit of seeing any players perform in game competition, Bill decided he and his family wanted to do something else. So Bill immediately took a new (and better) job on the West Coast, and the family's move allowed his hitting star son to begin playing baseball games year-round in San

Francisco. As professional ballplayers came home to the Bay Area in the fall after their baseball seasons ended, Bobby honed his skills playing against them in pickup games, as well as again excelling in American Legion competition, and even playing on two Bay Area semipro teams, all of which attracted the attention of scouts for the Yankees, Indians, and Dodgers. By his junior year at Galileo High School, Bobby started at shortstop, playing a major role in their march to the City Championship. The Cincinnati Reds scout in the Bay Area became so impressed that when the summer of 1941 arrived, sixteen-year-old Bobby Brown accepted the Reds' invitation to travel to Cincy to practice with their reigning championship team (which had beaten Detroit in the 1940 World Series) at home and in Chicago, and then watch their games from the bullpen alongside the veterans.[12]

The next year in the spring of '42, as captain of his high school team, Bobby led Galileo to its second consecutive San Francisco City Championship, knocking off not just the best high school area competition, but also beating the Stanford and Cal-Berkeley freshman teams. By that summer, Bobby's star had risen to the point that his dad sent his seventeen-year-old son east so he could spend his time working out with the Reds, Tigers, Dodgers, A's, and Yankees.

As important as baseball was in the Brown family, it did not interfere with Bobby's goals of pursuing education to its highest level. Refusing to sign with a big league team after high school graduation, he entered Stanford University in September 1942, turned eighteen in October, and proceeded to hit .463 in the spring while playing shortstop for the varsity, succeeding in competition as a freshman against not just West Coast college teams but also military squads loaded with professional ballplayers. Off the field during his first year of college, Bobby learned he didn't want to become a chemical engineer, decided to pursue a career in medicine, enlisted in the Navy, and was called to active duty on July 1, 1943.

On May 6, 1943, while still a freshman at Stanford, Brown and a group of his friends were relaxing at San Gregorio Beach one afternoon when a Coast Guard patrol plane, looking for Japanese submarines, flew

12 At that time, the Cincinnati Reds obviously believed in getting young teenagers involved with their team. In the context of having their roster decimated because of players serving in the military during World War II, they actually signed Joe Nuxhall to a contract, and had him pitch in a major league on June 10, 1944, before he reached his sixteenth birthday.

dangerously close to the beach, climbed over a promontory, turned west over the water, and then crashed into the ocean approximately 400 yards offshore. Seeing the nearby wreckage, Bobby and this friends saw an airman floating in the water near the plane, swam out to him, and towed the unconscious man ashore in very rough and cold (55-59° Fahrenheit) water. The rescue lasted an hour until they got the downed airman to shore, and they succeeded in saving his life. For his actions, Brown was awarded the U.S. Coast Guard's Silver Lifesaving Medal for Bravery.

Military service in the midst of World War II necessitated Bobby's immediately having to change colleges. After enlisting in the U.S. Navy on July 1, 1943, while at Stanford, he was soon assigned to the V-12 Naval Unit (officer-training program) at UCLA in the late summer of '43, where he stayed a year and completed his premed studies, participated in the training program, and starred on the Bruins' baseball team made up largely of service personnel. In that spring of 1944 at UCLA, he hit .444, was selected by his coach to serve as team captain on their Pacific Coast Conference championship team, and was named an All-Conference infielder.

After the '44 college season ended, the Navy assigned Bobby to the U.S. Naval Hospital in San Diego as a corpsman for five months, and then transferred him to the V-12 unit at Tulane University in New Orleans as a medical student, where he started med school in December 1944. The following spring, he made the Green Wave's baseball team, hit almost .500, and led his third college ball club (in three years) to a victorious season playing a schedule entirely against teams with rosters comprised of soldiers.

Following his final collegiate season, and with World War II ending in August 1945, when Brown was discharged from the Navy in January 1946, the Reds, Giants, Browns, Tigers, and Yankees all attempted to sign the hard-hitting infielder. Serving as his son's negotiator, Bill Brown accepted the highest offer of $52,000 paid over three years, made by the Yankees with their fully-loaded war chest. The contract provided Bobby with the second-highest bonus ever received by a young player as of that time. When the Dean of Tulane's Medical School learned of the bonus, he asked his prized student if the Yankees might like to endow a chair.

Life in the Pros: 1946-1954—Bobby Brown's minor league career began and ended in 1946 at Newark in the International League.

Playing with the famed Bears, the era's most dominant minor league team, which always had its lineup stocked with future New York Yankees, Brown roomed with Yogi Berra, led the league in hits, and batted .341 for the season, second in the league to Jackie Robinson's .349 average with Montreal. For Brown's spectacular play, the Newark Athletic Club named him the New Jersey Professional Athlete of the Year, and the Yankees called him up at the end of the '46 season along with Berra, Vic Raschi, and Frank Colman. The New York press immediately dubbed the Yanks' prized bonus baby "The Golden Boy," and he quickly went about proving his value. In the last week of the '46 season, with the Ted Williams-led Boston Red Sox having clinched the American League pennant, Brown and Berra each appeared in 7 games, with Bobby batting .333 (8 for 24) while Yogi hit .346 (8 for 22).

At spring training in '47, Brown battled popular right-handed-hitting Billy Johnson to a stalemate for the Bronx Bombers' starting third baseman position. Two weeks after Opening Day, Boston's hard-throwing southpaw, Mel Parnell, ended the season's platooning when he hit Bobby with a pitch on his hand, breaking a finger. By the time it healed, Johnson's hot hitting and consistent fielding had cemented his position in the Yankees' starting lineup, limiting Bobby's playing time largely to pinch-hitting for the rest of the '47 season. Playing in a non-starting, non-starring role for the first time in his life, Brown made the most of it, leading the American League in pinch-hits, and finishing the year with an even .300 batting average.

Bobby Brown's best moments as a player in his first full season with the Yankees came in the 1947 World Series, when his hitting performance earned him a new nickname—"The Wand." New York's manager, Bucky Harris, gave Brown 4 pinch-hit opportunities against the Dodgers, and the twenty-two-year-old achieved perfection, going 3 for 3 (2 doubles and a single) with a walk, and driving in 3 runs. In Game Seven, after hitting a double in the fourth inning to drive in a run, Brown stood on second base, heard the roar of the crowd, could sense that his team would soon become world champions, and looked into the stands in time to see his father sail a favorite hat into the sky. Bobby Brown smiled, knowing he had fulfilled the dream of his personal hero and greatest fan who, unlike Mutt Mantle and John Piersall, had always maintained the proper perspective between baseball and his son. Later that day, a proud Bill Brown told reporters,

Tommy Henrich on his teammate Bobby Brown's highest ever World Series batting average:
"He couldn't run, field, or throw, but with a million dollars on the line, he wouldn't choke up at the plate.
Either you have the attitude of a champion up there with the Series hanging in the balance, or you don't. Bobby had it."

"Bobby's not the best player on the Yankees, but he is the best son."

After missing 1948 spring training because of having to resume his studies at Tulane Medical School in the off-season, but nonetheless coming off his sensational performance in the World Series, Brown played more as a sophomore with the Yankees than he had as a rookie, again hit .300, stayed healthy, but still couldn't beat out Billy Johnson and break into the starting lineup on a consistent basis. As he would do for the next three years, after joining the team on Opening Day, Brown split his focus between baseball and medicine. Roommate Yogi Berra read Superman comic books while Brown read his medical textbooks (and Yogi famously asked his roomie as they turned out the light one night, "How'd your book come out in the end?"). The year 1948 would prove to be the only full season in Brown's active playing career when the Yankees failed to win the American League pennant, after being tied for first place with the Indians and Red Sox as late as September 23.[13]

Casey Stengel arrived as the skipper on the Yankee Stadium scene in 1949 after having managed 9 prior seasons in the big leagues without ever getting his teams to finish higher than fifth place. Casey surprised many by leading the Bronx Bombers to the pennant on the season's last day over the rival Red Sox, in a year immortalized in David Halberstam's *New York Times* bestseller, *The Summer of '49* (William Morrow, 1989). Stengel, the great platooner, followed predecessor Bucky Harris' strategy and continued to split the team's third base duties between the lefty-swinging Brown and the right-handed Johnson.

Under Stengel, Bobby had his most productive season as a major league player in 1949, hitting .283, while knocking in 61 runs in 104 games. Though he and Stengel had no memorable conversations, they established player-manager rapport through eye contact that Brown described in a 1999 *Elysian Fields Quarterly* interview with my friend Paul Rogers:

> If Casey wanted you to pinch hit he'd just say "go hit" and that was it. Usually if I saw that a pinch hitter was going to be needed an inning or two later, I'd get my bat and have it right in my hands sitting with me on the

13 He played slightly during the first half of the 1954 season after coming back from the Korean War and before starting his residency, in a year when the Indians won the pennant.

bench and I'd keep looking at him and every once in a while he'd look at me, and then he'd walk down the bench and look at everybody else and then he'd turn back and look at me and I'd be looking right at him, and finally when it came time for a pinch hitter, he'd say "go hit." I think Casey thought that he could read a base hit in a guy's eyes and I think some of his choices were made on that basis, on how the guy looked at him. I used to bet Gene Woodling all the time that I would hit ahead of him and Gene was one heck of a hitter. But I kept looking at Casey and Gene kept looking at the game, so I used to get to hit before he would a lot of times. Casey was just a funny guy.

In the 1949 World Series won by the Yankees in 5 games, Brown proved his '47 postseason heroics weren't a fluke, starting the last 3 games, going 6 for 12 (with 2 triples and a double), driving in 5 runs, and hitting the Series' key blow—a triple with the bases loaded to break open Game Four, a clutch hit made particularly sweet in light of (i) the Dodgers' decision to walk Joe DiMaggio intentionally so they could pitch to Brown, and (ii) Casey Stengel's decision to allow Bobby to bat against Brooklyn southpaw reliever Joe Hatten. Brown later told Commissioner Fay Vincent about the circumstances behind Stengel's decision:

> All season long, Casey never let me hit against lefties. In Game Four of the '49 Series, I kept waiting for him to go to Billy Johnson, but he didn't. For some reason, he let me hit; I hit a bases-loaded triple, and we won, 6-4. Somehow, Casey knew to let me hit against Hatten.

After the '49 season ended in triumph, Bobby again returned to New Orleans to resume his medical studies. Good fortune continued to shine on the World Series hero that winter when his sister introduced him to Sara French, who within the year would be named Sophie Newcomb College (Tulane's sister school) homecoming queen, and within two years would become Mrs. Bobby Brown.

The Yankees had another championship season in 1950, with Brown and Johnson again platooning at third base throughout the year.

Though Brown's average dropped slightly to .267, Casey Stengel knew his favorite medical student played his best baseball in the postseason, and handed him the starting position in the World Series against the Robin Roberts-led Whiz Kid Phillies. In Game One, Brown doubled and scored the game's only run. In Game Two, he hit a single off Roberts that has haunted Brown every single week of his life since then for over half a century because of his failure to turn it into a double.[14] In Game Three, his eighth inning ground ball smash produced the Series' most important moment, as Philadelphia shortstop Granny Hamner couldn't make the play on it, allowing the tying run to score. In Game Four, Brown hit a triple to knock in a key run in completing the Yankees' sweep of the Phillies.

After three Fall Classics, Bobby Brown's postseason batting average stood at a cool .481, and he had established himself as an authentic World Series hero for the Yankees. More significant in the long run than his Series performances, during the 1950 season, Brown became the first major leaguer ever to earn his M.D. degree as an active player, and then started his internship in San Francisco following the '50 Series against the Phillies, which prevented him from attending the Yankees' spring training in '51.

Brown's last full season with the Yankees proved to be 1951. Things started out that year going his way, as with medical school behind him, Brown could focus entirely on baseball. However, his hopes of playing every day during the season evaporated when the Yankees traded Billy Johnson to the Cardinals early in the year to give rookie Gil McDougald playing time at the hot corner, again depriving Bobby Brown of the opportunity to start every game. McDougal quickly emerged as a star (playing second base in the games Brown started at third) and was named American League Rookie of the Year.

Following his regular season's pattern, Casey Stengel played Brown and McDougald evenly as his third baseman in the '51 Fall Classic won by the Yankees in 6 games over the Willie Mays-Bobby Thomson Giants, with Brown having another great Series going 5 for 14 (.357) and leading the Yanks in hitting. Bobby's average would have been even higher if umpires hadn't botched a call in Game Four when, with his

[14] Proving that like most major league ballplayers of his "greatest" generation, Bobby Brown has a memory like an elephant, cuts himself no slack, and maintains high intensity whenever he competes.

back to the infield while running near the outfield wall, Willie Mays caught Brown's smash on the rebound off the ground. Because the centerfielder's back blocked the view of all the umpires, when his glove latched onto the ball, it appeared that the acrobatic Mays had managed to catch the ball on the fly. Sitting in the upper left field stands, Bobby's parents witnessed Mays' not making the catch, and his dad, Bill, almost jumped onto the field when the umpires blew the call.

America's intervention into the Korean War disrupted Brown's career from 1952 to 1954, allowing him to play only 29 games in '52, none in '53, and 28 in '54. Having completed his San Francisco internship on April 15, 1952, Bobby became eligible for the "Doctor's Draft," and soon became an enlisted army officer and doctor in the war. During the conflict, Brown served as the Battalion Surgeon for the 160th Field Artillery Battalion, 45th Division, in the Far East Command and later rotated to Japan.

Upon receiving his honorable discharge from the army, Brown returned to the Yankees in early May 1954 and played two months until his Internal Medicine residency began on July 1. Making $19,500 a year as a veteran player on a championship team, the time seemed right to retire from the game and become a full-time physician.

In his 1992 autobiography, Yankee teammate Tommy Henrich described Bobby Brown as a ballplayer. "He couldn't run, field, or throw, but with a million dollars on the line, he wouldn't choke up at the plate. In every pressure situation, Bobby was always the one in charge at the plate. It was the pitcher who was the one in trouble, not Bobby. You can't teach that attitude, and you can't practice it. Either you have the attitude of a champion up there with men on base and the pennant or World Series hanging in the balance, or you don't. Bobby had it."

Brown's hitting came naturally, but he improved it with constant practice. Teammate Irv Noren told author Dom Forker in his book, *The Men of Autumn* (Taylor, 1989), that when the Yankees were on the road, Brown "would call up the home team before the game to find out if he could come to the ballpark early and hit. For an hour-and-a-half, before a game, Bobby would just hit. That's how much he wanted it."

As for Paul Harvey's "rest of the story," his maligned fielding became Bobby Brown's Achilles heel, with much of the criticism deserved early in his career. When Casey Stengel first saw Bobby play third base, the Old Professor remarked, "Brown looks like he's been a hitter for twelve

During the Korean War, Bobby Brown served as a Battalion Surgeon in the 160th Field Artillery Battalion, 45th Division, in the Far East Command.

years and a fielder for one." Teammate Gene Woodling joked to his med student teammate, "Bobby, if I ever get sick, don't you dare show up, because I don't want your bad hands operating on me." Recognizing his playing deficiency, Brown worked hard to become a creditable infielder, and by 1950, his fielding average actually exceeded his platoon partner Billy Johnson's, who had always been regarded as having a solid glove.

Although never an everyday player on world championship teams during his career, Bobby Brown hit a solid .279 over parts of 8 seasons with an on-base percentage of .367, and became a bona fide star at crunch time in the World Series. In those Fall Classics, Brown hit more consistently than any of his esteemed teammates, and played a major role in the Yankees' winning all 4 Series. His lifetime .439 World Series batting average is the highest in baseball history for anyone with 20 or more at-bats, and his .707 slugging percentage is fourth highest in Series history, trailing only Reggie Jackson, Babe Ruth, and Lou Gehrig.

In his *Elysian Fields Quarterly* interview with Paul Rogers, Brown said his only regret about his baseball playing career was that he never achieved the status of being an everyday starting infielder on those championship teams.

> I would have liked to have had two or three years where I could have been like everybody else—where I could have gotten to spring training on time. I would have liked to play regularly every day just to see how well I could have done. The only time I played every day was at Newark, and I hit awfully well there, and I think I could have done that in the majors, too, if I'd gotten to play every day. None of us liked being platooned, but you couldn't fault the system. We had great teams, and you weren't competing against some guy who couldn't play. We could all really play.

The Doctor: 1954-1984—After his final game as a player at Boston's Fenway Park, Bobby Brown flew across the country overnight and began his three-year residency in internal medicine at the San Francisco County Hospital at 11 a.m. on July 1, not wasting one day to get started. During his residency, Brown decided to pursue a career in cardiology, preferring to specialize in the diagnosis and treatment of heart conditions rather than going the surgery route. His next step after twelve months in San Francisco was a return to Tulane for a one-year cardiology fellowship beginning July 1, 1957. While there, his medical school mentor and friend, Dr. Albert Goggans, persuaded Bobby to join him in practice in Fort Worth, and beginning August 1, 1958, they remained partners there for twenty-six years.

Brown practiced cardiology with the same intensity he demonstrated as a hitter in World Series competition, and the pressures were comparable. Bobby told Bruce Chadwick in a 1982 interview, "I learned in baseball how to respond to enormous pressure. As a doctor I find myself in the same pressure-filled situations." Later Brown drew other parallels between baseball and medicine for Robert L. Shook and Ramon Greenwood in their book, *The Name of the Game is Life* (Contemporary Books, 1992):

> Something that definitely carries over from baseball to medicine is the fact that you can't become discouraged when things are going badly. You can never give up until it's over—just like Yogi said, "It ain't over till it's over." There are many times in medicine when a situation looks utterly hopeless and you would like to throw up your hands and toss in the towel, but you can't do that. No matter how hopeless the odds appear, you make every effort and keep working as hard as you can to stay with it. You've got to tough it out and keep battling, and, if you do that, every once in a while you are going to get a miracle. You begin to see things turn and somebody fools you because he or she starts to respond. Somebody will pull through who you didn't think could. And when that happens it's like winning a World Series game. That's what keeps doctors going.
>
> In the last inning of a tight game, with 60,000-plus fans screaming as well as the opposing team's players trying to distract you, you've got to block everything out and do what you're supposed to do—and that's get a hit. The same is true during certain moments in the practice

As a practicing cardiologist, Dr. Bobby Brown could see parallels in dealing with high-pressure situations comparable to the ones he faced in four World Series.

of medicine. You must keep your concentration and do what you know must be done when everything around you is going to pot.

There are many cases in medicine when a teamwork effort requires several doctors to work together. For instance, a case might involve the joint efforts of an internist, a cardiologist, a surgeon, and an anesthesiologist. Each member of the team is responsible to do certain things. Each must do his or her part and, in turn, rely on the others to do theirs. Although certain doctors, like certain athletes, have big egos, they have to realize that they can't always be the star. Just like the great Yankee teams I played on, there are times when a physician must realize that his or her role is not the lead role.

While in Fort Worth, in addition to practicing cardiology and raising a family, Brown managed to find time to chair Fort Worth's Park Board, serve as a director of a major bank, and become one of the Amon Carter Foundation's three trustees.

The Baseball Executive: 1974, 1984-1994—During his extended career in cardiology, in 1974, Bobby Brown took a six-month break from practicing medicine to become president of the Texas Rangers, agreeing to help out his friend (and new Rangers owner) Brad Corbett for a period of one season. That summer, Brown reunited with former Yankee teammate Billy Martin who had become the Rangers' manager. Shocking the baseball world, with Bobby heading the front office while Billy called the shots on the field, the team went from a 57-105 last place season in '73 to a second place 84-76 record in '74, led by a rejuvenated Fergie Jenkins (who joined the ballclub and won 25 games after going 14-16 with the Cubs the prior year) and AL MVP Jeff Burroughs, who had the best year of his career, leading the league with 118 RBI's. Despite the Rangers' unexpected improvement, at the close of the '74 season, per his unwavering plan, Brown returned to his cardiology practice in Fort Worth where he would stay active as a physician for the next ten years.

In 1983, major league owners began their extended search for a replacement to succeed Bowie Kuhn as baseball commissioner, and called on Dr. Bobby Brown to interview for the position. He became a finalist, but lost out to Peter Ueberroth the following year when the Search Committee (headed by then Milwaukee Brewers' owner Bud Selig) decided what the game needed most in its new leader was proven business skills. Ueberroth had achieved international celebrity status as a businessman in making a huge success of the 1984 Summer Olympics in Los Angeles, which led to his being named *Time* magazine's "Man of the Year" in '84. By achieving such an outpouring of positive public recognition, it became impossible for the owners to deny Ueberroth the position once he threw his hat into the ring.

Baseball owners and league executives clearly had been impressed by Brown during their commissioner search and committed to find a high position for him in the game as soon as one became available. The wait was short. When American League President Lee MacPhail retired late in 1984, he and Bud Selig easily pushed through their personal choice of Bobby Brown to succeed him, because in MacPhail's eyes, "Brown had all the attributes necessary. Being league president is a baseball position. He knew how the game worked, both on the field and in the front office. I also knew he could get along with many people, and that's important, because he has to deal with the owners of teams who are usually top businessmen who think their way is the best."

For Bobby Brown, the decision to leave cardiology and return to full-time baseball was not difficult. He told author Tom Horton in a 1993 interview, "A cardiologist sees and experiences a great deal of bleak time in a patient's life and I decided it was time for me to leave, so I did. Becoming American League President was a once in a lifetime opportunity. When it knocked, I knew it would be the only knock."

Upon assuming his new position, Brown announced his goals for the job. In no set order, he wanted to (1) get more young kids playing the game, (2) have baseball become more integral in the inner city, (3) wage a campaign against the players' use of smokeless tobacco, and (4) assist owners in gaining control of expenses, thereby permitting economic survival for each team. As league president, in addition to pursuing those goals, Brown had primary responsibility for game scheduling, umpire relations, and imposing sanctions for misconduct by players and managers. Unlike third base during his playing days with the Yankees, the job of American League President proved to be a perfect fit on a daily basis for Bobby Brown with a baseball position. "It was a baseball job and I knew baseball, I enjoyed baseball, and I finally got to do it every day."

White Sox owner Jerry Reinsdorf spoke for the other owners in his evaluation of Brown during his tenure as AL President. "Everybody liked him. He was a true gentleman, and a low key individual who didn't cause confrontations, and kept the league running smoothly."

After Peter Ueberroth stepped down as commissioner in early 1989, National League President Bart Giamatti expressed a desire to move up to baseball's top executive position, while Bobby had no such ambition. Giamatti's friend, Fay Vincent, who later succeeded his boss as commissioner after Giamatti's fatal heart attack on September 1, 1989, in his book *The Last Commissioner* (Simon & Schuster, 2002), offered this perspective on how Bart Giamatti followed Ueberroth into the game's top executive position:

> Sometime in 1988, the word was out that Ueberroth would soon be stepping down as commissioner, and the owners wanted Bart to succeed him. He had a lot of support, particularly among the National League owners. Some of the American League owners wanted Dr. Bobby Brown, whom they had known forever and who of course had played baseball. Ueberroth wanted Brown, too. But a commissioner never gets to name his successor. Besides, Bart's political instincts were far sharper than Bobby's. Bart's ability to say the right thing at the right time with the right words was unmatched. The last sentence of Bart's formal bibliographical note in his last book, *Take Time for Paradise*, reads, "I owe the reference to Jane Austen to Charles Bronfman of Montreal." Charles Bronfman of Montreal was a major shareholder of Seagram's, the liquor company; he also owned the Montreal Expos. With a single sentence Bart had made a friend for life.

The former President of Yale and the former cardiologist immensely enjoyed working together during their time in baseball leadership positions, as evidenced by statements Giamatti made when he told the *New York Times* about the fun and chemistry of sharing his baseball duties with Bobby Brown:

> Last fall after the World Series, the rules committee met. Everybody in the room, with the exception of

myself, had spent his life in major league baseball. The conversation got long and interesting when we started talking about the strike zone—all these baseball people standing up trying to figure out just where the armpits are exactly. Then, because people thought the American public was not ready to hear on television "the nipple zone," we decided to define the strike zone as the middle of the chest.

Dr. Bobby Brown served as President of the American League from 1984 to 1994.

Dr. Brown was marvelous. Every time someone would propose an anatomically inoffensive term, like the breastbone, he'd explain that wasn't where we wanted the strike zone to be. So we ended up with "mid-chest to the knees," first to avoid the specious argument about where armpits are, and second, by lowering the strike zone we hope ... to get umpires to focus on the high pitch more.

As American League President throughout the four years Bart Giamatti dominated the baseball executive arena, Bobby Brown maintained his cardiologist perspective toward his new dynamic friend. Brown told me that he did approach Giamatti on one occasion and told his colleague at the start of the brief dialog, "Bart, we're only going to have this conversation one time," and then encouraged his friend to take better care of himself. Giamatti replied, "Bobby, thanks for your concern, but I simply cannot stop smoking." Brown abided by his word and never raised the subject again, and Giamatti proceeded to abuse his body mercilessly. Bobby Brown retired as President of the American League in August 1994, leaving in time to avoid the strike that caused the cancellation of the '94 World Series and the resulting demoralization in the game that hung over it for a year until Cal Ripken brought baseball back to life when he broke Lou Gehrig's consecutive game streak.

Never content to observe life from the sidelines, Bobby Brown quickly re-engaged in Fort Worth community service, joining the board of the Southwestern Medical Foundation, remaining a trustee of the Amon Carter Foundation, leading (along with best friend and former cardiology partner Dr. Albert Goggans) the $750,000 capital fundraising drive to benefit All Saints Hospital in Fort Worth, and speaking often to a wide variety of school and civic groups sharing funny stories of Yogi, Casey, and Mickey as well as lessons learned from his unique career. In addition, as Brown has done ever since his playing career ended, he has continued to maintain his status as an accomplished tennis player, playing doubles for years with former Wimbledon champion Chuck McKinley, former professional Ham Richardson, and Dallas' legendary businessman and philanthropist Ray Nasher, who are all now deceased.

The three successful careers of Bobby Brown are a testimony to his philosophy. "There's more to life than being an athlete. If you think otherwise, you miss a lot and spend too much time looking back. I never had to do that. Life has taught me to do the very best I can every single day." The man occasionally looks in his rear view mirror to tell a funny story about his salad days with the Yankees, but throughout his long life, Bobby Brown's eyes have kept their focus on the road ahead.

BOBBY BRAGAN: SINGING A JOYFUL SONG

Appropriately, I met Bobby Bragan early one evening at my church in the summer of 1992. As he has done thousands of times over the last four decades for the benefit of school groups, civic groups, church groups, retirement home groups, and every group in between, without charging a dime, Bobby came to Highland Park Methodist in Dallas to talk baseball, recite poetry, ask trivia questions, tell jokes, play the piano, and sing for our men's group. He quickly recognized he had a kindred spirit in his midst in the form of yours truly. As his program ended, I walked over to tell Bobby how much we had all enjoyed his presentation, and to my surprise, he invited me to Arlington the next day for his press conference (at the hotel nearest Arlington Stadium) being held in connection with the release of his baseball memoirs, *You*

In the Ebbets Field clubhouse, Bobby Bragan often entertained his Dodger teammates at the piano.

Can't Hit the Ball With the Bat on Your Shoulder as told to Jeff Guinn (Summit Group, 1992). Wild horses couldn't have kept me away from Arlington the next day, and after the press conference ended, at Bobby's invitation, we ate dinner together, and by the end of the evening, I found myself singing around the hotel's piano with the entire Bragan family.

In a few short days, I had devoured Bobby's book and found it so good that it prompted me to take action.[15] I picked up the phone and called the book editor for the *Dallas Morning News*, Bob Compton, who didn't know me from the man in the moon, and pleaded with Bob to let me, a total stranger to him, take a stab at reviewing *You Can't Hit the Ball...* for his newspaper. Probably sensing he would never get to hang up the phone if he answered in the negative, Bob said "okay," and the review became my first published article in the *Morning News* (the first of 62), which soon led to my writing columns, articles, and book reviews for other publications, which ultimately led to the writing of this book. So "Thank you very much, Bob Compton!" Here's my fateful review of Bobby's book:

––––––––––––––

While managing the Fort Worth Cats in the early '50s, Bobby Bragan instilled the teachings of mentor Branch Rickey into a cocky, teenaged outfielder named Dick Williams, who would later become the only manager in baseball history to lead three different teams to the World Series. While managing the Spokane Indians in the late '50s, Mr. Bragan transformed a journeyman bush league infielder named Maury Wills into a superstar player, who would become the National League's Most Valuable Player in 1962, by persuading him to switch hit, bunt, and steal more bases. While managing the Milwaukee Braves in the mid-'60s, Mr. Bragan guided young hurler Phil Niekro to abandon his traditional pitching repertoire and concentrate solely on his seldom-used knuckleball. Mr. Niekro heeded the advice and proceeded to win 300 games. While president of the Texas League in the late '60s, Mr. Bragan spearheaded the initial implementation of the designated hitter rule.

Despite these obvious successes in baseball, Bobby Bragan begins

15 My friend Don Jackson once commented, "Talmage doesn't read books. He devours them."

You Can't Hit the Ball With the Bat on Your Shoulder with his recollection of what would become his greatest lifetime achievement, which ironically arose during his worst season as a major league player.

In 1947, Bragan played in a total of 25 games and hit .194 as a backup catcher for the Brooklyn Dodgers. Notwithstanding his bench-warming status, that season changed Mr. Bragan's attitude forever in the midst of his encountering teammate Jackie Robinson in Branch Rickey's Noble Experiment, and learning that his Alabama-born-and-bred prejudice no longer had a place in his life.

In his first chapter, Bragan acknowledges his initial misgivings about having a black teammate. Through Branch Rickey's counseling, and by observing Jackie Robinson as a talented player and man of dignity, Bragan awakened to the reality that the baseball field should be level for all with the talent to play. After 1947, Messrs. Bragan and Robinson remained friends to the point of sitting next to each other at Rickey's funeral in 1965. Jackie Robinson's impact on the remainder of Bobby Bragan's life is established throughout the book as Hank Aaron, Orlando Cepeda, and others confirm that manager/coach Bragan treated his black and Latin players with total support and respect.

The book utilizes three innovative baseball-writing techniques. The first is a feature called "Between Innings," in which Bragan's peers give their perspective on the events in the previous chapter. These contributors include the likes of Joe DiMaggio, Stan Musial, Leo Durocher (in the final interview before his death), Roy Campanella, and Tommy Lasorda, and their comments add gravy to a thoroughly meaty book.

The second feature demonstrates Bobby Bragan's capacity to help the reader visualize yesteryear's heroes by comparing them to today's players. Harry "The Hat" Walker hit the ball hard to all fields like a young Rafael Palmiero. Mickey Owens performed as a durable, competent catcher like Mike Scioscia. Lee Walls had a perfect baseball physique like Ruben Sierra.

The final special feature is Bragan's ongoing discussion of the impact of money on professional baseball, and how it will always drive the game. As for the past, the Dodgers of the late '40s prospered because they annually received World Series revenues and held expenses down through the frugality of Mr. Rickey, the ultimate hardball contract negotiator. As for the present, today's game cannot survive financially without undergoing major changes in the rules of free agency, as discussed by Bragan and Texas Rangers managing partner George W. Bush (in the final "Between Innings" segment).[16]

Although his career .240 batting average will never get Bobby Bragan into Cooperstown, his book deserves a place there as a well-told account of baseball's last half-century.[17]

────────────

Not long after my review of Bobby's book appeared in the *Dallas Morning News,* he invited me to come to Fort Worth (roughly 40 miles west of Dallas) and be his guest for *The Fort Worth Star-Telegram's* annual book and author luncheon, where he would be one of the two featured speakers along with best-selling mystery novelist Mary Higgins Clark. With at least 700 people in attendance, including all the top brass from the *Star-Telegram,* after finishing his remarks about his book, Bobby stayed at the microphone. In his mind, given his compulsion for generosity, this was the right time to give a token of his appreciation to the fellow in attendance who had fulfilled one of his (till then) unspoken dreams for *You Can't Hit the Ball* ... "Out there," Bobby said,..."toward the back of this massive crowd, sits the man who caused my book to be reviewed in the *DALLAS MORNING NEWS*!!, and I have something I'd like to give him," at which point Bobby summoned me up to the podium so he could hand me a sharply framed, enlarged version of my book review. As the crowd applauded politely while I walked to the front of the ballroom to accept Bobby's gift, the *Star-Telegram* executives and journalists squirmed in their seats over the public tribute being paid at *their* sponsored luncheon to some stranger who had arranged for a book review to be published in the pages of *their* biggest newspaper competitor. Oh well! It sure made my day.

About the time of that luncheon, realizing more than ever that he had found an energetic and supportive ally for his many baseball and civic endeavors, Bobby named me to the Board of Directors of his Youth

────────────

16 Yes, the same man who nine years after giving the interview to Jeff Guinn for Bobby's book would be inaugurated as our nation's 43rd President.

17 Ironically (in light of my review's final sentence), less than a year after writing the review of Bragan's book for the *Morning News,* at Bobby's request I hand-delivered a copy of *You Can't Hit the Ball* ... to the National Baseball Hall of Fame and Museum in Cooperstown for the permanent collection of its library when I went there to do research on my first book.

From the time he first became a major league manager in Pittsburgh, Bobby Bragan always made sure he had fun. Here he clowns around with entertainer Joe E. Brown.

Foundation, which had just gotten off the ground. Since its inception, the Bobby Bragan Youth Foundation has been in the business of raising money in order to award $2,500 college scholarships for outstanding North Texas kids who have demonstrated well-rounded excellence by the eighth grade. The charitable philosophy (which has been proven sound over the last seventeen years) behind giving college scholarships to eighth graders is the belief that by affirming a good kid at that young age with financial aid for college, it provides him with a positive push upon his entry into high school, and will motivate him to maintain his existing high level of academic, civic, and athletic excellence through his next four years of schooling until graduation.

In my first year as a board member in 1992, the Foundation gave 4 scholarships (2 eighth graders from Dallas and 2 from Fort Worth), and in 2007, the number of scholarships awarded annually had steadily increased through the years up to 34. All winners actually receive their money after graduating from high school, at which time they designate their intended college, and the Foundation delivers a check payable to that school as a partial tuition payment. Through 2007, the Bragan Foundation has given over $1,000,000 in scholarships to over 400 area students, who have fulfilled the funding's mission by attending outstanding universities all over the country, from Stanford to Yale.

Beginning in '92, the Foundation's board determined that the primary means of fundraising to provide capital for the scholarships would be by organizing and hosting an annual Gala in Fort Worth on an autumn night, featuring a sports celebrity in attendance to receive our "Lifetime Achievement Award." Over the last seventeen years, recipients of the award have included Joe DiMaggio, Hank Aaron, Willie Mays, Tom Landry, Roger Staubach, Byron Nelson, Dr. Bobby Brown, Eddie Robinson, Gene Stallings, Dan Jenkins, Lou Brock, Brooks Robinson, and Bud Selig.

The most special Gala "Lifetime Achievement Award" winner for me, however, was when Rachel Robinson came to Fort Worth for our 2001 dinner. Since Jackie Robinson had been such a hero to me (see Chapter 3) my entire life, Bobby allowed me to pick up Ms. Robinson at the airport and drive her to the hotel where the Gala was held that night. Having the opportunity to spend time with Jackie Robinson's still beautiful and quietly dazzling widow became a surreal experience, and the circumstances that led to Bobby Bragan's choosing Rachel as his honoree at the Gala became a defining moment for me about the radiance in my friend's heart.

Early in 2000, Bobby's wife, Betty, had had some serious health problems (from which, thankfully, she later recovered) that required extended hospitalization. Knowing how badly this distressed Bobby, early one morning, I drove over to Fort Worth for coffee with him in hopes of boosting his spirits. Our conversation in the hospital's lobby soon focused on that year's Gala, still several months away, and who would be the best person to bring in that year as our headliner to receive the Lifetime Achievement Award.

From out of nowhere, Bobby expressed that he felt called to honor Rachel Robinson, not just in presenting her with the award, but also by making the commitment that if she would come to the Gala, he would present her with a check payable to the Jackie Robinson Foundation in the amount of $25,000.

As noted in my *Dallas Morning News* book review of *You Can't Hit the Ball*...(which appears earlier in this chapter), and as Bobby has always publicly acknowledged, he was among the small group of Jackie Robinson's 1947 Brooklyn teammates who definitely did not welcome baseball's trailblazer with open arms into the clubhouse at the outset of Branch Rickey's Noble Experiment. In fact, Bobby and a few others had to be addressed one-on-one by Mr. Rickey in spring training that year about the need for them to accept Robinson as a comrade if they wanted to remain on the Dodgers team.

In 1947, Bobby Bragan reluctantly agreed to Mr. Rickey's terms before the start of the season, and within a few months, seeing that Jackie Robinson was (i) the best player on the team, (ii) driving the Dodgers to the 1947 National League pennant, and (iii) clearly a highly intelligent and courageous man worthy of every thinking person's total respect, Bobby had an epiphany that extinguished racism from his mindset then and forever after. In his marvelous book, *Opening Day: The Story of Jackie Robinson's First Season* (Simon & Schuster, 2007), Jonathan Eig succinctly described Bragan's transformation in 1947 as a result of being Jackie Robinson's teammate:

> Bobby Bragan, one of the opponents of integration who had refused to back down when confronted by Rickey before the start of the season, still hadn't made any effort to reach out to Robinson, nor did he have any intention of doing so. But he had been thinking a good deal about him, and Bragan admitted to himself now that some of the things he'd worried about in spring training had been no cause for concern after all. He'd shared a locker room and a shower room with a black man, and neither he nor his parents had dropped dead from shock. A black man had joined a team of white players, and no riots had ensued. Robinson had taken a job that otherwise would have gone to a white man,

At the press conference in Milwaukee announcing the Braves' departure, manager Bobby Bragan told the crowd,
"The good news is I'm leaving town. The bad news is I'm taking the team with me to Atlanta."

and the nation's social structure had not collapsed. Bragan wasn't ready to join the NAACP or invite Robinson to dinner, but two things were slowly dawning on him. The first was that the world was changing. The second was that he could probably live with the change.

The year 1947 proved to be Bobby Bragan's final season as a big league player, though it ended on a high note, as Dodger manager Burt Shotten allowed him to pinch-hit in Game Six of the Fall Classic, and he lined a double to left in his only at-bat, giving him a cool career 1.000 batting average in World Series competition.[18] When the season ended, after it became clear Roy Campanella was poised to take over as Brooklyn's catcher in 1948, which meant moving '47 starting backstop Bruce Edwards into a backup role in the bullpen, thereby leaving no place on the roster for Bobby, team president Branch Rickey gave Bragan a chance to manage in the Dodgers farm system, making him the player-manager of the Fort Worth Cats in the Texas League. Jonathan Eig points out in *Opening Day* that all the negatives associated with Bobby's original reluctance to embrace Jackie Robinson had melted away by the time he became the manager at Fort Worth, as soon as he "developed a reputation as an equal opportunity employer, and was said to be especially good at working with black ballplayers."

Bragan's success as a minor league manager and his personal transformation in abandoning racism once and for all in 1947 caused his mentor, Branch Rickey (who left the Dodgers after 1950 and soon became the General Manager of the Pittsburgh Pirates), to give Bobby his first chance to manage in the big leagues, naming him the Pirates' skipper in 1956. As Lee Lowenfish mentions in his superb new biography, *Branch Rickey: Baseball's Ferocious Gentleman* (University of Nebraska Press, 2007).

---

18 As Jonathan Eig points out in *Opening Day*, after the double, Dodger manager Shotten sent speedy relief pitcher Dan Bankhead in to pinch-run for the notoriously slow-footed Bragan, thereby allowing Bankhead to become the second African-American to play in a World Series game.

It warmed Rickey's heart that Bragan quickly became a big advocate in integration, agreeing with him that only runs and hits are important in baseball, not color of skin. In a phone interview in May 2005 Bobby Bragan declared, "The three greatest men I ever met in my life were Jackie Robinson, Branch Rickey, and Billy Graham."

In summary, Bobby Bragan came a long way from resisting, for racial reasons, having Jackie Robinson as a Brooklyn Dodger teammate at 1947 spring training to becoming not only an equal opportunity minor and major league manager, but someone who by 2000 wanted to step up and pay tribute to Rachel Robinson on Bobby's single biggest night of the year, and make a generous contribution to the Robinson Foundation through donating a share of the proceeds from our annual Fort Worth Gala.

———————————

Two other mountaintop experiences come to mind from being Bobby Bragan's buddy, and both involved our trips together to Cooperstown for the 1997 and 1999 Baseball Hall of Fame Induction Weekends. Bobby decided he had to go in '97 because from his time spent playing and managing in the Dodgers organization form 1943 to 1952,[19] he developed a solid friendship with a young left-handed pitcher named Tom Lasorda, who of course would later become famous as "the Artful Dodger" in succeeding Walter Alston as the Los Angeles Dodgers manager at the end of the '76 season, and then lead them for the next 20 years, winning 8 NL West titles, 4 National League pennants, and 2 World Series. In Lasorda's first year of eligibility for the Hall of Fame, the Veterans Committee selected him for induction in 1997.

As Bobby planned for his trip to Cooperstown in July 1997, a wonderful blessing fell into his lap. Through the nineties, the Bragan Youth Foundation had developed as one of its strongest sponsors Pier One Corporation, under the leadership of its Chairman and CEO Clark

19 Bobby's last year to manage the Fort Worth Cats in Brooklyn's farm system was 1952.

Bobby with his beloved friend, Sister Francis, in Cooperstown for Nolan Ryan's 1999 induction.

Johnson. When Bobby mentioned his plans to attend Tom Lasorda's induction into the Hall of Fame, Clark offered Pier One's private jet to carry him and a small group of friends up to the festivities.

Fortunately, Bobby Bragan invited me to join his group, which included Clark Johnson, Bobby's wife, Betty, Pier One executive Marvin Girouard, and other Bragan Foundation leaders, John Esch and Darrell Barrett, and together we spent 48 hours in baseball heaven in the village of Cooperstown. While there, Bobby obtained special badges for all of us, enabling us to come and go at the Otesaga Hotel where only Hall of Famers get to stay during Induction Weekend, their privacy rigorously protected from the mass of adoring fans in town for the ceremonies. Being with Bobby and getting a Hall of Fame badge allowed this forty-three-year-old adoring fan from Texas to enter and converse with the baseball gods in their inner sanctum.

Most memorably, our merry band of Texans had breakfast at the Otesaga on the Sunday morning before the induction ceremonies, and Bobby reserved a table for all of us to dine with Tommy Lasorda on the day he entered the Hall of Fame. We had barely sat down to eat when, with great fanfare, a still vigorous Ted Williams was rolled into the dining room in a wheelchair, and he sat at the table next to ours along with Bobby Doerr.

As we ate breakfast, Bobby hailed down Sparky Anderson and Bob Feller to join us at our table. Then, after we finished eating, Bobby walked me across the room so he could introduce me to his old teammate Pee Wee Reese, and allowed me to enjoy a one-on-one chat with the fine gentleman from Kentucky, who had played such a key role in Jackie Robinson's entry into the major leagues. In looking around the Otesaga Hotel dining room on that July morning, it appeared I had truly died and entered baseball heaven, as my lifetime dream of sitting in the big middle of a room filled with genial Hall of Famers as an insider (unlike my 1989 Otesaga Hotel experience described in Chapter 6, where I was clearly an outsider) in a friendly, relaxed social environment had come true—thanks to arrangements made by my best baseball friend ever, Bobby Bragan.

In 1999, Bobby and I returned to Cooperstown for Nolan Ryan's induction, and this time we were joined by my wife and kids, my baseball soul brother, John Ledbetter, and his family, and a dozen other Dallas friends. On the front porch of the house we rented for the weekend (literally a stone's throw from Main Street where the Hall of Fame is located) on the Monday morning after the induction ceremonies, Bobby treated the Boston and Ledbetter children to his dramatic rendition of "Casey at the Bat," holding a plastic whiffle ball bat (that our kids had been playing with over the weekend) and thrusting it into the air at the right moments to emphasize the poem's key passages.

The actor DeWolf Hopper's constant performance of "Casey," beginning in 1892 for a period of over thirty years, in music halls all over the country had made Ernest L. Thayer's epic anthem become as much a part of our National Pastime as the song "Take Me Out to the Ballgame." I've heard Hopper's melodramatic interpretation of the poem many times (getting a recording of it on an old 78 record I purchased from a memorabilia dealer and had transposed onto a cassette tape sometime in the late eighties). In my unbiased opinion, on his best day, Mr. Hopper does not come close to Bobby Bragan's flawless version of "Casey," given Bobby's delivering it with the earnest tone of a man who knows and cherishes baseball, drama, and poetry. When Bobby does "Casey," it is as uplifting and powerful an American patriotic virtuoso performance as George C. Scott's opening monolog in the movie *Patton*.

Thus, on a sunny Monday July morning in Cooperstown, New York, the mythical "Birthplace of Baseball," on the front porch of a home just down the street from Doubleday Field, built on the site of Elihu Phinney's cow pasture where young Abner Doubleday and his buddies were once believed to have played the first baseball game, eighty-two-year-old Bobby Bragan, the "Mr. Baseball" of Texas for over four decades, gave a private performance of "Casey at the Bat" exclusively for the eyes and ears of my family and friends. It was as magical a baseball moment for me as our 1997 breakfast at the Otesaga Hotel in a dining room full of legends.

Bobby Bragan turned 90 on October 30, 2007, and still functions on all cylinders. He still recites "Casey at the Bat" for civic groups and retirement home residents, still plays and sings "You Can't Hit the Ball With the Bat on Your Shoulder" whenever he walks past a piano, still leads his foundation to provide 34 scholarships every year to great kids in North Texas, and still speaks frequently of the three greatest men he ever met in his life—Jackie Robinson, Branch Rickey and Billy Graham.

In the final paragraph of the prologue to his new biography on Branch Rickey, Lee Lowenfish concludes that Mr. Rickey, the man who

Bobby Bragan recites "Casey at the Bat" for family and friends on the Broses' front porch in Cooperstown.

mentored Bobby Bragan for fifteen years in the Brooklyn Dodger and Pittsburgh Pirate organizations and whose photo still hangs on the wall of Bobby's office, "communicated an unquenchable joy in life,... and was a man of outstanding energy and radical individualism." Those same characteristics fill the heart of Rickey's most enthusiastic disciple, my friend Bobby Bragan, whose lifetime of inspiration and generosity to others has provided a major extension of Branch Rickey's legacy.

One final thought on the subject of friends and baseball. Obviously, in each person's journey through life, some friends come through in providing emotional support at the times when we most need them, while others fail to deliver at the crunch time moments. In that respect, friends' commitments to each other resemble the careers of certain major league baseball players.

Some baseball superstars like Alex Rodriguez always play lights out in regular season games. Through 2007, in his 12 full big league seasons, A-Rod has averaged 44 homers, 128 RBI's, hit .306, and won 3 American League MVP awards during the months of April-September.

However, in October, since joining the New York Yankees, in the crunch time of postseason play, like a fair-weather friend, Rodriguez turns into jello. As a Bronx Bomber through 2008, participating in 24 postseason games, with 94 official at-bats, he has hit .245, with 4 homers and 14 RBI's. And, of course, because of his failure to deliver in the games when his bat is needed most, A-Rod's Yankee teams have never achieved their objective and, therefore, have never played in (never mind won) a World Series, and have gotten to only one ALCS (losing to the Red Sox in 2004).

Contrary to A-Rod's performance in postseason crunch, Lou Brock (in 21 games, going 34 for 87, a .391 clip), Dr. Bobby Brown (in 17 games, going 18 for 41, a .439 average), and Bobby Bragan (hitting a double in his only at-bat in the '47 Series) all played their best baseball in the World Series. Delivering when the pressure was on in baseball's most important games came naturally to these three wonderful men, just as it has in coming through as friends in our many encounters.

Alas, John Grisham never got to play in a World Series. But as a friend, he delivered at two critical times: first, when I needed a writing superstar to author a foreword to help me promote my first book; and later, when the State Bar of Texas leaned on me to help raise the attendance at the 2007 Annual Meeting by bringing in a blockbuster talent for our keynote speaker. Coming through as a friend, when he knew the pressure was on me in those two important situations, came as naturally to John Grisham as did hitting line drives in October (and being a steady friend) to Messrs. Brock, Brown, and Bragan.

Whether coaching our son's games or cheering for the Rangers with our daughter, baseball can and does bring a family together.

CHAPTER NINE

FIRST PERSON PERSPECTIVE
Time in the Sun with a Son and then Time by Myself

As mentioned in the Introduction, this book is not only about American baseball history since World War II, it's also the author's Baby Boomer baseball memoir. Mickey Mantle's and Jimmy Piersall's dads may have done it wrong, Carl Yastrzemski's and Nolan Ryan's dads may have done it right, but I did it my way, wrong and right, with my son, Scott, and thanks to him, it all came out okay in the end.

———————————————

E very fan has his favorite baseball experience. For some, it came when playing the game—for others it came when watching it. Mine was a hybrid (part playing, part watching) that came from the seven years of coaching my son, Scott, and his teams. There were many highs and a few lows, but always a personal hands-on connection shared between us until the day, in his junior year of high school, when he hung up his glove.

As with most extended parenting experiences, seven years provided ample opportunity for reflection (and thus, for writing) on what was really going on between Scott and me—and the game. This chapter covers the five most important thoughts that came to me in those times when we were together, and which are now locked into the green fields of my mind.

FADING FIELD: BASEBALL AS THE VICTIM OF TWO EPIDEMICS

It is most male baseball fans' favorite scene in a movie. At the end of *Field of Dreams*, middle-aged Kevin Costner realizes his life's ambition by finally getting to play catch with his reincarnated father. At long last, they connect. The scene captures the essence of baseball as a tool for generational connection, and why, once upon a time, the game was the National Pastime.

As its most devoted fans must now acknowledge, baseball started losing its appeal as the country's most popular sport in the late 1960's. Some suggest it was because the game doesn't televise well. Others point to the growing appreciation of faster-moving, more violent games. Both arguments are valid, but there are two other more socially important reasons.

During the past forty years, baseball became a victim of two epidemics. The first involved the dad disappearing act. Beginning in the late 1960's, America's divorce rate started skyrocketing, and with it, many boys found themselves without fathers except on alternate weekends. In the 1970's, many dads decided it was in their families' best interests to become workaholics and thereby be apart from their children on nights and weekends. By the 1980's, the number of unwed mothers escalated exponentially, a surge that will surely continue as female celebrities glamorize the lives of husbandless mothers.

A boy can shoot baskets in the back yard, run long distances, or lift weights all by himself, and feel as though he is improving in his chosen sport. But there are only so many times he can throw and catch a baseball off a roof or hit it off a tee. Unless he has a like-minded brother close in age, a boy's baseball options are substantially limited with no dad, and, therefore, no catch partner, no fungo hitter, and no one to help organize baseball games.

Which leads to the second epidemic that has caused the game's popularity to wane in recent years—the lack of safety in public places. Before World War II, when kids in urban areas had free time, they rode their bikes to the neighborhood park where their buddies played, and everything was safe. At the park in the spring and summer, most boys prior to the 1970's played baseball, and there were plenty of players available to field several teams ready to play from daylight to dark. Former New York Yankee great Tommy Henrich grew up in Massillon, Ohio, during the 1920's and said in his autobiography that it wasn't uncommon in those days for a boy to leave a park at dusk, having collected 50 hits in one day.

The days of Tommy Henrich's youth are gone. During the past 30 years, in most cities, no responsible parent would allow his young son to play in a public park without adult supervision. So instead of marathon pick-up baseball sessions in a field playing with other boys, essentially the only time kids have gotten around to playing the game since the late 1960's has been in structured youth league environments, typically organized by dads, where boys usually get to play 2 games a week, resulting in a maximum of 6 at-bats and maybe 4 hits if the kid is a slugger. In a span of decades, then, a talented player went from getting 50 hits in a day to 4 in a week, and the siren song of other sports grew louder.

As baseball loses popularity among the crowded field of youth sport competitors—basketball, football, soccer, and lacrosse—there's little hope for reversing the trend. We can't pretend that divorces, workaholism, and unwed mothers will be uncommon in the balance of the 21st century, that our city parks suddenly will become safe for kids when no adults are around, or that today's kids will all of a sudden start taking the initiative to organize their own sandlot games needing at least 12 participants.

Despite these contemporary realities, for those of us lucky enough to be married to the mother of our children and who find the time to take our children to the park where we can play catch, hit fungoes, and put together pick-up games, we know we are the lucky ones. The odds favor our having a bona fide connection with our kids in authentic green fields long before they reach middle age and start having to imagine connecting with a deceased dad in some make-believe field of dreams.

WHOSE BATTING AVERAGE IS IT?

Once the Super Bowl (and, therefore, football) is over in early February, and spring approaches, many begin preparing for the annual father-child obsession known as "youth baseball." Teams offering a variety of competitive levels are now being formed for boys and girls ranging in age from 4 to 18. Given my coaching experiences over the past five years, it is certain that some children participating on these teams will enjoy a positive experience, but many will not.

What spoils spring and youth baseball for too many kids are parents who subconsciously see the season as a chance to relive their childhood. But this time around, by golly, there better be some glory. Little Johnny darn sure ought to get a chance to pitch (even though he can't throw strikes on a consistent basis), catch (though his throws can't quite make it to second base), play infield (despite his propensity for dodging ground balls), or at least *start* in the outfield (though the paths of fly balls usually confuse him). Right. Whatever you say, Mr. Parent.

The smartest thing ever said in my presence about parents, kids, and baseball came during my first year of coaching when our son Scott was in the second grade. In watching dozens of Texas Ranger games, he had seen Julio Franco succeed as an outstanding major league hitter using a unique style holding his hands well over his head as the pitcher delivered the ball. If it worked for Julio, surely it would work for him.

As a coach supposedly knowledgeable about batting techniques, it seemed clear that starting the swing from such an awkward and distant position (unless blessed with super-human quickness like Julio Franco) would make getting his hands through the hitting zone in time to connect with the ball very difficult, and Scott's constant performance in swinging late confirmed my assessment. With each futile swing at batting practice, my temperature (and voice) rose as the advice to lower his hands went unheeded by our strong-willed child.

Finally, the boy had had enough. As I again started to give my high octane spiel about bringing his hands down after another late swing, Scott turned hard on me with a look as serious as a heart attack, and said to me in an icy tone, "Dad, it's my batting average. Not yours." A 30-30 rifle shot between the eyes would have done less damage to my psyche.

For those parents about to embark on a youth baseball spring with hopes of Junior's impressing friends and neighbors by his baseball prowess, the advice here is to step back now and think a little before the games begin. Two conflicting images come to mind as the predominant perspectives that may make or break a child's experience with our National Pastime over the next few months. A father's and mother's attitude toward their child on the diamond can be symbolized by either a tightly-clenched fist or a relaxed open hand, and the choices of hand positions in the metaphor will determine whether or not the kid has a fun spring playing the game.

This was confirmed recently at a dinner party in a conversation with my friend Larry, whose boys have played baseball for many years,

From an early age, Scott had the wherewithal to stand up for himself. "Dad, it's my batting average. Not yours."

and I asked him where they would be playing this spring. Larry said they would play only for their small private school's team, and would not be joining other leagues because it would interfere with some non-sports activities that became available to them that summer. "My boys are pretty good players, but they're not good enough to play professional baseball or even at the college level unless they go to a small school. So we had to sit down and ask ourselves where all of this is going."

Larry's closing thought on the subject speaks volumes: "I'll tell you one thing, though. Ever since I backed off of them about the game, they sure seem to enjoy playing baseball a whole lot more."

GETTING PAST CHOPSTICKS

To play or not to play. That is the question ... and it's a tough one for parents of children participating in competitive sports.

For most kids, hand-eye coordination (or the lack thereof) has surfaced by the age of six. If it appears that Little Johnny likes to play ball and can really throw, catch, or hit, then mom and dad have a choice. Either the child will be given the chance to extend his athletic gifts to their fullest or he won't. As with most important parenting decisions, the prudent course is not necessarily the convenient one.

A musically gifted child will not develop his piano skills by playing only "Heart and Soul" over and over again. A young virtuoso emerges by taking on increasingly challenging pieces, under the instruction of a capable and demanding instructor. Obviously, the responsible parent wants his child to become the best he can be, so no second thought is given to arranging for the best music lessons and recitals available.

The situation in parenting the young athlete is both similar to and different from that of raising the budding musician. Similar in that Little Johnny will not refine and grow his sports talents by playing against weak teams in the least competitive league with unhelpful coaching. Maintaining a .600 batting average against unchallenging competition with a dad-coach is the equivalent of mastering "Chopsticks."

Like the advancing music student, the young ballplayer will fulfill his potential only through the instruction of a competent coach who can teach the game's increasingly sophisticated techniques, played against tough competition in game situations. Fathers as coaches, though well-intentioned ("Keep your eye on the ball!"), rarely have the capacity to take a child past the basics and up to the next level.

The difference between developing the young athlete and pianist is in the logistics. The musician can work on his craft at home. The best-played ballgames take place on the road.

Welcome to the world of children's select baseball leagues where practices three times a week are the norm, games are played constantly at divergent locations, and weekend tournaments devour all notions of family time. One family with three talented baseball playing sons just finished a summer attending 194 games. A North Dallas family recently decided to interrupt a four-day vacation to Disneyland by having the father and son fly home for one regular-season baseball game, then rejoin the clan in California. Dangling in the shadows, presumably, is the possibility that Little Johnny might become Wally Pipp, who in 1925 missed one game with a headache, allowing Lou Gehrig to step into the starting lineup for the next 14 years.

The rational parent asks, "What are the alternatives?"

One is to insist that a child avoid or quit the select leagues, and have Little Johnny dominate the uncompetitive teams, which typically cut off when a kid reaches twelve. Then, when he reaches high school, he can try out for his school's teams and compete against the kids who have stayed in the select leagues and played in the weekend tournaments. Little Johnny's chances of making the school baseball team under these circumstances? Slim to none.

If parents cause their child to drop out from the select leagues, and then he later fails to make the school teams, Johnny will probably abandon competitive sports, and have more time to pursue academics. In that scenario, sometimes he will actually bite into the books with a new level of dedication. Sometimes.

If Johnny stops playing sports, however, he surely will have extra time to be home alone or to spend with those kids who are not athletic. Some of those teenagers are into good things and some are not. At least when adolescents are at practice and games, we know where they are, whom they're with, and what they're doing.

There's no easy solution here. Answers vary based on each family's unique circumstances. Clearly, the intense baseball path should not get traveled if the child is, in fact, a marginal player or doesn't enjoy the competition. A detour also needs to take place if the select league is being joined for the primary purpose of allowing a father to live out his prime time fantasies through his son.

When the competitive youth baseball path is pursued for the right reasons, however, with a sensible parental attitude, i.e., don't run out on Disneyland and fly across the country just to play one game, in guiding a child who thrives on competition, then the decision to play in select leagues makes sense, albeit inconvenient sense.

When the decision to participate in select leagues is made for the right reasons, yes, odometers spin, fast food restaurants thrive, other social commitments go unscheduled, and potential is fulfilled.

GOING ON DOWN THE ROAD

There comes a time in the life of every red-blooded American male when he admits to himself he will never become a major league baseball player. That day is not a good day.

Then, thirty or forty years later, the time comes when that same American male admits to himself that his son will not become a big league ballplayer. That day is also not a happy time, though it comes at different times for different dads. For some, it comes when the boy is 10; for others, when he's 16; for a few, when he's 20. Regardless of the exact time, for dads in our neighborhood (with the exception of Chris Young's[1] and Clayton Kershaw's[2] fathers), the day *does* come.

When that fateful time arrives, a walk through the house becomes a trip down Memory Lane. The dad looks in his son's drawers and spots the old uniform shirts; then stumbles on an outgrown pair of cleats littering the laundry room floor; then opens the hall closet and finds the dusty bag of old baseballs scuffed up from last year's batting practice; then sees on the bookshelf the framed photo of his son hurling a fastball.

He closes his eyes and remembers the weekend tournaments at Cowtown Park in Burleson; the year his boy's team won the North Dallas

---

1 National League All-Star pitcher for the 2007 San Diego Padres.

2 Los Angeles Dodgers #1 pick in the 2006 player draft, who joined the Dodgers' starting rotation at midseason 2008.

Chamber championship; all the trips to Dallas Baseball Academy of Texas for pitching and hitting lessons; the games when his teams had too many players and the ones when they had too few; and the hassle of rainouts, makeup games, and finding practice fields.

The father then thinks of all the men he coached with on the same team or in the same league where his son played; the parents who took ballgames too seriously and those who didn't care enough; the boys who cried when they struck out and those who turned cartwheels after hitting a home run; and the point in time when girls started coming out to watch the games.

Mainly though, he remembers playing catch with his son in the front yard, trying to throw strikes to him in the cage, hitting fungoes clear across the park, and how the boy loved the game for a while, and talked as though he planned to go as far as he could with it. The dad recalls the days his son played well, when his pitches moved around the strike zone, and his fielders made plays behind him.

When the end comes, and the high school coach posts the list of those who made the team, and it doesn't have the son's name, the father talks to the boy to see how he's handling it. He says, "Dad, it's okay; I'm ready to move on." It is then that the man knows this crisis shall pass,

When the day comes for a son to hang up his glove from competitive baseball, the father can hopefully look back and thank God for the memories.

the seasons of life have changed, a new day with new challenges has arrived, and, on a going forward basis, things will work out just fine.

On that day, the father looks deep into his son's eyes and thanks God for the memories and for having a boy-turned-young-man capable of moving on down life's highway despite the occasional bump in the road.

The obligatory team photo. This was our championship year, and former major league pitcher Ray Burris served as the Twins' head coach.

Along the parenting trail and the bumps that shoot up unexpectedly on the road's surface, here's a final piece that involved my son and football, but actually addressed the universal subject of how things can often go awry (as they did in the Mantle and Piersall families, as described in Chapter 1) when a dad imposes his own sports dream on his son. Here is our story and the lessons we learned when this father (and writer) second-guessed his son's self-awareness and good judgment.

FATHERS AND SONS AND FOOTBALL

My 97-pound eighth grade son, Scott, lay on the football field in agony, holding his left thigh and groaning, "Dad, I broke my leg." As coaches and referees hovered over the boy waiting for the ambulance, two words from my high school Latin teacher exploded in my brain—*mea culpa* (my fault).

Four weeks before, shortly before school started, we had had what I thought was one of our best conversations ever. Lying on a high-jump landing pad at a nearby track that summer evening, I opened the conversation: "Mom says you don't think you want to play football this year."

Scott's response will haunt me the rest of my life: "Well, Dad, I'm kind of small, and I'll probably get hurt."

Having grown up in Texas and spent most of my life here, I have come to understand the unique stature football has in the mentality of our state. Playing it is something of a rite of passage. It is the stuff of lifelong memories, good and bad, but authentic. My own father had not been athletic, and had never encouraged me to play it beyond the sixth grade. Given that in high school the scouting report on me would have been, "he's small, but at least he's slow," I had not pursued it on my own, and always regretted not being in that special "arena," as Teddy Roosevelt would have called it.

When Scott was born and developed an early love for the game, and showed some promise with a strong and accurate passing arm to offset his genetic lack of youthful size and speed, Ol' Dad was pleased. Attending a small private school then opened up the opportunity to pursue the game beyond the YMCA youth level.

Seventh grade football went well, as Scott had some good moments against bigger schools with larger squads, though he had been taken out of two games with minor leg injuries that healed quickly. Everything seemed rosy heading into this season.

Then something changed. Scott fell in love with the game of golf. The summer after seventh grade was devoted almost entirely to time on the municipal links with his buddies. He developed a genuine passion for the game, and on the golf course his lack of size and foot speed did not matter.

So as we lay on the high-jump pad in early August, Scott explained,

"Dad, you know I'm not going to play football in high school. So I'd like to spend the fall focusing on baseball and golf since those are the two sports I'm going to try to play next year."

I responded, "Life is made up of memories that usually come from shared experiences. All your close friends at school will be playing football this fall and they will all sweat together, win together, lose together, ride the bus together, and make memories that will probably stay with them the rest of their lives. Do you want to miss out on that? Besides, you didn't get hurt much last year. This year probably won't be any different."

We continued to talk that summer night. Scott came around to see my point, and decided to accept Dad's advice. Amazing. The kid actually listened and changed his mind. Real father-son communication. Eureka!

Early football practices went well, as fellowship and sweat melded, just as I had predicted. The first game against another small school ended in defeat, but things had gone reasonably well. Our team's biggest kid weighed in at a whopping 136 pounds, but the boys seemed scrappy enough to hold their own for the most part.

Then came the fateful day. As we arrived at the field in Fort Worth, a sense of foreboding came upon us. The other team had some players who were fully developed young men. One defensive end stood 6' 2" and weighed 190 pounds. Two others looked even bigger. As someone observed later that night in the hospital emergency room, during the nine months of eighth grade, boys come in many widely varying sizes, depending on which end of the puberty scale they land. Clearly, for that game in Fort Worth, our team and particularly my son, Scott, were on the wrong side of the scale.

By the time the second quarter started, we were down 14-0, with a total blowout in the making. As our team got the ball, the play called was a sprint right pass, and after Scott released the ball, the huge defensive end slammed into him and the impact snapped his femur. Our school's coach had the good sense to stop the game immediately before anyone else got hurt.

For those fathers out there encouraging sons (for whatever reasons) to stick with football beyond grade school recreational leagues, hear my plea. Evaluate your boy's size compared with those against whom he'll be competing. With early weight training programs, better nutrition, evolutional/genetic mixing, or whatever reason, there are some really big, fast, hard-hitting young adolescents playing football in this state, and they are guided missiles capable of doing serious damage to a pre-pubescent boy. Some middle school players today are bigger than linemen in the National Football League during the 1950's. It is a different world.

I have been blessed in many different ways during my life, but in the context of the end of our son's football career, two blessings stand out. First, he is expected to make a full recovery from his injury, such that his future days of playing golf and baseball should not be jeopardized. Second, in the days since breaking his thigh bone, as he slowly gets around on his crutches and wheelchair and sees my sadness over his situation, not once has he looked at me and said, "Dad, I told you so."

Scott is now thriving in college. Though these days his favorite sport is golf, he still enjoys watching baseball games, and will occasionally humor his crazy dad by playing catch or hitting fungoes. In early 2007, our positions reversed themselves as he prepared me for the once-in-a-lifetime opportunity of attending the St. Louis Cardinals Legends Camp, a magical experience that proved to be the straw that broke the camel's back in overcoming my past impulses to never write another book. At the age of 53, just as in my Little League days, I remembered that playing baseball can still produce days of bliss, as I tried to capture in this final first person essay.

THE BOYS OF JANUARY

Once upon a time in this country, most red-blooded boys aspired to grow up and be one (and only one) thing—a major league baseball player. And for those in Texas and the Midwest, one team's uniform stood out—the red and white of the St. Louis Cardinals, whose games were beamed over more airwaves than any other ball club.

For some of us, that childhood dream refused to fade, though our playing days ended in adolescence. Ultimate career paths may have veered off the diamond, but our hearts never left the green field in the sun.

American ingenuity understands supply and demand. If legions of

As a batter at St. Louis Cardinals Legends Camp in January 2007, at least I had a good snarl at the plate, though it intimidated none of the pitchers.

grown businessmen have unrequited love for the image of themselves adorned in a St. Louis uniform, playing on a manicured ballfield and then yukking it up in the locker room with guys whose Cardinal heroics once filled the sports pages, then by golly, there ought to be an opportunity for making those would-be players' dreams come true.

As a poster child for the person described above, in January 2007, I attended the St. Louis Cardinals Legends Camp in Jupiter, Florida. The time spent there shall henceforth be known as "Days of Bliss."

Upon arrival at the Cardinals' spring training complex, each camper is directed to his locker, where he finds his home and away St. Louis uniforms, bearing his name on the back along with his chosen number. Since Roger Maris ended his career in St. Louis, yours truly selected "9" in hopes that clothes would make the man.

After suiting up beside former Cards standouts Joe Magrane and Lee Smith, and receiving a pep talk from retired ace reliever Al "the Mad Hungarian" Hrabosky, we entered the great outdoors where trainers led us through stretching exercises in hopes of minimizing injuries to this overachieving band of 120 grown-up kids, all itching for their first at-bat.

Then the games began, with 10 teams assembled, each "coached" by 2 former Cardinals. Thankfully, Legends Camp rules allow games to flow—4 outfielders, no stealing, short leadoffs, no pick-off throws, maximum 7 runs per inning, and a 2 hour per game time limit. A radiology entrepreneur, business consultant, toy designer, plumbing company owner, saloonkeeper, marketing executive, retired chemical company executive, 3 lawyers and 2 guys whose day jobs remained a mystery—residents of places ranging from Seattle to Palm Beach—made up my team.

Our band of brothers was coached by Danny Cox (12 year veteran pitcher, who at 6 '4", 250 pounds, is literally a mountain of a man) and Tito Landrum (consummate utility infielder and outfielder, who played his best under postseason pressure). In a period of 3 days, each team played 5 games against other campers, and a final 3-inning game facing the Cardinal "Legends." As each game progressed, bending over lessened, shoulders tightened, and "running" on tired legs slowed to a trot. Yet none of the physical decline dimmed the Field of Dreams mindset, allowing us to play through pain over the course of each hotly contested game.

At night, we listened to yesteryears' stories from Hall of Famers Bob Gibson, Lou Brock, and Orlando Cepeda, as well as longtime Cards skipper Whitey Herzog. ESPN commentator Tim Kurkjian says in his new book, "Baseball is a hard game played by hard men." The stories confirmed that. Baseball people have total recall memories, laced with laser beam sarcasm, and a recurring tendency to retaliate in the spirit of righting perceived wrongs. Every man who steps onto a major league diamond knows that this rough-justice attitude goes with the territory.

By Sunday afternoon, even the most diehard campers had had their fill of the National Pastime. We had made plays, committed errors, lined hits, and struck out. But in those Days of Bliss, we wore our Cardinals uniform with the same pride as Stan Musial once did. Color this boyhood dream fulfilled.

EPILOGUE

In October 2007, midway through the postseason, the Boston Red Sox and the Cleveland Indians had each won 3 games in the American League Championship Series, and it was thirty minutes before the start of Game Seven. Obviously, as a lifelong Bosox fan eager for my team to prove that 2004 had not been a fluke, and that the Curse of the Bambino had been permanently exorcised, I hoped for a victory. To square the series though, the Sox had had to come back from a 3-1 game deficit, and the odds of winning 3 consecutive games against the very solid Indians seemed remote. To add further uncertainty to the situation, Boston's starting pitcher in the series' final contest was scheduled to be Daisuke Matsuzaka, who had not exactly inspired confidence in his prior postseason appearances.

Like many fans, anticipating a Game Seven in a postseason series involving one's favorite team is for me one of life's most delicious pleasures, and the hours before the first pitch provide the time for in-depth analysis of each competitor's strengths and weaknesses, leading to a strong sense of the keys to victory or defeat.

My review of the pertinent information that day had brought me to a stalemate of the competing relevant factors between these two high-powered and evenly matched teams, sending me into an anxiety funk, finding myself unable to ascertain which ballclub was most likely to win the series' climactic game. What to do to solve this problem?

After our son, Scott, broke his femur playing eighth grade football, which ended his days on the gridiron, and then wasn't selected to play on his high school's baseball team during his junior year, which ended his days on the diamond, I feared that those two very unpleasant experiences might cause him to lose his enthusiasm for those two sports. Not to worry. His enthusiasm after those setbacks was not dampened, and Scott remained a committed student of both football and baseball, to such an extent that he is the most consistently effective predictor of game outcomes I have ever known.

What to do about gaining a confident hunch before the first pitch of the 2007 American League Championship Series' Game Seven as to its likely outcome? Of course! Pick up the phone and call Scott! Even though he's in college and away from home, this extraordinary situation involving the fortunes of our family's favorite (and namesake) team obviously merited an immediate father-son discourse on this fundamental subject so urgently important to both of us.

Walking across our home's downstairs in search of a phone, I had just located it across the room when it rang. Our daughter Lindsey, always closest to the telephone, answered it quickly and said, "Dad, it's for you. It's Scott."

Most people have better phone manners than I do, and when handed a telephone, they speak first, and say something polite like "Hello" or, when they know who's on the other line, open with something like "Hey son. How are you doing?" But this was Scott, and I am me, and it was almost time for Game Seven in the ALCS to start at Fenway Park. So when Lindsey handed me the phone, and I pulled it up next to my ear, I opened the conversation with my most urgent thought at that critical moment: "Who's gonna win?"

Scott chuckled a second and then replied, "I was calling to ask you the same question."

There it is. This book started with a story of two great major league players who struggled through serious emotional problems because of having baseball-driven, dysfunctional relationships with their fathers. Now it shall end on a hopeful note. Although Scott and I never played in the major leagues, we have something better than that. As evidenced by our hitting fungoes to each other in a neighborhood park to get Ol' Dad ready for the St. Louis Cardinals Legends Camp and our extra-sensory-perception, meeting-of-the-minds phone conversation before the seventh game of the 2007 American League Championship Series, baseball's vital juice runs through our veins. And thanks to the image created by Bart Giamatti, in our minds we play together on the same green field in the sun.

ACKNOWLEDGEMENTS

—————————

MY WIFE CLAIRE, SON SCOTT, AND DAUGHTER LINDSEY have all
accepted their plight of having a husband and father who does what
he does in obsessing over all things baseball—and have done it with a
gracious spirit every step of the way. Thanks to the three of you for your
extraordinary support these many years. And over the course of my
lifetime, my parents Paul and Mary Jean Boston, in their own unique
way, have also allowed me to follow my baseball dreams.

This book came to be because of Rue Judd, publisher of Bright Sky
Press. She believed in this project and me, and committed her
wonderful team to it—most notably Leslie Little, Carol Cates, editor
Dixie Nixon, and book designer Ellen Cregan.

It also came to be because of these persons along the way who have
given me opportunities to write for publication: Stephen Lehman at
Elysian Fields Quarterly; Len Oszustowicz at the Summit Group; Steve
Harding and the good folks at the Nolan Ryan Center; Bob Moos, Cheryl
Chapman, and Bob Compton at the *Dallas Morning News*; Reid Slaughter,
Glenn Arbery, and Wick Allison at Park Cities People; and Huntley Paton,
Glen Hunter, and Kerry Curry at the *Dallas Business Journal*.

To make sure this book resonated with readers other than the
author, I asked Bill LaForge, Joe Vonder Haar, Fred Bowers, Randy Flink,
Dr. John Ledbetter, Michael Wakefield, Dr. Bobby Brown, Mike Capps,
and Jeff Angus to give me feedback on each chapter. Their comments
definitely made this a better book, and they are all special friends.
Finally, thanks to Dr. Jim Beckett for his help with the title and subtitle
of this book.

Frank Deford not only wrote an inspiring foreword, he also gave me
critical input that kept me on track. Lou Brock, one of my all-time
favorite players who has become one of my all-time favorite people,
raised my spirits with his preface. Those who blessed the project
through their dust jacket comments—John Grisham, Tim McCarver,
Dan Shaughnessy, Tim Kurkjian, Sharon Robinson, David Maraniss,
and Rob Neyer—lifted me up to the top of the mountain with their
kind words. In addition, John Horne at The National Baseball Hall of

Fame Library and historian Bill Deane helped me find the right photos for this book.

My assistant, Cathy Leslie, maintained a positive attitude throughout these 80,000 words and the many revisions that had to take place before they were put into final form.

Finally, I thank all the nice people over the last sixteen years who have encouraged me to keep on writing. No author can keep producing without a steady stream of positive reinforcement, and you, the reader, have kept me going.

Talmage Boston
October 1, 2008

PERMISSIONS

A few of the materials in this book have been previously published, and permission to use them has come from the following:

1. *The Dallas Morning News* has given permission as to my using my past Op-Ed Viewpoints columns published in that newspaper.

2. *People Newspapers* has given me permission to use my past columns published in their newspapers.

3. *The Scribner Encyclopedia of American Lives: Sports Figures* is now the property of Cengage Learning in Belmont, California, and Cengage has given me permission to use the biographical essays of Carl Yastrzemski, Bart Giamatti and Lou Brock that I wrote for the encyclopedia.

4. The Nolan Ryan Foundation gave me permission to use the essays I authored which appear on the walls of the Nolan Ryan Center on the campus of Alvin Community College in Alvin, Texas.

INDEX